Constructing *The Wicker Man*:

Film and Cultural Studies Perspectives

Edited by

Jonathan Murray, Lesley Stevenson,

Stephen Harper and Benjamin Franks

University of Glasgow, Crichton Publications
2005

University of Glasgow
Crichton Publications

General Editor
Mark G. Ward

Rutherford/McCowan Building
Crichton University Campus
Dumfries, DG1 4ZL
Scotland

First published 2005

ISBN 0 85261 818 2

Contents

Foreword   v
Robin Hardy

Introduction   1
Jonathan Murray, Lesley Stevenson, Stephen Harper and
Benjamin Franks

1   **Straw or Wicker? Traditions of Scottish film criticism
and *The Wicker Man***   11
Jonathan Murray

2   **Religion in *The Wicker Man*: Context and
representation**   37
Steven J. Sutcliffe

3   **Demotic Possession: The hierarchic and anarchic in
*The Wicker Man***   57
Benjamin Franks

4   **'Here On Official Business': Production, patriarchy
and the hazards of policing a pre-industrial utopia**   75
Belle Doyle

5   **'The Game's Over'. Breaking the Spell of Summerisle:
Feminist discourse and *The Wicker Man***   91
Gail Ashurst

6   **Sightseeing in Summerisle: Film tourism and *The
Wicker Man***   107
Lesley Stevenson

7   **Things that go Clunk in the Cult Film Text: Nodes and
interstices in *The Wicker Man***   123
Justin Smith

8   Now a Major Motion Picture? *The Wicker Man*
    Novelisation   139
    Mark Jones

9   Mister Punch as Sacrificial Victim in *The Wicker Man*   157
    Melissa Smith

10 'The Other Coppers': Uncanniness, identity and *The*
    Wicker Man audience   173
    Stephen Harper

11 *The Wicker Man*, The Uncanny, and the Clash of Moral
    Cultures   189
    Stefan Gullatz

    Notes on contributors   207

    Index   211

Foreword

Robin Hardy

In July 2003 I delivered the keynote speech at a conference held at the University of Glasgow's Crichton Campus in Dumfries, on a film which I directed: *The Wicker Man* (1973).[1] The film, as is widely known, was given a 'no press' launch and effectively 'buried' by the new management of British Lion, after Peter Snell, the film's producer, had been unfairly forced to resign as President of our production company. Happily, thanks to the enterprise of Christopher Lee, a print found its way to Le Festival des Films Fantastique et Science Fiction in Paris, where it won the Grand Prix. The British critics then insisted on seeing *The Wicker Man* and gave it wide praise. *The Financial Times* said that it evoked 'a vision of *The Bacchae*' (we took that as positive), while *Variety* wrote that the Grand Prix was well deserved, and referred to the film's 'boffo business' (good box office). 'You're unlikely to live to see a review this good again', Peter Snell told me. Neither of us could have known then that we were going to see thirty more years of reviews that were all that good: right up to the recent DVD launch and on and on with every television repeat (usually on New Year's Eve).

In America, it took one great review of *The Wicker Man* to launch the film and sow the seeds of its future mythology. The review was I think almost unique, in that it occupied the entire issue of one of the trendiest of film magazines, *Cinefantastique*. The headline on the cover, over the familiar picture of Christopher invoking the blessing of the gods as the Wicker Man burns, read: 'The *Citizen Kane* of Horror Films'. In Hollywood, the great Orson Welles movie is a yardstick against which any producer can only dream of having his work compared. And so it went, from city to city, around the USA. Our distributors – far too poor to finance a blanket release across hundreds of cinemas – had to storm into each American town, one after the other.

---

[1] An edited version of Hardy's keynote speech – 'The Genesis of *The Wicker Man*' – and the transcript of Hardy's interview with Jonathan Murray at the conference are available in Franks, Harper, Murray and Stevenson, eds., *The Quest for 'The Wicker Man'*.

In San Francisco, the film's growing fame attracted an invitation to open at the Castro theatre, a huge art deco cinema, with a benefit function in aid of America's Cinematec. Every critic attended the press conference before the show and Christopher was on every local radio and TV channel that morning. Queues snaked around several city blocks, hoping to get tickets. Woad-painted Pagans, swathed in chains, demonstrated against the film for giving their religion a bad name. The press adored it and embroidered any controversy to epic proportions. 'The film they didn't want you to see!' became a persistent theme in America and, later, in Britain, when the press there picked up on the 'little British picture wows them Stateside' angle. *The Wicker Man*'s long run beat the record at the downtown Lumière cinema in San Francisco, and was to do the same at the Orson Welles cinema in Boston, a little later in that amazing tour. In Kentucky, we received the most unusual of critical praise – pastors and priests advising their flocks to go and see the film; this after screenings to lively prayer breakfasts in Holiday Inns. 'It is rare in a movie', one minister said, 'to see so clear an invocation of what resurrection really means'. Those words spoken from a pulpit in Peebles would, I imagine, cause scarcely a ripple in the local multiplex's box office receipts; but in Kentucky it meant full houses, and the boffo business reported in *Variety*. Both Christopher and I were rewarded by being made Kentucky Colonels, just like Harland David Sanders (of Kentucky Fried Chicken fame).

We rather hope for a similar transatlantic reception for a film we plan, based on my new novel, *May Day*, whose plot is quite different to that of *The Wicker Man*, but whose story inhabits similar territory (like *The Wicker Man*, *May Day* concerns the vulnerability of the 'innocent abroad'). If the themes and concepts of *The Wicker Man* continue to inform my own creative work, this volume attests to their continuing fascination for film and cultural critics.

Bibliography

Franks, B., S. Harper, J. Murray and L. Stevenson, eds., *The Quest for 'The Wicker Man': Historical, folklore and Pagan perspectives* (Edinburgh: Luath, 2005).

Introduction

Jonathan Murray, Lesley Stevenson, Stephen Harper and Benjamin Franks

The essays collected in this volume represent a cross-section of contributions to an interdisciplinary conference on Robin Hardy's film *The Wicker Man* (Hardy, 1973), held at the University of Glasgow's Crichton Campus in Dumfries in July 2003. The purpose of that gathering was to bring together academics from a variety of disciplines to analyse and discuss this enigmatic and under-researched film. The conference papers and the discussions they provoked provided a forum – rare in these days of academic specialisation – for multi-disciplinary intellectual exchange. Through their engagement with the film's production context, its representational strategies, and its critical and audience reception, the papers collected here provide fascinatingly diverse insights into the film's cultural import, past and present.

The contributors' readings of the film are various, engaging with the film's problematic aspects (such as its arguably stereotypical representations of nationalist tropes) and its progressive elements (including its subversion of received patriarchal gender roles). But the scope of these essays extends beyond textual analysis, situating the debates raised by (and within) the film in the social and political context of the early 1970s and charting the film's critical fortunes, audience negotiations, and social uses throughout the last three decades.

The first two essays locate *The Wicker Man* in its critical and historical contexts. Jonathan Murray analyses the film's deployment of the 'Scotland as island' motif, reading its conflict between native/communal and Modern/atomised ideological values in the light of other Scottish-themed films, such as *Whisky Galore!* (Mackendrick, 1949) and *The Maggie* (Mackendrick, 1954). The stereotypes of 'Scottishness' presented in these films have been variously interpreted. For Scottish cinema studies in the 1980s, the images of Scotland in 'metropolitan' films such as *The Wicker Man* testified to Scotland's 'discursive colonisation' by American and British cinemas. Changing contexts of film production and criticism in the 1990s, however, rendered such critiques problematically complicit with colonial discourse. The rather rigidly structuralist film criticism of the 1980s, Murray argues, became a critical straw man for postcolonial critics. Jane Sillars, for example, argued that an anti-authoritarian impulse towards self-conscious deconstruction is central to cinematic representations of Scotland. This enables the colonised 'locals' to participate in a strategic masquerade which, as in *The Wicker Man*, turns the colonisers' arsenal of stereotypes on its previous owners. Murray suggests, however, that such arguments too often depend on recuperations of 'whimsical' national stereotypes, such as those identifiable in *The Wicker Man*, for essentially commercial purposes, despite a misleading veneer of politicised rhetoric. At the expense of radical innovation in filmmaking and criticism, postcolonial criticism of films like *The Wicker Man* can become an ostensibly progressive (but, in fact, blandly reformist) form of national identity politics.

While Murray is concerned with the relation between *The Wicker Man*'s representational strategies and successive paradigms of film criticism since the 1970s, other contributors examine its ideological relation to contemporaneous cultural debates. Steven Sutcliffe, for example, locates *The Wicker Man*'s 'religious' problematic in the popular culture of the early 1970s. Sutcliffe analyses the film's intersection with several interweaving currents in 'popular religion' of that period: the haemorrhage in Christian identity and practice, the celebration of the occult, a revived interest in folklore and traditions, and moral panics over the proselytising of new religions. He argues that these multiple constraints produce a deeply ambivalent film that dichotomises, through a series of binary oppositions (ascetic/hedonistic, repressed/uninhibited, celibacy/sex, etc.), the emergent religious heterogeneity in Anglo-American culture into a 'culture war' between 'Christians' and 'pagans'. Thus Sergeant Howie's death can be read either as martyrdom in a new post-Christian culture or sacrifice in the pre-Christian symbolic order. But Sutcliffe also shows how the film can be taken as a warning against the structuralist tendency to reduce the diverse culture of the 'long sixties' into a series of binary oppositions. The ambiguities of *The Wicker Man* problematise dichotomising interpretations of its cultural milieu, suggesting the interrelatedness of such apparently oppositional terms as 'counterculture' and 'religion'.

Benjamin Franks is also concerned with the struggle between various social groups over *The Wicker Man*'s meanings. The film, he notes, was intended as a critique of totalitarianism, on the basis that freedom and the democratic distribution of power is a product of Enlightenment Reason, and that irrationality leads to authoritarianism. Thus the film can be seen to privilege the bureaucratic rationality embodied by Sergeant Howie and to advance a dramatic argument based on a Weberian understanding of the relationship between political power and the authority to rule. Nonetheless, alternative readings of the film are possible. Franks investigates the problematic aspects of the film for anarchists (such as Summerisle's hierarchical structure, capitalist economy and rigid division of labour). Focusing on a spoof article about the film's influence on anarchists in *Hate Mail* (a free newspaper parodying the socially conservative tabloid *The Daily Mail*), he explores the subversion or 'détourning' of *The Wicker Man* by anti-capitalist activists to promote a revolutionary, anti-hierarchical politics. Franks shows that just as the Summerislanders undermine the policeman's arguments at every turn, so too the *Hate Mail*'s parody of right-wing rhetoric about pagans and other social scapegoats illustrates the prejudices and limits of liberal understandings of legitimate authority.

Belle Doyle explores *The Wicker Man*'s gender politics, showing how Howie represents a system that prides itself on its control of both the means of production and reproduction, and how the Summerislanders scandalise the policeman's patriarchal worldview. As Doyle points out, the traditional allocation of gender roles is reversed on the island: the men do not seem to be particularly productive, even when they have professional roles such as doctor or chemist, while the female librarian, the landlord's daughter and the schoolteacher 'are all seen as taking their roles to extremes'. Doyle also explores the film's deployment of the notion of masculine 'parade'. In accordance with Steve Neale's observations about the homoerotic subtexts of patriarchal narratives, Howie must exert 'masculine' control or be punished; yet this is more difficult than might be imagined, as the policeman is transformed from an active investigator into a passive victim. Finally, Doyle sets these observations about *The Wicker Man* within a wider cultural-historical context, linking its implicit critique of patriarchal reproductive modes to other horror films about domestic and family crisis in the 1970s, such as *The Exorcist* (Friedkin, 1973), *The Omen* (Donner, 1976), and *Carrie* (De Palma, 1976). The appearance of Rowan Morrison as a symbol of the island's future at the end of the film, and the suggestion of Lord Summerisle's inevitable sacrifice, both suggest the end of patriarchy. Doyle concludes that the horror of *The Wicker Man* derives not from its representations of paganism, but from its threat to patriarchal structures.

Gail Ashurst also finds a critique of patriarchy in *The Wicker Man*. While recognising that the film mobilises several 'myths of femininity', she discusses it as a radical text that exposes male-centred constructions of femininity. According to Ashurst, the film subverts patriarchal narrative strategies though a number of techniques, in particular a bold and self-conscious use of the game of the 'hunter leading the hunted', which in *The Wicker Man* involves a reversal of traditional gender roles. Drawing on narratology and the feminist theories of Cixous, Mulvey, Butler and Doane, Ashurst points out that *The Wicker Man* not only reverses the binary logic of gender (as in, for example, the fairy-tale reversals of Angela Carter), but also disrupts and destabilises that logic by demonstrating the performativity of gender in a self-conscious and ludic fashion. Thus the cunning manipulations of the women in *The Wicker Man* reveal the constructedness of femininity in a way that resonates strikingly with some of the critical strategies of poststructuralist feminism.

While many of the contributors mentioned so far focus on the film's ideological constructions, others focus on its public status and its promotional currency among contemporary audiences and organisations. Lesley Stevenson explores the relationship between the absence of references to *The Wicker Man* in tourism literature about Dumfries and Galloway and discontent among local residents with the film's shooting in the region during 1972. This local displeasure focused on the film's perceived support for pagan values and its purportedly unsympathetic representation of the region's cultural life. While these objections might suggest a

Introduction

Jonathan Murray, Lesley Stevenson, Stephen Harper and Benjamin Franks

The essays collected in this volume represent a cross-section of contributions to an interdisciplinary conference on Robin Hardy's film *The Wicker Man* (Hardy, 1973), held at the University of Glasgow's Crichton Campus in Dumfries in July 2003. The purpose of that gathering was to bring together academics from a variety of disciplines to analyse and discuss this enigmatic and under-researched film. The conference papers and the discussions they provoked provided a forum – rare in these days of academic specialisation – for multi-disciplinary intellectual exchange. Through their engagement with the film's production context, its representational strategies, and its critical and audience reception, the papers collected here provide fascinatingly diverse insights into the film's cultural import, past and present.

The contributors' readings of the film are various, engaging with the film's problematic aspects (such as its arguably stereotypical representations of nationalist tropes) and its progressive elements (including its subversion of received patriarchal gender roles). But the scope of these essays extends beyond textual analysis, situating the debates raised by (and within) the film in the social and political context of the early 1970s and charting the film's critical fortunes, audience negotiations, and social uses throughout the last three decades.

The first two essays locate *The Wicker Man* in its critical and historical contexts. Jonathan Murray analyses the film's deployment of the 'Scotland as island' motif, reading its conflict between native/communal and Modern/atomised ideological values in the light of other Scottish-themed films, such as *Whisky Galore!* (Mackendrick, 1949) and *The Maggie* (Mackendrick, 1954). The stereotypes of 'Scottishness' presented in these films have been variously interpreted. For Scottish cinema studies in the 1980s, the images of Scotland in 'metropolitan' films such as *The Wicker Man* testified to Scotland's 'discursive colonisation' by American and British cinemas. Changing contexts of film production and criticism in the 1990s, however, rendered such critiques problematically complicit with colonial discourse. The rather rigidly structuralist film criticism of the 1980s, Murray argues, became a critical straw man for postcolonial critics. Jane Sillars, for example, argued that an anti-authoritarian impulse towards self-conscious deconstruction is central to cinematic representations of Scotland. This enables the colonised 'locals' to participate in a strategic masquerade which, as in *The Wicker Man*, turns the colonisers' arsenal of stereotypes on its previous owners. Murray suggests, however, that such arguments too often depend on recuperations of 'whimsical' national stereotypes, such as those identifiable in *The Wicker Man*, for essentially commercial purposes, despite a misleading veneer of politicised rhetoric. At the expense of radical innovation in filmmaking and criticism, postcolonial criticism of films like *The Wicker Man* can become an ostensibly progressive (but, in fact, blandly reformist) form of national identity politics.

While Murray is concerned with the relation between *The Wicker Man*'s representational strategies and successive paradigms of film criticism since the 1970s, other contributors examine its ideological relation to contemporaneous cultural debates. Steven Sutcliffe, for example, locates *The Wicker Man*'s 'religious' problematic in the popular culture of the early 1970s. Sutcliffe analyses the film's intersection with several interweaving currents in 'popular religion' of that period: the haemorrhage in Christian identity and practice, the celebration of the occult, a revived interest in folklore and traditions, and moral panics over the proselytising of new religions. He argues that these multiple constraints produce a deeply ambivalent film that dichotomises, through a series of binary oppositions (ascetic/hedonistic, repressed/uninhibited, celibacy/sex, etc.), the emergent religious heterogeneity in Anglo-American culture into a 'culture war' between 'Christians' and 'pagans'. Thus Sergeant Howie's death can be read either as martyrdom in a new post-Christian culture or sacrifice in the pre-Christian symbolic order. But Sutcliffe also shows how the film can be taken as a warning against the structuralist tendency to reduce the diverse culture of the 'long sixties' into a series of binary oppositions. The ambiguities of *The Wicker Man* problematise dichotomising interpretations of its cultural milieu, suggesting the certain lack of distinction between film settings and film locations, Stevenson shows that local discontent continues to the present day, as attested by the controversy surrounding the first Wickerman Festival in 2002. Nonetheless, she also argues that, despite a lack of promotional support emanating from Dumfries and Galloway itself, the film's cult status has recently generated significant tourist activity in the region. Drawing upon Urry's notion of the 'tourist gaze' and existing literature on 'movie-induced tourism', she contends that conventional film tourism trends, which have been invariably derived from research on films which were box-office successes, are of little relevance to *The Wicker Man.* Stevenson concludes that the life-cycle commonly associated with movie-induced tourism does not apply to films such as *The Wicker Man* which benefit from a cult following.

The cult aspects of the film are also the concern of Justin Smith, who provides a concise summary of the film's chequered production and distribution history (itself a prime source of 'cult' appeal among *Wicker Man* fans). Smith also identifies certain 'nodes' in the text – elements of playful dissonance including symbolic references, 'over-acting' and body language (as in, for example, Christopher Lee's stiff posture throughout the film), camp elements, music and the juxtaposition of certain camera shots – which, he argues, appeal to the cultist. Smith contends that the film's jarring, discordant and often cartoonish elements disrupt narrative verisimilitude, undermine the accretion of suspense typical of mainstream horror films, and thereby delimit the affective investments upon which the success of the horror genre depends. While these techniques confound conventional modes of horror film spectatorship and frustrate critical attempts to categorise the film as a horror movie, they are nonetheless anticipated with relish by cultists.

Questions of cultural distinction also inform Mark Jones's discussion of *The Wicker Man*'s novelisation in 1979. Jones sees the publication of the novel as part of the gradual reclamation of the film from obscurity. While most novelisations of films are contracted out to career novelists, this novel was written by the film's director and writer, providing an alternative and supplementary view of the celluloid text's events, characters, and themes. Jones draws on theories of adaptation and cultural production to show the significance of the novelisation in precipitating the reinvention of *The Wicker Man* as the authentic British horror film at the very moment of the film's greatest obscurity in the UK. He also explores the differences between the two textualisations. The novel differs from the film, argues Jones, by emphasising Howie's self-consciousness about his policing methods and his reservations about his own officiousness and stridency. The novel also presents Howie as an anti-racist with egalitarian principles. While such qualities may not be entirely inconsistent with Howie's cinematic characterisation, they are certainly not mentioned in the film. As a result of its relatively sympathetic representation of Howie, the novel, Jones contends, is far less ambiguous than the film in its condemnation of paganism.

Melissa Smith is also concerned with the film's literary contexts in her exploration of the significance of the figure of Punch in both *The Wicker Man* and traditional sources. Starting with the presentation of Punch in Neil Gaiman and Dave McKean's graphic novel *The Comical Tragedy or Tragical Comedy of Mr. Punch* (1995), Smith discusses Punch as a figure who blurs the boundaries between the binaries of life and death, individual and collective, morality and immorality. In versions of the Punch story such as that of Gaiman and McKean, Punch kills the Devil and proceeds to beat and murder an array of characters. At first sight the presentation of Howie/Punch in *The Wicker Man* is quite different to Gaiman and McKean's. Yet whereas the film's revision of Punch sees him as a victim rather than a villain, Smith argues that the sacrifice of the 'virgin fool' Howie in fact produces similar consequences to the violent actions of other Punches, unwittingly erasing Christian culture's established notions of right and wrong and opening up previously unimaginable realms of moral and spiritual possibility.

The final two essays here concentrate on *The Wicker Man*'s often-noted 'uncanniness'. Stephen Harper draws on Freud's essay 'The Uncanny' (1919) to argue that Freud's work may be as strong an influence on the film as Frazer's *The Golden Bough*. The film replicates many of the elements of uncanniness mentioned in Freud's essay, including specific details such as severed limbs, tropes such as that of the 'double', and the indeterminacy of the boundary between the animate and the inanimate. These elements give *The Wicker Man* a distinctly Modernist sense of depth and perhaps confer upon it a certain cultural value. Together with the film's self-conscious use of mirror imagery to reflect Howie's increasingly fractured identity, these uncanny elements also facilitate a certain critique of Howie's inauthenticity (experiences of uncanniness, in Freud's schema, are symptoms of repression). This critical perspective, Harper suggests, would have been readily available to a countercultural audience in the early 1970s, which can be expected to have had a strong interest in psychology and psychoanalytical concepts. For such an audience, Harper argues, *The Wicker Man*'s uncanny motifs undermine Howie's unreflective self-image and constitute a dire warning against the dangers of ignorance and repression.

Stefan Gullatz also concentrates on the uncanny aspects of the film, this time from the perspective of Lacanian psychoanalysis. In a reading informed by Idealist continental philosophy, from Schelling to Žižek, Gullatz argues that the islanders' trickery in luring Howie to his sacrificial death has the same structural function as the oracle in *Oedipus Rex*, or the prophecy in Nicolas Roeg's film *Don't Look Now* (1973, the 'companion' film of *The Wicker Man* at its London premiere): it is the device through which the hero fulfils his symbolic destiny. For Gullatz, the wicker effigy at the end of the film is a Phallic 'fatal signifier', which restores the questing Howie to his proper place in the socio-symbolic order. Gullatz also discusses the film in the light of pagan and Christian notions of 'evil'. The film's artistic integrity, and its 'sublime-uncanny effect', he suggests, lies in its chilling, but ontologically faithful depiction of the pagan islanders as lacking in any sense of 'radical' or diabolical evil. A lesser director than Hardy, Gullatz concludes, might have succumbed to sensationalism, ascribing to the islanders 'a satanic Evil'.

While all of the contributions here contain a certain amount of theory and associated terminology, the editors hope that they are accessible to a non-academic readership. Nonetheless, the contributions of Gullatz and Sutcliffe, in particular, raise contentious issues of terminology, particularly around the terms 'Paganism', 'pagan' and 'neo-Paganism'; therefore, a brief explanation of these terms is necessary. The capitalised versions ('Pagan' and its derivatives) are used to describe the identifiable set of spiritual practices or coherent set of beliefs concerning magic, pantheism and derived moral principles. The upper-case term is applied both to systematised pre- and non-Christian groupings (some authors, however, prefer to use the term 'neo-Pagan' for these post-war religious movements; this has been respected in their individual contributions). The lower case 'pagan', meanwhile, is mainly used in reference to religious or mystical beliefs that lie outside standard monotheism.

The conference at which early versions of these papers were delivered was made possible by the efforts of many people. Particular thanks must go to Steven Gillespie, Dr Helen Loney, Dr Donald MacLeod, Professor Rex Pyke, Frank Ryan and Professor Rex Taylor. The editors are also grateful for the input and encouragement of Robin Hardy. In addition, we wish to express our appreciation to all those who attended and supported the conference for their enthusiastic participation and to those organisations who provided sponsorship and commercial assistance: Canal+, Dumfries and Galloway Council, Dunfermline Building Society, South West Scotland Screen Commission and the University of Glasgow. Special mention must be made of Nick Jennings and Tina Worsey who administrated the conference so successfully, and of the invaluable assistance of Dr Belle Doyle, formerly of the South West Scotland Screen Commission, who set up a parallel horror film festival.

For their editorial work and support for this collection, thanks are due to Professor Mark Ward, Ms Phillipa Crowson and Ms Maureen Robertson, of University of Glasgow, Crichton Publications. Finally, the editors would like to thank the contributors to the volume for the outstanding quality of their submissions and for their patience and co-operation during the editing process. Readers seeking further analyses of *The Wicker Man* may wish to refer to a second volume of essays on the film,

The Quest for 'The Wicker Man' (Edinburgh: Luath, 2005). That collection contains contributions (also based on papers delivered at the conference) written from a range of disciplinary perspectives, with a particular emphasis on anthropology, archaeology, history, and folklore. The editors do not claim that either of these two volumes represents the final word on *The Wicker Man*; yet we do hope that they redress the absence of serious critical work on the film.

Straw or Wicker? Traditions of Scottish film criticism and *The Wicker Man*

Jonathan Murray

Introduction

The fact that you are reading this volume (and that I am contributing to it) testifies to the enduring attraction exerted by *The Wicker Man* (Hardy, 1973) upon film buffs and cinema scholars alike. Hypotheses seeking to explain this phenomenon are almost as numerous as the film's acolytes. Taking one example, Christopher Lee, *The Wicker Man*'s co-star, has explained its evergreen fascination for audiences by arguing that the film's macabre tale 'could take place anywhere; it happens to take place in Scotland. But it's an international story'.[1] Now, crossing Lord Summerisle is, as we all know, a dangerous business. Yet I willingly intend to play the Fool throughout the course of this essay. I wish here to outline the terms of my own interest in *The Wicker Man*. They flatly contradict Lee's lordly assertion. For it is undoubtedly the case that this film's ingenious narrative conforms, in near-classical fashion, to a hegemonic representational paradigm within which 'Scotland' and 'Scottishness' have been repeatedly constructed in narrative feature film. In what follows, I begin by illustrating the extent to which this is so.

Second, however, the essay's central contention is that consideration of *The Wicker Man* enables a remarkably vivid mapping of the changing ways in which the ideological impact of popular cinematic representations of 'Scotland' have been understood within the academic disciplines of Film Studies and Scottish Cultural Studies at various junctures over the last quarter century or so. While it is true that the quintessential filmic narration of 'Scotland' remained remarkably stable throughout the twentieth century, the dominant ways in which such images are routinely interrogated have altered dramatically since the late 1970s. Of Scottish cinema's academic study, one might argue that the textual ball often remains roughly the same shape and colour, while the conceptual goalposts towards which it is kicked

---

[1] Quoted in Bartholomew, '*The Wicker Man*', p. 40.

have shifted dramatically. This essay is concerned to investigate and illuminate the terms of that disjunction.

In brief: the 1980s and early '90s were dominated by despairing diagnoses of Scottish culture's ideological 'colonisation' by more powerful, external loci of cultural, political and economic authority. Specifically, 'successive waves of discursive hegemony exercised on Scotland'[2] by American and British metropolitan societies and cinemas were detected and castigated during this period. Yet over the last decade, a far more optimistic reading of popular cultural stereotypes of 'Scotland', and their potentially radical ideological meanings and use-value for inhabitants of the Scottish sphere, has become increasingly fashionable. With specific reference to *The Wicker Man*, this essay traces the terms of that collective intellectual shift. In addition, some of the methodological and political issues that may be at stake in it are briefly outlined.

'The Wilds of Scotland'™

In a biographical study of the Scottish-American filmmaker Alexander Mackendrick, Philip Kemp astutely points out that *The Wicker Man* can be read as a remake, whether conscious or not, of Mackendrick's celebrated Ealing comedy *Whisky Galore!* (1949). Kemp goes so far as to argue that the former film 'could stand in for the horror movie that Mackendrick never made'.[3] The narrative and thematic parallels between the two texts are indeed striking. Not least among these, both films open with ironic framing devices that purportedly construct their respective depictions of regional Scottish cultures as actuality, not fiction. In *The Wicker Man*, an arch intertitle acknowledges thanks to Lord Summerisle and the islanders for their co-operation during filming; *Whisky Galore!*'s opening sequence is narrated by an omniscient male voiceover that parodically recalls the formal conventions and patrician condescension of the 1930s Griersonian documentary.

Further homologies abound. *Whisky Galore!* was adapted from Compton Mackenzie's 1947 comic novel of the same name. The

---

[2] McArthur, 'The Scottish Discursive Unconscious', p. 82.
[3] Kemp, *Lethal Innocence*, p. 40.

latter was in turn based upon an actual incident that took place during WWII. In 1941, a cargo ship, the *SS Politician*, ran aground off the Inner Hebrides. Unpatriotic, drouthy locals looted its precious cargo of whisky, which had been destined for export to America in order to prop up Britain's parlous national balance of payments.[4] In both Mackenzie's literary and Mackendrick's filmic retelling of these events, an incoming representative of civilised, juridico-legal authority, the English commander of the local Home Guard, Captain Paul Waggett, vainly attempts to combat flagrant local disregard of mainland law on the island of Todday, a thinly fictionalised version of Barra. Like *The Wicker Man*'s Sergeant Howie, *Whisky Galore!*'s Waggett is appalled by what he sees as an orgy (although here, not a literal one) of native bacchanalian exuberance and superstition. So devoted to *uisge beatha*, or the water of life, are the islanders that a dram comes to possess miraculous healing properties. Whisky instantaneously escorts those at death's door back to the land of the living. It is not simply an alcoholic 'spirit'. Like Howie, Waggett is systematically mocked and seamlessly manipulated by the far shrewder, scruple-free locals. He too becomes a sacrificial Fool, transported for interrogation on the mainland at the film's climax, having been framed for the theft of the whisky. In *Whisky Galore!*'s justly famous final sequence, Waggett is literally laughed off the island, 'the intensity of [his] humiliation and destruction [...] deliriously realiz[ed] at the level of the *mise-en-scène*'.[5] If Waggett is not actually immolated, then like Howie, both his individual authoritative status and the wider institutional equivalent he personifies are wholly destroyed, in a paganistic but ruthlessly efficient maelstrom of native excess.

It is also worth noting, for the purposes of this kind of quasi-structuralist argument, the context in which Kemp is prompted to link *Whisky Galore!* and *The Wicker Man* in the first place. He is reacting against the narrow terms of received genealogical accounts of Mackendrick's subsequent influence within British cinema. These typically saw and continue to see the filmmaker's

---

[4] For a detailed and entertaining historical account, see Hutchinson, *Polly: The True Story Behind Whisky Galore.*

[5] McArthur, *Whisky Galore and The Maggie*, p. 54.

imprimatur most clearly manifested in the first four 1980s Scottish features of writer/director Bill Forsyth. Thus, around the time that Forsyth's most internationally successful and best-known feature, *Local Hero* (1983), was released in British cinemas, John Caughie argued of it that 'the film's success [...] is like the more ambiguous success of the crew of *The Maggie* [Mackendrick, 1954], or like the success of the communit[y] of *Whisky Galore!*'.[6] More recently, in an historical study of the reception of British films in the USA, Sarah Street argues that '*Local Hero* can [...] be related to Ealing with its story of the impact of an American oil company on a small Scottish village'.[7] Such categorisations draw authority from an admission by Forsyth himself, at the time of *Local Hero*'s original theatrical run:

> I didn't see *The Maggie* till it was on television
> after we had finished filming *Local Hero* [...] I
> felt quite touched that I had unconsciously
> followed the same kind of progression on from
> *Whisky Galore!* as Sandy Mackendrick did.[8]

To clarify: in Mackendrick's 1954 Ealing comedy *The Maggie*, an incoming representative of international corporate capital, American businessman Calvin B. Marshall, arrives in Scotland. Here he plans to build a remote Highland holiday home in an attempt to save his foundering marriage. Marshall is, however, seamlessly manipulated and humiliated by the native crew of a small, antiquated cargo vessel, the ship of the film's title. They ultimately, albeit inadvertently, destroy the materials for and contents of the never-to-be-built dream home, in transit to the northwestern seaboard. In Forsyth's *Local Hero*, MacIntyre, an American corporate asset stripper, arrives in Highland Scotland intending to purchase an entire village on the same stretch of Scottish coastline. It is to be razed to the ground, making way for a massive oil refinery financed by US capital. The entire local community shamelessly gulls him, however. They masquerade a

---

[6] Caughie, 'Support whose Local Hero?', p. 45.

[7] Street, *Transatlantic Crossings*, pp. 195-96.

[8] Quoted in Brown, 'A Suitable Job for a Scot', p. 159.

quasi-feudal, avowedly non-materialistic way of life, in order to drive up the price credulous American executives will pay to separate them from it.

A pattern begins to emerge. *The Wicker Man*, like the other well-known Scottish-themed films briefly referenced here, conforms in significant degree to the terms of a quintessential cinematic narration of 'Scotland', which in its myriad individual variants proceeds roughly as follows. Somewhere in 'The Wilds of Scotland'™ there unfolds a perverse conflict between Modernity and Tradition. Isolated representatives of the former are trounced or seduced at every turn by an amoral gaggle of adherents to the latter. This is so notwithstanding diametrically opposed, long-term historical and cultural shifts experienced and acceded to elsewhere in the Occident. Such a national-representational 'base' underwrites a range of apparently incompatible narrative, generic and aesthetic 'superstructures' encountered in the body of films that construct 'Scotland'. This state of affairs entails that, contrary to seeming logic, 'the delightful absurdities of *Brigadoon* (Minnelli, 1954) are not unrelated to the nightmarish foreclosures of *The Wicker Man*'.[9] For, according to *The Wicker Man*, *Whisky Galore!*, *The Maggie*, *Local Hero* and more films than it is possible to cite here, Scotland is both a place and a mindset definitively out of kilter with Western rationality. *The Wicker Man* is emphatically not, as Christopher Lee erroneously suggests, 'a story that happens to take place in Scotland'. Rather, it both instantiates and reiterates *the* classic 'Scottish story' re-run time and time again in popular cinema.

Part of my own interest in the film lies, therefore, in tracking its deployment of a national identity template only too familiar to students of Scotland's cinematic representation. This constructs archetypal oppositions, whether utopian or dystopian, between traumatised American or British Modernity and its sanguine, quasi-feudal Celtic precursor. Moreover, *The Wicker Man* also mobilises an equally well-worn 'Scottish island' or 'Scotland as island' narrative and ideological motif within which to set its familiar representational project. As Duncan Petrie notes, key to

---

[9] Riach, *Representing Scotland in Literature*, p. 198.

Scotland's hegemonic portrayal in British and American cinemas
has been a pre-meditated depiction of the nation as:

> A distant periphery far removed from the
> modern, urban and cosmopolitan social world
> inhabited by the kind of people involved in the
> creation of such images [...] central to this is
> the idea of remoteness – physical, social, moral
> – from metropolitan rules, conventions and
> certainties... another central trope [...] is the
> literal and metaphorical figure of the 'island', a
> space in which remoteness and isolation is
> enhanced by virtue of its detachment from the
> mainland.[10]

For fresh corroborating evidence in support of this analysis, the
reader is referred no further than the May 2003 British theatrical
release of the low-budget Scottish road movie (and please note
the title) *The Last Great Wilderness* (Mackenzie, 2002). In this
film, two jaded urbanites traverse the Scotland-England border,
eventually stalling at an isolated Highland community that is the
fiefdom of an unsettlingly eccentric rogue psychotherapist,
perhaps loosely modelled on the figure of R. D. Laing. As one
contemporary reviewer noted of the unorthodox local therapeutic
interventions on display here, 'accumulating hints of Pagan
ritualism brace us for sinister conspiracies to rival those of *The
Wicker Man*'.[11] Indeed, *The Last Great Wilderness* was marketed
in its accompanying publicity campaign as '*The Wicker Man*
meets *Straw Dogs* [Peckinpah, 1971]'. Even if, or perhaps in part
precisely *because*, now self-consciously and ironically referenced
by filmmakers, the dominant cinematic trope of 'Scotland' (The
Lasting Great Wilderness?), represented *par excellence* by *The
Wicker Man*, remains alive and well in contemporary film
culture.

---

[10] Petrie, *Screening Scotland*, p. 32, p. 35.
[11] Richards, 'The Last Great Wilderness: review', p. 49.

Mapping the Scottish cinematic 'Wilderness' I: 1980s rhetorics of colonialism

That said, what *have* indubitably shifted over the past two decades are the key axioms and signature priorities driving the changing critical paradigms within which apparently stable hegemonic constructions of 'Scotland', as pre- and/or anti-Modern wilderness, have been interpreted. To my knowledge, *The Wicker Man* has received no sustained attention within the fragmentary body of literature that comprises Scottish cinema studies. This is ironic. I would like to argue that the film offers an especially productive textual vehicle allowing a comprehensive tracing of that discipline's methodological history, a task I attempt to perform immediately below.

The major factor that makes Scotland near-unique within Anglophone and/or European cinemas is the remarkably delayed emergence of a substantive indigenous production infrastructure.[12] Writing in 1976, three years after *The Wicker Man* was first released in UK cinemas, David Bruce argued that film as an expressive medium itself was not 'something that belonged here [in Scotland] [...] one that always had to be imported as a finished, packaged article' from other national cultures.[13] Of course, assessing the 'national' character of individual film texts is a contentious exercise. Yet we can perhaps identify the first 'truly' Scottish film after the silent era, that is, one wholly created, produced *and* financed by domestic personnel and capital, as late as Bill Forsyth's *That Sinking Feeling* (1979). That film was accurately described by its maker as 'the first narrative feature made by someone living in Scotland, perpetrated by someone – house-produced so to speak – from the resources of the country'.[14]

Although a meaningful amelioration thus began to gather pace around the beginning of the 1980s, the historical fact of Scotland's persistent film industrial underdevelopment had a profound intellectual corollary for the pioneering Scottish film criticism that also began to emerge in significant volume at this

---

[12] For a comparative discussion of Scotland and Ireland in this regard, see Murray, 'Sibling Rivalry? Contemporary Scottish and Irish Cinemas'.
[13] Bruce, 'Feature Film-Making: Realities and Prospects', p. 40. My insert.
[14] Quoted in Stein, 'The Forsyth Saga', p. 55.

time. For many contemporary critics, David Bruce's idea of 'importation' signified an infrastructural vulnerability lamentable because it simultaneously illustrated and entailed certain profoundly regressive ideological and cultural conditions of existence for Scottish society as a whole. The first academic writers on Scottish cinema in the late '70s and early '80s[15] typically explained the puzzling absence of an adequate infrastructural framework within which an indigenous feature cinema might have emerged by proposing that Scotland had been subject to long-term, inter-locking processes of discursive and industrial colonisation at the hands of American and British metropolitan cinemas. Given the provenance of its creative talent and production capital, a film like *The Wicker Man* could easily have been presented by critics writing at this time as microcosmic evidence of these much wider processes at work.

1980s Scottish cinema criticism therefore sought both to explain the historical roots, and diagnose the contemporary consequences, of a traditionally uncontested external saturation of the local commercial cinema marketplace by British and American-produced representations of Scotland. The key argument developed with regards to the latter concern was that distorted domestic understandings of Scottish history, culture and identity had been incrementally imposed upon the national sphere via the fruits of other cinemas, in a kind of national cultural equivalent of Chinese Water Torture. For Colin McArthur, writing in 1983, the available reservoir of Scottish cinematic images typically 'fitted the needs of others rather than the needs of Scots'.[16] Alastair Michie argued some three years later that the lamentable history of indigenous Scottish feature cinema's 'non-existence' had been one where, in symbiotic industrial and ideological senses, 'we can put together a picture of a people losing control of their film representation from the word go'.[17]

Consequently, so the argument ran, generations of Scots had internalised self-understandings of their history and identity manufactured at both a geographic and cultural remove from their own national sphere. And, such hegemonic 'foreign'

---

[15] The seminal publication in this regard is McArthur, ed., *Scotch Reels*.

[16] McArthur, 'Tendencies in the New Scottish Cinema', p. 33.

[17] Michie, 'Scotland: Strategies of Centralisation', p. 253.

understandings were profoundly regressive ones. They were unable, and indeed unconcerned, to fully reflect the actual complexity of lived experience within Scottish society past or present. This ideation of both Scottish cinema specifically and Scotland's representation in film more generally saw these as both expressive metaphors for, and influential enabling mechanisms of, a stunted modern-day national culture. Scottish audiences, as well as the country's historical and creative resources, had been subjected to pervasive waves of ideological and economic colonial exploitation. Such assaults had been facilitated to a significant degree through the monopolisation of the infrastructural and economic means of film production and representation by elite constituencies resident within other national societies.

Given the nature of this contemporary intellectual backdrop, a 'typical' 1980s reading of *The Wicker Man* would very probably have concentrated its attention upon the text's conscious ascription of colonial and feudal discourses to its anti-hero, Lord Summerisle. Indeed, Summerisle's explanation to Sergeant Howie of the reasons for his family's absolute dominion over the native islanders echoes, to a striking degree, the terms of early Scottish film criticism's key debates, for example, its quest to identify and isolate specific, originary historical moments of ideological and economic 'colonisation' by individual agents and institutions from other national societies. As Summerisle explains to Howie, in 1868, the former's grandfather 'rous[ed] the people from their apathy by giving them back their old Gods', thus cynically rendering the island economically productive for the dynasty. Early '80s Scottish film critics would have very likely seized upon these elements of *The Wicker Man* as over-determined, symptomatic references to the troubled cultural and historical legacies of Scotland's ambiguous, quasi-colonial relationship with the British State and global Imperium post-1707.

Moreover, Summerisle and Howie's initial confrontation also appears to speak with salutary clarity to 1980s criticism's desire to highlight the extent to which deeply regressive ideations of Scottish identity had – so it was believed – become internalised and essentialised by colonising and colonised national formations

alike. This was allegedly so long after the material roots of such
ideations in the social, political and economic needs and struggles
of a given historical moment had been all but obscured and
forgotten. Summerisle appears to gloss just such a material
historical process for Howie's benefit when he explains,
paradigmatically enough, that 'what my grandfather had started
out of expediency, my father continued out of love [...] to
reverence the music, the drama, the rituals of the old Gods'. The
absent figure of Summerisle's grandfather is clearly constructed
here as colonial entrepreneur, manipulating indigenous cultural
beliefs and natural resources to meet the ends of an externally
imported, unspoken project of economic rationality. Crucially,
however, the actions and professed beliefs of his progeny cannot
be understood with such unambiguous ease. The extent to which
Summerisle Junior, the modern islanders' enthusiastic High
Priest, has himself become, like his father and the islanders they
apparently manipulate, interpellated by the repressive colonial
apparatus created by their forebear, remains to *The Wicker Man*'s
denouement tantalisingly unclear.

The attraction of *The Wicker Man* for early Scottish cinema
critics might, then, conceivably have proved two-fold. In an
immediately obvious sense, it firstly involves the text's external
articulation and imposition of a purportedly 'colonising'
representational trope ('Scotland' as Anti-Modern Island
Wilderness). Well into the 1990s, for example, Colin McArthur,
the doyen of 1980s Scottish film criticism, continued to
confidently term Scotland, at least 'on the filmmaking front', a
'Third World country'.[18] Yet it might also be noted that the
insertion of *The Wicker Man* into the 'The Wilds of Scotland'
paradigm is complicated substantially once a process of close
textual analysis is begun. Then, the film appears a paradoxically
fractured text, as much a metacommentary on the 'Wilderness'
paradigm as it is a striking example of it in action. Key here is
The Wicker Man's apparently self-conscious allegorisation,
through Summerisle's explicatory monologue, both of the kinds
of reasons why such colonial representational models of

---

[18] McArthur, 'In Praise of a Poor Cinema', p. 30.

'Scotland' were formulated in the past, and why they stubbornly endure into the present.

Yet, having now reconstructed a hypothetically representative 1980s Scottish film critical reading of *The Wicker Man*, it might even be possible to go yet further, generating an actively sympathetic reading of this film. The most optimistic textual analysis of all would be one in which *The Wicker Man* deliberately invokes and inhabits, as opposed to unconsciously if vividly exemplifying, hegemonic film and popular cultural constructions of 'Scotland', with the express intent of destroying these from within. After all, it is possible to argue that, rather than simply being colonised dupes, the islanders in fact calculatedly masquerade certain aspects of their 'primitivism'. This is done in order to entrap and sacrifice Howie, a figure ostensibly empowered and protected through his status as authoritative representative of civilised Modernity, in the very specific manner required.

This latter (strategically selective) allegorical reading is not simply one in which a confident and cohesive Scottish culture is seen to subvert and ultimately appropriate the colonial shackles of a historically oppressive, externally dictated national-representational apparatus. It is also one predicated on the belief that such a liberating national cultural advance is most readily achieved through covert sabotage and ironic inhabitation, not overt destruction and outraged recantation, of an historic armature of 'Scottish' stereotypes encountered in cinema and other popular cultural forms. I highlight the possibility of such a reading of *The Wicker Man* at this point because it illustrates the material critical approach to both questions of national representation and industrial development within Scottish film culture that came to assume the mantle of critical orthodoxy with the advent of the 1990s.

Mapping the Scottish Cinematic 'Wilderness' II: 1990s rhetorics of postcolonialism

From the early 1990s, a locally based Scottish production industry expanded rapidly in the wake of key international commercial and/or critical successes such as *Trainspotting* (Boyle, 1996) and *Ratcatcher* (Ramsay, 1999). Against and

encouraged by this contemporary cinematic backdrop, an
increasing number of critics have argued (often in rather patchily
theorised terms) that both Scottish film and national cultures are
belatedly entering a 'postcolonial' phase.[19]

Many such '90s usages of the postcolonial metaphor applied to
Scottish culture, filmic or otherwise, stressed both the necessity
and increasing actuality of radical, celebratory re-evaluations of
what increasingly came to be seen as a 'victimised' national-
cultural history, to date part-critically disparaged, part-critically
ignored. Symptomatically, Robert Houston and William Knox,
editors of a recent major anthology surveying the entire
chronological sweep of Scottish history, begin their introduction
to that volume by quoting the early twentieth century African-
American novelist James Baldwin: 'If you know whence you
came, there is really no limit to where you can go'. 'More than
most Europeans', Houston and Knox contend, 'the Scots can
identify with Baldwin's sentiments.'[20] The inference can only be
that this is because '*the* [sic] Scots' and African-Americans have
each endured comparable, generations-long histories of
systematic exclusion on the grounds of ethnic discrimination,
from wider, 'alien' national historiographic traditions and social
structures, within which they were originally subsumed by
historical accident and/or misfortune, but certainly through no
fault or wish of their own. Michael Coyne illustrates, with
specific reference to the history of Scotland's cinematic
representation, the same general contemporary ideation of
modern national history and identity when he asks, with blithe
rhetorical certainty:

> Is there any real difference between the eye-
> rolling antics of [the late Scottish character
> actor] John Laurie (1897-1980) and those of
> Stepin Fetchit (1902 - 1985) [the late African-
> American character actor ostracised by many

---

[19] See, for example, Morgan-James, 'Postcolonial Reflections of Scottish
Landscape in cinema'.
[20] Houston and Knox, 'Introduction: Scots and their Histories', p. xiii.

African-Americans due to his racially
offensive, stereotypical screen persona]?[21]

If critics like those quoted directly above are to be believed, both
communities currently contend with, but are in the process of
overcoming, roughly equivalent senses of cultural and racial
inferiority. The historic 'colonisations' of Scots and African-
Americans by other ethnic groups relied upon, and therefore
aimed to inculcate, such collective self-abnegation.

The assertions of Houston, Knox and Coyne are as
methodologically problematic as they are representative of
certain recent Scottish intellectual fashions. Ironically, such
intemperate effusions look less like a convincingly 'postcolonial'
reframing of modern Scottish history and culture, and more like
the last, mendacious gasp of North British Imperialism. Here, it is
the intellectual and cultural resources of an oppressed diasporic
ethnic community (for example, James Baldwin's prose and the
ideas it expresses) that are rapaciously plundered and
appropriated by individual mouthpieces of authority within First
World societies, academic 'Scotsmen on the Make'.

Yet for the very specific purposes of this essay, the rise of a
celebratory, albeit often under-theorised, postcolonial rhetoric
within the study of Scottish culture is significant for a more
modest reason. It is the increasing fashionability of the
postcolonial paradigm that explains the radical reformation of
Scottish cinema criticism's governing theoretical axioms and
methodologies from the early '90s onwards. We have already
seen that the pioneering 1980s theorists of the relationship
between Scotland and cinema generally framed their conclusions
within an overtly stated colonial paradigm, identifying Scottish
culture and society as entities oppressed, culturally and
industrially, by the institutions and texts of metropolitan British
and American film industries. Yet while a set of diffuse colonial
and/or postcolonial metaphors held fairly consistent sway in
Scottish film criticism as the '80s gave way to the '90s, the
institutions and texts most often identified as the key perpetrators

---

[21] Coyne, 'Review: *Brigadoon, Braveheart and the Scots*', p. 314. My inserts.

of Scottish cinema and national cultures' perceived subjugation
have changed radically.

The broad terms of this transformation proceeded roughly as
follows. As noted above, during the 1980s, an endemically
distorted modern Scottish national culture and identity was most
commonly believed to be due to the alleged ideological impact of
a massive corpus of externally produced cinematic and popular
cultural representations of 'Scotland'. In the 1990s, by contrast,
the prime instruments of Scottish culture's still-assented-to
'oppression' increasingly came to be seen as precisely such
earlier theorisations. What was believed during the 1980s by its
protagonists to be an oppositional contestation of national cultural
colonisation was re-evaluated in the 1990s, and 'unmasked' as an
insidious form of internally generated and policed colonial
oppression in and of itself. In other words, the terms in which an
earlier generation of critics diagnosed Scottish film and national
cultures' central problems in turn *became* just those burdens in
the minds of the former's immediate successors.

Adrienne Scullion, writing in 1996, neatly glossed this tectonic
shift within the study of Scottish culture as one that
contemporarily perceived a 'crisis not of the national culture *per
se* but of the critical agenda'[22] within which the former's
achievements (including its persistent inability to produce a
sustainable indigenous feature cinema) had been despairingly
assessed in past times. In an equally pithy and representative
distillation of the same quintessential 1990s argument, David
McCrone stated that the most historically pervasive and distorting
constructions of Scottish culture and identity were not to be found
in a range of externally-produced stereotypes of 'Scottishness',
filmic or otherwise. Rather, the real culprits were 'the limited
discourses adopted by Scottish intellectuals in their analysis of
[Scottish] culture'.[23] Here he has the work of the first prominent
Scottish cinema critics such as Colin McArthur explicitly in
mind. Elsewhere, Craig Beveridge and Ronald Turnbull
specifically attacked McArthur's 'colonial' categorisation and
theorisation of Scottish cinema and national culture. For the

---

[22] Scullion, 'Feminine Pleasures and Masculine Indignities', p. 202. My insert.
[23] McCrone, *Understanding Scotland*, p. 189.

former, the bitter irony of the latter's position is that it itself becomes an instrument through which the oppression of Scottish culture was perpetuated, rather than, as was McArthur's conscious intention, diagnosed and contested. For Beveridge and Turnbull, McArthur's reduction of Scotland's relationship with cinema to one of helpless indigenous oppression at the hands of international popular cultural forms and producers 'accords perfectly with the governing image of Scotland as a dark and backward culture,'[24] which the latter misguidedly claimed he was trying to destroy.

Such radical reassessments by the Scottish intelligentsia of its own critical heritage began to find their way into Scottish cinema studies proper. Discussing the relationship between film costume and British national identity, Pam Cook, for example, recuperates the historically inaccurate, mythically archetypal, Hollywood studio-financed 'kilted western' *Rob Roy* (Caton-Jones, 1995). This is another film that draws heavily and premeditatedly on the 'Last Great Wilderness' trope. Crucially, Cook reads *Rob Roy* sympathetically not despite, *but precisely because of*, the major representational debt owed by its construction of Scottish history and identity. The deliberate acceptance of this debt by *Rob Roy*'s key Scottish creative personnel, screenwriter Alan Sharp, producer Peter Broughan and director Michael Caton-Jones, can in retrospect be rationalised as a deliberate local perpetuation of an over-familiar image of 'Scotland' in order to access American production capital and global exhibition markets, thus making the project economically viable.[25] However, ignoring such germane financial/industrial considerations, Cook prefers in her reading to instead explicitly dismiss the originary 'discursive colonisation' thesis of early Scottish cinema criticism, arguing that:

> Nostalgia might play a productive role in national identity, releasing the desire for social change or resistance [...] This idealised version of [Scottish/British] history may appear to have

---

[24] Beveridge and Turnbull, *The Eclipse of Scottish Culture*, p. 14.

[25] For an explanation and illustration of this thesis in the words of *Rob Roy*'s key creative personnel, see the detailed account of the film's development, financing and production practices in Finney, 'Rob Roy: Case Study No. 3'.

> little to do with 'reality', past or present [...]
> [but] it seems more pertinent to investigate the
> emotional appeal of reliving the past and the
> part this plays in popular imaginings of
> community and resistance at specific historical
> moments.[26]

Elsewhere, but in a manner equally symptomatic of
contemporary critical fashion, the same author praises the
representation of Scotland in Michael Powell and Emeric
Pressburger's *I Know Where I'm Going!* (1945). This film is, of
course, another utopian variation on the 'Wilderness' paradigm,
albeit remarkable for its heady degree of aesthetic and narrative
accomplishment. Again, with regard to *I Know...*'s textual
construction of 'Scotland', Cook encourages readers to view the
film's pre-meditated artifice, inauthenticity and self-conscious
appeal to mythic archetype as essentially progressive, not
regressive, discourses:

> A series of visual and auditory puns introduce
> *IKWIG*'s Scotland as entirely a mythical
> construction... It is tempting to view these
> playful strategies as a deconstruction of
> stereotypes, and to see *IKWIG!* as contributing
> to a debate about representations of
> Scottishness... [through] its concern with the
> relationship between illusion and reality, and
> with the power of myth...[27]

In a near-identical vein, Duncan Petrie, easily the most prominent
contemporary Scottish cinema scholar, asserts of *The Wicker
Man* itself that:

> The religious practices depicted are [...]
> subject to creative license, comprising a pot-
> pourri of elements drawn from a variety of

---

[26] Cook, *Fashioning the Nation*, p. 26. My insert.
[27] Cook, *I Know Where I'm Going*, p. 33.

> pagan rituals and including some very English
> motifs, such as the maypole and the figure of
> Mr Punch. But to criticise the film for its lack
> of authenticity is a pointless exercise.[28]

Unfortunately, the justification for a definitive dismissal of 'pointless' concerns with issues of authenticity and accuracy in national cultural representation remain somewhat unelaborated within Petrie's argument. One suspects that the unspoken reason, one that Cook makes overtly clear in her discussion of *Rob Roy*, involves the pressing desire to disavow in doctrinaire terms the signature methodologies and conclusions of an earlier school of Scottish film criticism.

Perhaps the most sophisticated example of the self-transformation of such criticism that I am attempting to identify and describe here can be detected in an essay by Jane Sillars. She identifies two broad generic, aesthetic and thematic traditions of representing 'Scotland' in popular audiovisual cultures. These Sillars labels 'Naturalism' and 'Whimsy', and in terms of the long-sought-after goal of constructing industrially sustainable and culturally progressive Scottish film and television production sectors, she is at pains to sing the praises of the latter. Sillars argues that Whimsy's distinguishing generic mark is its signature ironic construction of 'Scotland' as a skewed local variant upon the Arcadian myth. The Whimsy genre's textual strategies characteristically work, Sillars argues, 'through comic reverse', embodied in whimsical texts' knowing quotation of historically established, externally produced iconographic and narrative templates of 'Scottishness'.

In the context of the steady post-1990 expansion of local audiovisual production activity, one potential attraction of Whimsy's keynote strategy of quotation is that, according to Sillars, it allows for the fruitful local subversion of what were previously understood to be predetermining, externally imposed 'dominant models'[29] of Scottish national identity, the 'Wilderness' paradigm key among these. For, in Whimsy,

---

[28] Petrie, *Screening Scotland*, p. 49.
[29] Sillars, 'Drama, Devolution and Dominant Representations', p. 250.

cinematic 'Scotland' is a land populated by natives who sidestep
repressive prescriptions of gender, class and other forms of social
and national identities, both in their relationships with each other
and in the transformative effects they wield over visitors from
other cultures: 'if naturalism proposes that people are shaped by
their environment, then whimsy presents means by which they
negotiate their placing'.[30] Thus, the central progressive aspect of
this Scottish representational tradition as proposed by Sillars is its
fundamentally anti-authoritarian impulse. It is hopefully no great
leap to see how yet another hypothetical reading of *The Wicker
Man*, for example, could easily classify it as a 'Whimsical' text
and cite it as evidence for this representational tradition's
historical existence and material influence.

But Sillars also suggests another attraction to a strategy of local
quotation and recreation of whimsical stereotypes of
'Scottishness' traditionally articulated within other national
cinemas. This is that it forms a lucrative marketing tool at the
disposal of an infant Scottish audiovisual production sector: 'the
use of heavily stereotypical depictions of Scotland works to
market an exportable product'.[31] Sillars implies that the nation's
aspirant film producers can learn economically valuable lessons
that run parallel to the ideologically progressive ones purportedly
offered both to fictional characters within and material audiences
for Whimsical film and television texts. Whimsy's typically
reductive national imagery can thus be seen to primarily
prefabricate profitably exportable cultural commodities, as
opposed to problematic ideological conundrums, for
contemporary Scottish film and national cultures.

For Sillars, this is so because the characteristic, heavily ironic
framing of national stereotypes within contemporary indigenous
variants of Whimsy precludes their damaging, unconscious
internalisation by Scottish viewers. A domestic audience is
instead prompted to consciously participate in a lucrative national
masquerade, 'invited to share in the process of playing up to
stereotypes in pursuit of gain'[32], as do the villagers of Forsyth's
Local Hero, for example (and this is not to mention the

---

[30] Sillars, 'Drama, Devolution and Dominant Representations', p. 250.

[31] Sillars, 'Drama, Devolution and Dominant Representations', p. 251.

[32] Sillars, 'Drama, Devolution and Dominant Representations', p. 251.

Summerislanders of *The Wicker Man*). Knowing local appropriation of, and strategic, feigned acquiescence within, established representational traditions of 'Scotland' is therefore claimed as an industrially fertile, but ideologically sterilised, developmental agenda for Scottish cinema. The 1995 film epic version of the Rob Roy myth noted above, written, produced and directed by Scots bankrolled by Hollywood capital, might be one quintessential example of this strategy in action, as would the slyly misleading invocation of *The Wicker Man* by the makers of *The Last Great Wilderness*.

The appeal of *The Wicker Man* to this latterly dominant model of Scottish film criticism is, then, as follows. Firstly, in ideological terms, the film can be read as an anti-authoritarian parable *par excellence*. When Sergeant Howie, the figure of apparent external authority and identity, warns Miss Rose, the local schoolteacher, that, 'I hope you don't think I can be made a fool of indefinitely', her delayed, but ultimately damning, answer is: 'for all eternity'. For a parallel, late '90s film industrial/commercial perspective, the belief that an indigenous Scottish feature cinema could create a reliably lucrative international market for its textual products by concentrating collective creative energies on a subversive, because apparently quiescent, recycling of Scottish identity stereotypes was certainly seductive. Might not gullible overseas audiences (excepting those with second degrees and/or substantial personal experience of Scotland) be thus 'fooled', at least for the foreseeable future, if not quite 'for all eternity'? Extrapolating Sillars' implicit argument that the thematic lessons of Whimsical texts have close industrial analogues for contemporary Scottish filmmakers, and hypothesising that *The Wicker Man* might conceivably be read to exemplify her point, the islanders' hideously successful deception thus becomes metaphorically resonant. It could be seen to challenge traditionally accepted assumptions regarding the supposedly Manichean distinctions between the respective amounts of cultural and political capital available to the Scottish national sphere and to those external national formations previously asserted to have tailored popular cultural representations of 'Scotland' solely to their own economic and ideological needs.

Thus, within this representative kind of contemporary critical discourse, *The Wicker Man*'s elaborate textual deceptions and reverses would become powerfully emblematic. They might be seen to indicate the extent to which Scotland's oft-asserted 'discursive colonisation' across a range of popular cultural forms, including cinema, would be best symbolised by a man made of straw, not wicker. For, in a suggestive precursor of Sillars' ideologically *and* industrially privileged concept of domestic whimsical masquerade, *The Wicker Man* could be taken to proselytise on behalf of subversive, carnivalesque processes of cross-cultural encounter. Here, in Summerisle's words, it is 'the hunted leading the hunter [...] we who have found you and brought you here and controlled your every thought and action'. Consequently, even if forced to accept that British metropolitan and American cinemas unquestionably dominated the twentieth-century cinematic representation of Scotland in industrial terms, the national-cultural consequences of this historical process come to seem far less damaging, ideologically speaking, than they once did.

Such a belief relies on two key propositions. First, as with nearly all 1990s and '00s Scottish film criticism, there is a conviction that classic externally-produced, ostensibly colonising cinematic constructions of 'Scotland' should now be recognised as far more ideologically fractured, multifaceted and ultimately recuperable than first given credit for. Indeed, this essay has itself attempted to demonstrate ways in which *The Wicker Man* might be engaged with in this regard. Even Colin McArthur has recently conceded, in accordance with the general trend noted directly above, that:

> [My] historical polemic against aspects of *Brigadoon* has eased to the point where [I] now better appreciate its charm and its far from negligible aesthetic qualities while still finding its representation of Scotland and the Scots problematic.[33]

---

[33] McArthur, *Brigadoon, Braveheart and the Scots*, p. 5.

There is certainly something to recommend this collective shift away from certain originary strictures of 1980s Scottish film criticism. It is useful to acknowledge that the critical orthodoxy of that period was too rigidly structuralist. Its individual textual analyses often made films forcibly conform to the pre-existing 'discursive colonisation' thesis. The possibility that individual texts might – as *The Wicker Man* seems to – instead complicate, qualify or simply provoke further elaboration of that paradigm was overlooked.[34] This omission can now be rectified on a film-to-film basis.

However, the second argument underlying recent criticism's downgrading of both the validity and scope of the traditional 'colonisation' thesis is far more contestable. In the most optimistic prognoses, the belated rise of an indigenous Scottish cinema is taken to indicate that previously dominant external industrial and cultural formations, American and British metropolitan cinemas, have ultimately proved to be, as Miss Rose might put it, but 'king for a day'. In Sillars' reading of contemporary Scottish film and television cultures for example, the stereotypical arsenal of historic cultural colonisers has been hijacked by hitherto oppressed natives, who, with poetic justice and an eye for a discreet *coup d'theatre*, turn them on their previous owners. Such contemporarily influential, diffusely 'postcolonial' reasonings neatly circumvent Ellen-Raïssa Jackson's anxiety regarding much recent Scottish cinema, namely that while 'the traumatic search for a modern identity is a familiar postcolonial problem, [it is also] one that is complicated in a cinematic context by the commercial attraction of a ready-made brand [of 'Scottishness']'.[35] After all, the methodological attractiveness and sophistication of Sillars' representative model of criticism is that (as with Cook's reading of *Rob Roy*) it cleverly rationalises the 'commercial attraction' of regurgitated national cinematic stereotypes into an ostensibly progressive form of postcolonial national identity politics.

Of course, it cannot be argued that such contemporary approaches are wholly without precedent within Scottish and

---

[34] See Caughie, 'Representing Scotland' for the most authoritative example of this general argument.
[35] Jackson, 'Dislocating the Nation', p. 125.

British cinema studies. After all, as early as 1977, Charles Barr could be found arguing that *Whisky Galore!* (the text we began by aligning *The Wicker Man* with), in its knowing exploitation/deconstruction of stereotypical Scottish identities:

> keeps confronting us with surfaces, appearances to be interpreted [...] an English audience, at least, is drawn into the film in the manner of the English sergeant [Sgt. Odd, an incomer who marries into the island community at *Whisky Galore!*'s climax]... [the island] embodies an ancestral Celtic shrewdness and toughness, from which we could learn, from which we should learn, from which the Sergeant learns. Waggett does not...[36]

The central point, however, has to do with scale. Between the late 1970s and the present, individual peccadilloes like Barr's have been reified into an increasingly powerful disciplinary orthodoxy. This has directly affected the conclusions typically reached and, perhaps even more fundamentally, the questions typically asked, in the contemporary study of Scottish cinema and Scotland's representation on film.

In conclusion, there are serious questions to be asked of this orthodoxy. Positions like those of Sillars, Cook, Petrie and others neither significantly bemoan nor dissent from the traditional thesis that the terms of Scotland's representation in audiovisual culture have always been markedly curtailed, through their blanket subjugation to a painfully limited range of externally dictated, albeit recently locally re-inflected, generic and ideological prototypes. Rather, they claim – not wholly without justification – that the problem has been to do with the markedly and monotonously hostile way in which that historical-cultural phenomenon was previously interpreted by key theorists of Scottish cinema and national culture. Present-day critics are quite understandably more exercised by the immediate possibility of a

---

[36] Barr, *Ealing Studios*, p. 115, p. 118.

reformist qualification of Scottish cinema's industrial marginality in both British and international contexts, a prospect that quite simply seemed impossible as little as a decade-and-a-half ago. Yet their typical arguments, for all the surface bullishness, appear implicitly to concede that, in order to compete effectively on one terrain – industrial and economic development – another, more ostensibly politicised one – radical creative innovation within traditions of national-cultural representation and debate – has to be ceded definitively. At very best, the representational terrain is to be contested in a very narrow range of ways, through piecemeal guerrilla operations. In other words, if one were being especially uncharitable it might seem that indigenous filmmakers are left little to do other than fiddle cannily with hoary Scottish stereotypes.

Indeed, the possibility of such a scenario is at least countenanced by certain prominent Scottish producers and commissioners, even if not by their academic counterparts. For example, in 2004 the recently-retired Controller of BBC Scotland, John McCormick, had this to say of that broadcaster's long-running Sunday evening popular television drama *Monarch of the Glen* (a prime example of Sillar's lucrative Highland Whimsy in action if ever there was one):

> *Monarch of the Glen* does raise interesting issues. I just came back from Australia where it's playing on a Saturday at 7.30 and getting record audiences. And you have that kind of feeling like 'is that what they think contemporary Scotland's like?'[37]

To be fair, McCormick elsewhere argues (like Sillars and others) that contemporary audiences are now largely inured to the more deleterious side-effects of stereotypical representations of 'Scottishness'; he also maintains that commercial successes like *Monarch* are vital in creating and maintaining the industrial conditions in which more aesthetically and thematically challenging material can be produced from Scotland. What he

---

[37] Geraghty and Goode, 'An Interview with John McCormick', p. 280.

does not do, however, is present the whimsy of *Monarch* as a progressive intervention within the Scottish national sphere *simply in and of itself*; rather, he sees it as a potentially facilitating factor in the creation of such interventions elsewhere within the Scottish production sector. Yet much current Scottish film criticism seems determined to obscure such complex industrial and political considerations and qualifications. The suspicion is that commercial necessity is repeatedly misrepresented as national-cultural virtue in recent work by influential academic commentators on Scottish moving image cultures.

Here, yet again, *The Wicker Man* hoves into view. Part of this film's interest lies in its complex warning about the dangers inherent in internally coherent but unself-reflexive belief systems reliant upon unverifiable articles of faith. Despite the otherwise wholly antinomic opposition that the film constructs between them, the discourses of both Sergeant Howie and the Summerislanders are comparably flawed and vulnerable in this regard. The doctrinaire, quasi-postcolonial optimism that has overtaken much recent writing on Scottish cinema's industrial prospects and national-cultural significance is itself similarly compromised. We should apply *The Wicker Man*'s lessons about the dangers of ecstatic certainty to much contemporary film criticism emanating from the culture that the film itself so famously imagines.

Bibliography
Barr, C., *Ealing Studios* (London: Cameron and Tayleur, 1977).
Bartholomew, D., '*The Wicker Man*', *Cinefantastique,* 6.3, Winter (1977), 4-18; 32-46.
Beveridge, C. and R. Turnbull, *The Eclipse of Scottish Culture: Inferiorism and the intellectuals* (Edinburgh: Polygon, 1989).
Brown, J., 'A Suitable Job for a Scot', *Sight and Sound*, 52.3, Summer (1983), 157-62.
Bruce, D., 'Feature Film-Making: Realities and prospects', in *The Scottish Review*, 1. 4, Autumn (1976), 38-43.
Caughie, J., 'Support whose Local Hero?', *Cencrastus*, 14, Autumn (1983), 44-46.

_____, 'Representing Scotland: New questions for Scottish cinema', in *From Limelight to Satellite: A Scottish film book*, ed. by E. Dick (London/Glasgow: BFI/SFC, 1990), pp. 13-30.

Cook, P., *Fashioning the Nation: Costume and identity in British cinema* (London: BFI, 1996).

_____, *I Know Where I'm Going* (London: BFI, 2002).

Coyne, M., 'Review: *Brigadoon, Braveheart and the Scots*', *Journal of British Cinema and Television*, 1. 2, (2004), 212-15.

Finney, A., 'Rob Roy: Case Study No. 3', in A. Finney, *The State of European Cinema: A new dose of reality* (London: Cassell, 1996), pp. 192-202.

Geraghty, C. and I. Goode, 'An Interview with John McCormick', *Journal of British Cinema and Television*, 1. 2, (2004), 275-86.

Houston, R. A. and W. W. J. Knox, 'Introduction: Scots and their histories', in *The New Penguin History of Scotland: From the earliest times to the present day*, ed. by R. A. Houston and W. W. J. Knox (London: Penguin, 2001), xii-lviii.

Hutchinson, R., *Polly: The true story behind 'Whisky Galore!'* (Edinburgh: Mainstream, 1998).

Jackson, E.-R., 'Dislocating the Nation: Political devolution and cultural identity on stage and screen', *Edinburgh Review,* 110 (2002), 120-31.

Kemp, P., *Lethal Innocence: The cinema of Alexander Mackendrick*, (London: Methuen, 1991).

McArthur, C., *Brigadoon, Braveheart and the Scots: Distortions of Scotland in Hollywood cinema* (London: I. B. Tauris, 2003).

_____, 'In Praise of a Poor Cinema', *Sight and Sound*, 3.8, August (1993), 30-32.

_____, 'The Scottish Discursive Unconscious', in *Scottish Popular Theatre and Entertainment: Historical and critical approaches to theatre and film in Scotland*, ed. by A. Cameron and A. Scullion (Glasgow: Glasgow University Library, 1996), pp. 81-89.

_____, ed., *Scotch Reels: Scotland in cinema and television* (London: BFI, 1982).

_____, 'Tendencies in the New Scottish Cinema', *Cencrastus*, 13, Summer (1983), 33-35.

_____, *Whisky Galore and The Maggie* (London: I. B. Tauris, 2003).

McCrone, D., *Understanding Scotland: The sociology of a stateless nation* (London: Routledge, 1992).

Michie, A., 'Scotland: Strategies of centralisation', in *All Our Yesterdays: 90 years of British cinema*, ed. by C. Barr (London: BFI, 1986), pp. 252-70.

Morgan James, A., 'Postcolonial Reflections of Scottish Landscape in cinema', in *European Cinema: Inside out, images of the self and the Other in postcolonial European film*, ed. by G. Rings and R. Morgan-Tamosunas (Heidelberg: Universitätsverlag, 2003), pp. 119-32.

Murray, J., 'Sibling Rivalry? Contemporary Scottish and Irish Cinemas', in *Ireland and Scotland: Culture and society, 1707-2000*, ed. by L. McIlvanney and R. Ryan (Dublin: Four Courts, 2005), pp. 144-63.

Petrie, D., *Screening Scotland* (London: BFI, 2000).

Riach, A., *Representing Scotland in Literature, Popular Culture and Iconography: The masks of the modern nation* (Basingstoke: Palgrave Macmillan, 2005).

Richards, A., '*The Last Great Wilderness*: Review', *Sight and Sound*, 13.6, June (2003), 49.

Scullion, A., 'Feminine Pleasures and Masculine Indignities: Gender and community in Scottish drama', in *Gendering the Nation: Studies in modern Scottish literature,* ed. by C. Whyte (Edinburgh: Edinburgh University Press, 1996), pp. 169-204.

Sillars, J., 'Drama, Devolution and Dominant Representations', in *The Media in Britain: Current debates and developments*, ed. by J. Stokes and A. Reading (Basingstoke: Macmillan, 1999), pp. 246-56.

Stein, E., 'The Forsyth Saga', in *American Film*, 10.2, November (1984), 54-57.

Street, S., *Transatlantic Crossings: British feature films in the USA* (New York and London: Continuum, 2002).

Religion in *The Wicker Man*: Context and representation

Steven J. Sutcliffe

Introduction: Popular religion

In this chapter I treat *The Wicker Man* (Hardy, 1973) as a symptom of broader cultural change by focusing on the discursive context of the film's production: that is to say, I want to explore how the film – and in particular, its representations of 'religion' – becomes the *product* of a particular set of historical and cultural forces. My intention is to contextualise the script and imagery of the film within wider discourses on 'religion' in an emergent post-Christian culture of the late 1960s and early 1970s. I hope to show how a *popular* mode of representation, at work in both 'authorial' intention and audience reception, mirrors a wider hermeneutic turn towards 'the popular' in the period in question. In this era 'religion' increasingly becomes both an object of social critique, as it is for the filmmakers here, and a 'potent cultural resource'[1] for new identity-making practices, as evidenced in Pagan reclamations of the film.

My wider perspective is the politics of category formation in 'religion', by which I mean simply the comparative history and ethnography of how, when, where, why and by whom 'religion' gets defined, enacted, legitimated, transmitted and contested in the many specific ways that it does.[2] Defining, practising and representing 'religion' in a post-Christian era can be highly politicised activities, whether undertaken by academics or practitioners.[3] In particular, I am interested in *popular* practices and representations of 'religion'. By 'popular' I mean the practice and representation of 'religion' in everyday contexts by non-specialist practitioners[4] who appeal to variegated and diffuse sources to authenticate and legitimate how they do 'religion', and not just (sometimes not at all) to ecclesiastical doctrine and expert theology.

---

[1] Beckford, *Religion and Advanced Industrial Society*, p. 170.
[2] See Smith, 'Religion, Religions, Religious'.
[3] Baird, *Category Formation and the History of Religions*; McCutcheon, *Manufacturing Religion*.
[4] Compare Sutcliffe, *Children of the New Age*, on 'New Age' seekers.

In an influential etymological essay, Raymond Williams argues that 'popular' derives from Latin *popularis*, a legal term meaning 'of or belonging to the people'.[5] 'Popular' in the sense of 'widely-favoured', he writes, emerged around the late eighteenth century, with the connotation of 'well-liked' following in the nineteenth. Williams claims that 'popular' by the early 1970s implied demotic culture: a set of practices and preferences made and validated by people for themselves. Although this is only implicit in Williams' account, culture is heterogenous rather than homogenous. For him, it is a site of struggle rather than stasis, a politicised arena in which rivalrous identities and practices are simultaneously realised, critiqued and suppressed. This was so for 'religious' discourses, no less than for those of class, gender, sexuality or ethnicity (to cite just some of the spectrum of cultural identities 'coming out' in the 1960s).[6] The filmmakers' portrayal of 'religion' on Summerisle, derived conceptually from a particular antiquarian source (J. G. Frazer's *The Golden Bough* [1890-1922]) and constructed in a very specific historical context of religious decline and innovation marked by popular, mass-media representations of witchcraft and paganism, is one kind of 'popular' representation of 'religion'; the Pagan audience reclamation of the film, following its original unhappy release, is another.

My argument is in three stages: first, I map specific 'Christian' and 'Pagan' representations in the film; second, I briefly contextualise these within the cultural history of the late 1960s and early 1970s; third, I examine the tension between the authorial (*auteur*) irony of the film's creators, principally director Robin Hardy and screenwriter Anthony Shaffer, and the popular Paganism of later audience interpretations. The chapter as a whole has two overall aims: first, it contextualises, historically and materially, *The Wicker Man,* both as a celluloid product of its time and place, and as the object of a particular 'cult' audience (Pagan) act of appropriation; second, it contextualises the film's representations of 'religion' within an expanding series of

---

[5] Williams, *Keywords*, pp. 198-99.
[6] For fuller discussion of 'culture' in relation to 'religion', see Masuzawa, 'Culture', and Lincoln, 'Culture'.

popular reconfigurations of cultural institutions during a
particular historical period.

'Christians' and 'Pagans' in *The Wicker Man*

Representing 'religion' in general, and 'Christian' and 'Pagan' in
particular, is a central concern of *The Wicker Man*, made plain in
the opening caption, in which the producers thank the people of
Summerisle for allowing 'privileged insight into their religious
practices'. The first frames of the director's cut version of the
film continue the trope, where Howie and McTaggart walk past
the 'Jesus Saves/Jesus Lives' graffiti, McTaggart commenting in
a dry voice, 'Ah now, there's a message, Sergeant!', and Howie
retorting soberly, 'A message for us all'. Almost immediately we
overhear the constables gossiping over Howie's celibate
engagement to his betrothed, followed by scenes of Howie taking
Communion and reading from the Bible in church.[7] This lampoon
of a testy evangelical man in a rapidly-secularising culture is
further strengthened by Howie's very first words in the film (to
McTaggart): 'Get your hair cut!' The 'square' significance of
appropriate male hair length would not be lost on an early 1970s
audience, for whom growing one's hair long had become, for
men in particular, a popular symbol of cultural dissent.

But not only is Howie, the 'Christian copper' (Lord
Summerisle's sarcastic trope), seemingly at odds with secularised
mainland culture; he soon clashes with the hedonistic, sensual
culture on Summerisle. 'This is still in theory a law-abiding

---

[7] The scene of Howie taking a Communion wafer at the altar implies that he is
participating in either an Episcopal Eucharist or Catholic mass. Yet a lay reader
would not be reading from the New Testament story of the Last Supper before the
Eucharist in Episcopal and Catholic traditions, as we see Howie do. The
constable's Virgin Mary joke – an obvious Catholic reference – and Howie's stern
moralism – a popular Free Church stereotype – multiply the denominational traits
inscribed in Howie's cartoon persona, undermining the historicity of the film's
'Christianity' and reinforcing Howie's presentation as a composite Christian
stereotype. Although director Robin Hardy recently rationalised this as a
screenplay weakness – 'we'd spent less thought on Howie's Christian face', he
admitted during his July 15th 2003 talk at the University of Glasgow's Crichton
Campus, Dumfries – this authorial 'lapse' actually makes a point about the
immediacy and accessibility of popular representations. For an edited version of
Hardy's keynote speech see 'The Genesis of *The Wicker Man*' – and Murray,
'Interview with Robin Hardy'.

Christian country – however unfashionable that may seem', he
remarks to The Green Man's landlord, on the pub's drinking
culture. Alternative religious imagery and practices multiply as
Howie explores the island, from graveyard inscriptions and
decorations to public nudity and sexual behaviour. The woman
breastfeeding in a ruined church, and the shining maypole against
its backdrop, are poignant images of the rise (or return) of a new
(or old) 'Pagan' order. The island setting itself reinforces this
sense of Pagan revival, fitting into a tradition in British occult
films where rural landscapes, including standing stones, function
to evoke not just pastoral innocence but an alternative order of
'pre-Christian agrarian religious practices'.[8] In any case, by the
time Miss Rose, the school teacher, tells Howie that Christianity
is of interest to the islanders 'only in the geography of
comparative religion', the norm has been (ironically) reversed,
and it is clear that Howie's evangelical Christian testimony must
be in tension with *both* of the film's competing cultural
paradigms: secular/mainland and religious/island.

    The film's final image can be read both from a secular
perspective – the burning of a policeman symbolising the
authority of law – and as a religious sacrifice or martyrdom,
depending on audience sympathies. Motifs such as those
discussed above, then, graphically symbolise Howie's double
transgression and would have carried considerable 'symbolic
capital [...] for the 1970s counterculture', as Krzywinska correctly
points out.[9] The contemporary symbolism of burning a 'Christian
copper' is reinforced when we consider political events which
prefigured the film, from the May 1968 uprisings in France to the
Baader-Meinhof group's anti-capitalist bombing campaign in
West Germany in the early 1970s. More recently, a comparable
symbolism was evident for a renewed post-hippy, Pagan audience
for the film in the UK, with reference to the 1985 'battle of the
beanfield' at Stonehenge, where the 'Peace Convoy' of 'New
Age travellers' heading for the summer solstice festival was
broken up by police.[10] At the same time, however, the film's

---

[8] Krzywinska, *A Skin for Dancing In*, p. 78, p. 84.
[9] Krzywinska, *A Skin for Dancing In*, p. 105.
[10] Chippendale, et al., *Who Owns Stonehenge?*; Hetherington, *New Age
Travellers*.

polysemic narrative leaves the precise interpretation of events to
the viewer, although director Robin Hardy – as we shall see – has
repeatedly disclaimed any 'countercultural' intent on his part,
which seems to dispense with at least one reading. However, the
evidence of tension between authorial voice and audience
interpretation means that assessment of the film's representations
of 'religion' requires attention be paid to both standpoints. I
return to this point below.

Howie's brief but intense exchange with Lord Summerisle in
the castle encapsulates the screenplay's combative politics of
religious representation. This set piece, in which Howie confronts
Lord Summerisle on the fate of Rowan Morrison, is effectively
constituted as a popular debate on Christian and Pagan doctrine.
The following excerpts from their exchange instantiates the point:

> **Summerisle**: We don't commit murder around
> here. We're a deeply religious people.
> **Howie**: Religious? With ruined churches, no
> ministers, no priests, and children dancing
> naked?
> **Summerisle**: They do love their divinity
> lessons.
>
> [...]
>
> **Howie**: Oh, what is all this? I mean, you've got
> fake biology, fake religion... Sir, have these
> children never heard of Jesus?
> **Summerisle**: Himself the son of a virgin,
> impregnated – I believe – by a ghost?
>
> [...]
>
> **Summerisle**: It's most important that each new
> generation born on Summerisle be made aware
> that here, the old gods aren't dead.
> **Howie**: And what of the true God, for whose
> glory churches and monasteries have been built

on these islands for generations past? Now, sir,
what of him?
Summerisle: He's dead. He can't complain. He
had his chance and, in modern parlance, he
blew it.[11]

In this and other key sequences of *The Wicker Man*, 'religion' is
appropriated and contested amongst the protagonists through
similar popular tropes and acts to those that obtained in Anglo-
American cultural formations of late 1960s and early 1970s. But
it is no level playing field: in the interrogative structure of the
dialogue and the relative complexity of its discursive content, the
screenplay establishes who is on the back foot here, asking the
questions (the Christian), and who is in charge, giving the
answers (the Pagan). This is clearly a reversal of the traditional
'flow' of religious authority, but one increasingly plausible to a
mid-1970s audience. So although Howie (the Christian) initiates
the encounter, Summerisle (the Pagan) dominates, speaking two-
thirds of the dialogue. Summerisle's position is given extra
weight in the exchange quoted from above by his authoritative
commentary on the symbolism of the girls' naked bonfire dance,
seen through the window. Howie, in contrast, is merely reactive
(and, for Pagan audiences, reactionary), equating Christianity
with the Immaculate Conception and evangelical faith in Jesus,
both markedly 'square' positions to take in 1970s religious
controversies,[12] while seeming to locate its triumphs solely in the
past. Simultaneously, both Howie and Lord Summerisle
negatively equate Christianity with 'ruined churches' and absent

---

[11] Transcribed from *The Wicker Man – Special Edition Director's Cut* (2002).

[12] The Anglican Bishop John Robinson explicitly mentions the 'virgin birth', an
article of faith in both the Apostles' and Nicene creeds, only in passing in his
popular critique of 'supernaturalistic Christianity'; see *Honest to God* (and also
Robinson and Edwards, *The Honest to God Debate*). But it is implicitly a target of
his humanistic revisionism insofar as he attacks all 'Father Christmas' views of
deity, the notion that 'God took a space-trip and arrived on this planet in the form
of a man' (*Honest to God*, p. 66). The Virgin would become an explosive popular
controversy for Archbishop David Jenkins in 1984, when, in a *Credo* programme
on BBC1, he expressed personal doubts on the virgin birth, initiating a torrent of
sensationalistic media headlines, e.g. 'Doubting Bishop - Jesus not Born of a
Virgin' - and over 4,000 letters on the subject (Jenkins, *Free to Believe*, p. 2, pp.
24-5).

clergy, a resonant trope for the film's audiences in the face of a widely-remarked decline in church membership in the UK from the 1960s onwards. Furthermore, the exchange seems to establish that Christians uphold a creed no less 'fake' than 'parthenogenesis', as Summerisle puts it, and worship a 'dead' god. Conversely (and once again, ironically), Paganism is normativised, the measure of a 'deeply religious' culture, advocate of the 'old Gods' and at the core of Religious Education in schools. Nakedness in Pagan ritual is positively re-coded as a mark of fertility and religious virtue, with connotations, familiar to early *Wicker Man* audiences, of controversies from the 'swinging sixties'[13] and the 'permissive society'[14]: from the high-profile trial (and acquittal) of Penguin Books in 1960 for publishing an unexpurgated edition of D. H. Lawrence's sexually-explicit novel, *Lady Chatterley's Lover* (1928), [15] to the public nudity in the London shows *Oh, Calcutta!* and *Hair* in 1968-9.[16] Howie is not allowed to make any real critique stick against Paganism. Summerisle has the first and last word, and the better of the exchange throughout. Howie – presumably like other cultural conservatives amongst 1970s audiences – can only express indignation.

Popular images and stances dominate this 'doctrinal' exchange. Howie and Lord Summerisle are demotic mouthpieces: self-appointed, 'lay' spokesmen for their respective 'religions'. Their references are simple, direct and unambiguous, and their positions are dialectical. They confront at least one 'other', rival system: in Lord Summerisle's case, Christianity, in Sergeant Howie's, both island Paganism *and* mainland secularism.

The 'Long Sixties': Revolution or carnival?

In the period in which *The Wicker Man* was conceived, scripted, cast and filmed – the 'long sixties' or 'c.1958-1974'[17] – all commentators agree there was a dynamic collision of cultural forces. But there is considerable debate on the enduring social

---

[13] Masters, *The Swinging Sixties*.
[14] Hoggart, et al.., *The Permissive Society*.
[15] Rolph, *The Trial of Lady Chatterley: Regina* v. *Penguin Books Limited*.
[16] Marwick, *The Sixties*, p. 343, pp. 357-58.
[17] Marwick, *The Sixties*.

and political significance of the decade. Was it a 'cultural revolution'[18] or merely an 'exploratory curriculum, a range of experiences and exposures'[19] in which, as John Lennon put it in *Rolling Stone* magazine in 1970, 'nothing happened except that we all dressed up', with 'the same bastards in control, the same people running everything'?[20]

While the rhetoric on 'the sixties' remains often bold and heady, real outcomes and effects are disputed.[21] Musgrove's emphasis on a heuristic 'exploratory curriculum' coupled with Martin's identification of an 'expressive ethic' can be confirmed by other accounts of the function of drugs, sex and psychotherapy in various 'anti-institutions' of the day.[22] But while revolutionary fervour and antinomian values marked certain tendencies within the counterculture, others embraced entrepreneurship and free-market libertarianism,[23] with uncertain long-term political and institutional effects.

These larger questions apart, at least three currents in Marwick's 'long sixties' constrain representations of religion in *The Wicker Man*. First is the question of the decline of discursive Christianity. In the case of 1960s Britain, Callum Brown finds a very rapid decline – a 'haemorrhage' – in 'subscription to [Christian] protocols of personal identity' among the population at large.[24] In oral history narratives he finds evidence of a baffled loss of Christian identity amongst the older generation in particular, amounting to a 'discursive bereavement', with largely secular narratives of identity replacing it amongst younger generations. Quantitative evidence over the last quarter of the twentieth century from church membership figures (down to just 10% of the UK population by 2000)[25] and opinion polls[26] amply

---

[18] Marwick, *The Sixties*.

[19] Musgrove, *Ecstasy and Holiness*, p. 19.

[20] Cited in Moore-Gilbert and Seed, (eds.) *Cultural Revolution? The Challenge of the Arts in the 1960s*, p. 3.

[21] Moore-Gilbert and Seed, (eds.), *Cultural Revolution? The Challenge of the Arts in the 1960s*.

[22] Musgrove, *Ecstasy and Holiness*; Martin, *A Sociology of Contemporary Cultural Change*; Green, *All Dressed Up*.

[23] Neville, *Playpower*.

[24] Brown, *The Death of Christian Britain*, pp. 12-13.

[25] Bruce, *God is Dead*, p. 67.

support Brown's qualitative thesis and underscore the societal base for *The Wicker Man's* cartoons of Christian identity in rapid decline.

At the same time, 'new' and 'alternative' forms of religion were gaining ground. This is the second set of cultural forces at work on the film, and it consisted of both a negative attitude 'against' religion, and specific institutional innovations 'in' religion. In the first place, a diffuse yet pervasive rhetoric grew against 'organised religion' and 'churchianity'. A typical example comes from 1975, in the directory *Alternative Scotland*, one in a series of 'alternative' UK directories based on Nicholas Saunders' self-published prototype, *Alternative London* (1970). The entry on 'religion' in *Alternative Scotland* begins by repeating a bitter pastoral joke to the effect that 'everybody in Scotland has a church to stay away from', and goes on to bemoan the 'pettiness and sheer "un-Christianity" [...] so rife in the Kirk these days'.[27] The entry ends by noting that, in Scotland as well as in England and Wales, 'there is an increasing number of groups simply interested in borrowing from any religion or none for the purpose of developing the potential of the individual',[28] an observation borne out by other well-documented surveys and resources on the period, such as Kenneth Leech's *Youthquake: Spirituality and the growth of a counter-culture* (1976 [1973]) and Stephen Annett's *The Many Ways of Being: A guide to spiritual groups and growth centres in Britain* (1976).

Some of this new 'spirituality' was fed by a parallel celebration of occult and magical powers in both countercultural and popular publishing. The *Directory of British Alternative Periodicals 1965-1974*[29] lists more than thirty specifically 'occult' and 'pagan' publications alongside the more staple political and community products of the underground press, while *Alternative England and Wales*[30] carried 23 pages on 'mystical' religion (the only kind of 'religion' it deemed legitimate). In paperback publishing there was high consumption of popular texts on

---

[26] Field, "'The Haemorrhage of Faith?'".

[27] Wright and Worsley, *Alternative Scotland*, p. 113.

[28] Wright and Worsley, *Alternative Scotland*, p. 114.

[29] Noyce, *The Directory of British Alternative Periodicals*.

[30] Saunders, *Alternative England and Wales*.

astrology, psychic powers, esotericism and reincarnation;[31] in the USA, paperback publishing on 'occult' topics rose over 500% between 1968 and 1971.[32] Occult and esoteric material was also disseminated and reproduced idiosyncratically across a spectrum of cultural practices, from elite, experimental arts to everyday vernacular practices, or 'superstitions'.[33]

In addition to this diffusion of a non-aligned discourse on 'alternative' religion, a growing range of non-Christian religious groups and organisations were emerging, both migrant and homegrown, as the gap between ascriptions of 'deviant' and merely 'variant' behaviour shrunk. Some of these so-called 'cults'[34] were active proselytisers within youth and countercultures, triggering a series of moral panics, and giving rise to an 'anti-cult' movement of self-styled 'de-programmers' of 'brainwashed' converts, ready to tackle the perceived menace.[35] In the UK the principal movements of Asian origin were the Unification Church, known as 'Moonies' after their Korean founder, Sun Myung Moon, and the Hindu-based International Society for Krishna Consciousness, or 'Hare Krishnas'. An indigenous American human potential movement, the Church of Scientology, was also a notorious presence. Of direct relevance to *The Wicker Man*, particularly in view of its subsequent successes amongst Pagan audiences, were the indigenous recreations of Druidry and Wicca: Druidry through the formation of the Order of Bards, Ovates and Druids in 1964 and the British Druid Order in 1979,[36] Wicca via the publication of Gerald Gardner's *Witchcraft Today* in 1954, *The Wiccan* newsletter from 1968, and the formation of the Pagan Federation in 1971.[37] These latter re-creations of erstwhile 'indigenous' practices were to play a significant role in the 'Paganisation' of the film, as we shall see. Although out of proportion to actual

[31] Truzzi, 'The Occult Revival as Popular Culture'.

[32] Galbreath, 'The History of Modern Occultism'.

[33] Campbell and McIver, 'Cultural Sources of Support for Contemporary Occultism'. Webb, *The Occult Establishment,* pp. 417-87. Abercrombie, et al., 'Superstition and Religion'.

[34] Martin, *The Kingdom of the Cults*; Evans, *Cults of Unreason*.

[35] For a critical sociology of 'brainwashing', see Barker, *The Making of a Moonie*.

[36] Carr-Gomm, *The Druid Renaissance*.

[37] Hutton, *The Triumph of the Moon*.

numbers involved, the public profile of new and alternative religions in the 1970s and 1980s was nevertheless such that, in 1988, a Home Office-funded educational charity, INFORM (Information Network Focus on Religious Movements), was established in London to broker public information on these 'cults' or 'new religious movements' in the face of various polemics and media panics.[38] In the wake of the 'long sixties', religion was back on the agenda with a vengeance, often taking the form of an impatient, youthful dialectic against tired, unfashionable 'organised religion': which meant Christianity.

The third and final current shaping representations of religion in *The Wicker Man* (and of direct impact on both authorial intention *and* audience reception) was a burgeoning, reflexive interest in 'folklore' and the recovery of 'traditions': festival days and customs of place; dances, songs and rhymes; folk medicine; old monuments, earthworks and tracks. Nevertheless, many of the antiquarian beliefs and practices gathered and interpreted earlier in the century by bodies such as the Folklore Society[39] and now disseminated in popular publications were, in fact, not especially 'ancient'. Rather, they were a product of modern economic forces and cultural fashions, as Ronald Hutton[40] has conclusively demonstrated. Of especial import was the significant population shift from countryside to city that followed the Industrial Revolution, which in turn stimulated a nineteenth-century Romantic eulogisation of 'nature'.

The immense popularity of *The Wicker Man*'s main source – J. G. Frazer's *The Golden Bough: A Study in Magic and Religion*, which since its first edition in 1890 has gone through numerous expanded, complete and abridged editions – demonstrates the persistent allure for the twentieth-century British imagination of a folkloric and antiquarian hermeneutic. Despite Frazer's rationalist agenda in explaining scientifically the ultimate fate of the folkloric 'survivals' he so painstakingly (and sometimes erroneously) documented, his readers were surely often reading his tome *against* the grain of his declared intentions, and *for* the thrill of the details of 'taboo' magic and 'exotic' religion that

---

[38] Barker, *The Making of a Moonie.*
[39] See Dorson, *The British Folklorists.*
[40] Hutton, *The Stations of the Sun.*

drive the book. This returns us to the point about the principles of simplicity and accessibility which underpin popular modes of interpretation. It is a short step from reading Frazer's data – for example, the comparative material on fire festivals in Chapters 62 and 63 of *The Golden Bough* (already decontextualised and spliced from secondary sources) – to using it in one's own imaginative constructions or re-constructions of 'ritual' and 'tradition'. This is what director Robin Hardy and Pagan audiences both do, to rather different ends. Such re-constructions, as Hutton points out in relation to the specific rituals featured in *The Wicker Man*, 'can be put together really easily by reading just two or three books that were really popular about the time of the early 1970s'.[41] Mentioning three main sources – Celtic/Druidical lore (for the sacrificial effigy itself), English folklore (for the sword-dance) and Wicca (for the naked fire-jumping) – Hutton comments: 'You put the lot together, and within about three or four hours of reading, you've got yourself a movie'.[42]

Accounting for the existence and cross-pollination of these three contemporary currents – discursive Christian bereavement, the resurgence of 'alternative' religion, the allure of folklore – problematises grand narratives of counterculture as a distinct, pure, revolutionary force, and reveals a far more frayed and internally-contested spectrum of popular practices and beliefs. Audience studies such as Janice Radway's *Reading the Romance*, which examines housewives' strategic use of the romantic fiction genre, or Penny Summerfield's *Reconstructing Women's Wartime Lives*, which explores how memories are actively constructed in the present moment, illustrate cultural 'materials' (books, discourses, memories) are put to work by practitioners for immediate needs and ends. These uses may or may not accord with the dominant or 'respectable' culture (where, in these examples, romantic fiction is popularly considered 'the lowest of the low', and memories mere 'nostalgia').

It is no different with that sphere of culture we conventionally separate out as 'religion': hence my broader aim of representing popular 'religious' practices as part of a wider ethnography and

---

[41] Cited in the documentary television programme *Burnt Offering*.
[42] Cited in *Burnt Offering*.

history of culture, with *The Wicker Man* as a case in point. Moore-Gilbert and Seed caution against tidy interpretations of the 'long sixties': 'there was no single monolithic counterculture, or cultural opposition with a coherent programme'.[43] The crude dichotomisation of 'religion' into a 'culture war' between Christians and Pagans is achieved at the expense of compressing and polarising the heteroglossia of the 'long sixties' into a contest between 'uptight virgins' and 'libidinous heathens'. This kind of structuralist closure conceals the fluid and destabilising historical forces of popular religion. Cultural formations of the late 1960s and early 1970s, of which the film is symptomatic, were, as always, fluid and ambiguous.

Director's Cut or Audience Take?

Still, in aesthetic contexts, the question of authoritative interpretation persists, not least amongst cult film fan bases. Here, the forces of dichotomisation may resurface in the form of the question of authorial intent *versus* audience reception. Put simply, do we favour 'director's cut' or 'audience take'? Whichever position we choose can lead to radically different interpretations of the film, as I will very briefly show, and these can be summed up as a choice between attitudes of 'ironisation' and 'Paganisation' respectively.

First, the *auteur*'s view. Recently Robin Hardy has re-emphasised watching the film through his, and screenwriter Anthony Shaffer's, eyes, for the film's sources, he said, 'come out of one's own life'.[44] He is particularly keen that the authorial approach should *not* be read as either pro-Pagan or, more generally, pro-counterculture. On the first point, he said that he and Shaffer had not met any Pagans before filming, and claimed that his first encounter with 'real' Pagans had been at a launch of the film in San Francisco, although the group had been 'too stoned' to pursue their complaint that the film exploited Pagans. Hardy's views on historical Paganism are powerfully expressed

---

[43] Moore-Gilbert and Seed, *Cultural Revolution*, p. 1.
[44] Unless otherwise stated, all subsequent quotations, and my glosses, are from Robin Hardy's talk on July 15th 2003 at the University of Glasgow's Crichton Campus, Dumfries. Some of these themes are addressed also in Murray, 'Interview with Robin Hardy'.

in a 1977 interview in the film journal *Cinefantastique*, where he said that Paganism 'keeps people in the thrall of superstition':

> Maybe it's not too big a connection to make between the final scene of *The Wicker Man* and the Nuremburg rallies in Germany. It was no accident that Hitler brought back all those pagan feasts in his rise to power.[45]

Similarly, Hardy was anxious to disclaim any affinity with feminism, such as a reading of the film, based on the sexually and politically empowered religion of Summerisle women, might encourage. On the contrary, he claims in retrospect that he and Shaffer were 'bemused' by 'the militant feminism' of the period.

This repudiation of 'alternative' commitments has led to a sceptical authorial stance in which Hardy describes his own religious position as 'a deep and comforting agnosticism' and his preferred reading of the film as 'an intriguing entertainment'. His relationship to the film's subject material is in this sense similar to J. G. Frazer himself, whose complete edition of *The Golden Bough* Hardy had to hand during filming ('it's all in Frazer'). Like Frazer, Hardy is fascinated and intrigued by the romance of cultural 'survivals' in the modern world, but ultimately takes refuge in a distanced intellectualism. We hear this ironic voice in Hardy's account of the genesis of the film. Although he acknowledges the contemporary appeal of the horror film genre and its leading British star, Christopher Lee, for himself and Shaffer, he claims that they maintained a critical, sceptical distance: 'we enjoyed *analysing* [its] *camp* world' (my emphasis). As a result, the authors tried to write the film as 'anti-Hammer'.

Since 1962 Hardy and Shaffer had been close business partners in advertising, and through long acquaintanceship indulged in what Hardy calls 'revenge games' or 'dog-eat-dog jokes' between themselves.[46] It would seem that some of this male gamesmanship infused the 'mind games' in Shaffer's script for

---

[45] Cited in Hardy, Krzywinska, *A Skin for Dancing In*, pp. 83-84.
[46] Quotations come from Hardy's conference address but details of his account of games-playing are available in Hardy, 'The Genesis of *The Wicker Man*'.

Sleuth (1970), and Hardy admits that 'the importance of *Sleuth* as an antecedent to *The Wicker Man* can hardly be exaggerated'. Also 'on the horizon', as Hardy put it, were the critically successful plays of Shaffer's twin brother Peter, including *Royal Hunt of the Sun* (1964) and *Equus* (1973). The authorial circumstances infusing *The Wicker Man*, it would seem, were male competition amongst close friends and family, resulting in a generalised attitude of 'outwitting' the other. Just as Hardy and Shaffer, the principal protagonists in *Sleuth*, and Howie and Summerisle, all aim to outwit each other, so *The Wicker Man* as a whole can be read as an *auteur*'s spectacle designed to outwit its audience. Deciphering various symbolic clues in *The Wicker Man* (the woman holding the egg, breastfeeding at a ruined altar) then becomes 'part of the entertainment', as Hardy put it, and if you do not 'get' these references, you 'lose'.

This authorial ploy clearly had mixed results. On the one hand, the film was a commercial disaster. Without proper marketing and support on initial release, it did not reach the 'arthouse' audience of urbane, erudite, playful viewers it dearly needed. It was only with the achievement of 'cult movie' status – where identification and celebration, rather than ironic distance, are the order of the day – that the film came to prosper. Significant in this regard is the gradual 'Paganisation' of the film: its reclamation by avowedly Pagan audiences, who form 'a significant component of the cult audience for the film', according to Judith Higginbottom's UK research.[47] Higginbottom's analysis, based upon interviews with Pagan informants, suggests that this constituency reverses authorial intentions by interpreting the film as a 'drama in which knowledge of Pagan spirituality is key to understanding the outcome'.[48] A key element in the film's Pagan appeal is its 'depiction of sexual rites as central'; its 'positive, permissive attitude to sexual expression [...] accords very closely with the worldview of most Pagans'.[49] In contrast, Howie 'encapsulates for Pagan audiences everything they dislike about Christianity: a repressive morality, an overwhelming insistence that he is always

---

[47] Higginbottom, 'Do as Thou Wilt', np.
[48] Higginbottom, 'Do as Thou Wilt', np.
[49] Higginbottom, 'Do as Thou Wilt', np.

right, and a censorious intolerance of the beliefs of others'.[50] His
peculiar tragedy is that, although offered 'knowledge' by the
islanders that will 'save' him, his 'repeated rejection of the
feminine' makes him 'wilfully ignorant'.[51] Ironically (from the
authorial perspective), Pagan audiences find an 'overall Pagan
sensibility' in the film: it is 'the only film they know of in which
the action takes place in a Pagan context, where Paganism is the
norm rather than a transgressive, exotic practice, and where the
validity of Pagan belief is accepted'.[52]

This 'Paganisation' of *The Wicker Man* amongst cult audiences
has in turn infected popular media representations of the film, as
can be seen from the title of one recent television documentary,
Burnt Offering: The cult of 'The Wicker Man' (2001). The
opening shots depict film critic Mark Kermode beside the stumps
of the wicker man effigy in Wigtownshire, where he refers to the
'popular notion' that the film's dramatic revival demonstrates
'something genuinely magical about this most unholy of British
chillers'.[53] Other principal protagonists develop this theme on
camera. Shaffer says of the film, 'it *is* a spell' and adds, 'I look
forward to the day when we *are* Pagans again... I think we'd have
a lot more fun... a lot more belief, a lot more faith'. Christopher
Lee says that the burning of the effigy on set was itself 'a Pagan
religious service' and affirms 'there is a touch of Paganism in all
of us'. Kermode takes up this trope magisterially:

> The burning of the colossus itself lifted the
> endeavour out of the everyday, and into the
> realm of magic. For though [the construction
> crew] had in theory built nothing more than a
> vast movie prop, the sight of that gigantic fiery
> angel blazing away on a cliff head stirred
> primal emotions in the cast and crew, and also
> in the generations of viewers who would
> subsequently be caught up in *The Wicker
> Man*'s ghastly spell.

---

[50] Higginbottom, 'Do as Thou Wilt', np.
[51] Higginbottom, 'Do as Thou Wilt', np.
[52] Higginbottom, 'Do as Thou Wilt', np.
[53] This and subsequent quotations are my own transcriptions from *Burnt Offering*.

These and other popular 'paganisations' of the film are clearly a long way from Hardy's authorial interpretation. But beyond the dichotomy between ironised distance – the 'director's cut' – and Paganised embrace – the 'audience take' – a more nuanced reading of the film, derived from detailed knowledge of its historical context, finds ambivalent, unresolved attitudes in the screenplay. These cannot be reduced to a binary polarity without parodying the complex cultural matrix in which the film gestated. In this sense *The Wicker Man* is emblematic of its time and place in depicting the complexities of an emerging post-Christian culture. Contextualising the particularities of the film's cultural production supports a wider agenda of re-theorising religion as an incomplete, impure domain of popular practice and representation – with all the interpretative ambiguities this must entail.

Bibliography

Abercrombie, N. et al., 'Superstition and Religion: The God of the gaps', in *A Sociological Yearbook of Religion in Britain 3*, ed. by D. Martin and M. Hill (London: SCM, 1970), pp. 93-129.

Annett, S., *The Many Ways of Being: A guide to spiritual groups and growth centres in Britain* (London: Abacus/Turnstone, 1976).

Baird, R., *Category Formation and the History of Religions* (The Hague: Mouton, 1971).

Barker, E., *The Making of a Moonie: Brainwashing or choice?* (Oxford: Blackwell, 1984).

_____, *New Religious Movements: A practical introduction* (London: HMSO, 1995[1989]).

Beckford, J., *Religion and Advanced Industrial Society* (London: Unwin Hyman, 1989).

Brown, C., *The Death of Christian Britain: Understanding secularization 1800-2000* (London: Routledge, 2001).

Bruce, S., *God is Dead: Secularization in the west* (Oxford: Blackwell, 2002).

Burnt Offering: The Cult of 'The Wicker Man' (Nobles Gate/C4 Television, 2001).

Campbell, C. and S. McIver, 'Cultural Sources of Support for Contemporary Occultism', *Social Compass*, 34.1 (1987), 41-60.

Carr-Gomm, P., ed., *The Druid Renaissance: The voice of druidry today* (London: Thorsons, 1996).

Chippendale, C., P. Devereux, P. Fowler, R. Jones and T. Sebastian, *Who Owns Stonehenge?* (London: Batsford, 1990).

Dorson, R., *The British Folklorists: A history* (London: Routledge and Kegan Paul, 1968).

Evans, C., *Cults of Unreason* (London: Harrap, 1973).

Field, C., '"The Haemorrhage of Faith?" Opinion Polls as Sources for Religious Practices, Beliefs and Attitudes in Scotland since the 1970s', *Journal of Contemporary Religion*, 16 (2001), 157-76.

Frazer, J. G., *The Golden Bough* (New York: Macmillan, 1963 [1922]).

Galbreath, R., 'The History of Modern Occultism: A bibliographical survey', *Journal of Popular Culture*, 5 (1972), 726-54.

Green, J., *All Dressed Up: The sixties and the counterculture* (London: Jonathon Cape, 1998).

Hardy, R. 'The Genesis of *The Wicker Man*', in *The Quest for 'The Wicker Man': Historical, folklore and Pagan perspectives*, ed. by B. Franks, S. Harper, J. Murray and L. Stevenson (Edinburgh: Luath, 2005).

Hetherington, K., *New Age Travellers: Vanloads of uproarious humanity* (London: Cassell, 2000).

Higginbottom, J., 'Do as Thou Wilt: Contemporary Paganism and *The Wicker Man*'. Conference paper, forthcoming in *The Quest for 'The Wicker Man': Historical, folklore and Pagan perspectives*, ed. by B. Franks, S. Harper, J. Murray and L. Stevenson (Edinburgh: Luath, 2005).

Hoggart, R. et al., *The Permissive Society: 'The Guardian' Enquiry* (London: Panther Modern Society, 1969).

Hutton, R., *The Stations of the Sun: A history of the ritual year in Britain* (Oxford: Oxford University Press, 1996).

_____, *The Triumph of the Moon: A history of modern pagan witchcraft* (Oxford: Oxford University Press, 1999).

Jenkins, D., *Free to Believe* (London: BBC Books, 1991).

Krzywinska, T., *A Skin For Dancing In: Possession, witchcraft and voodoo in film* (Trowbridge: Flicks Books, 2000).

Leech, K., *Youthquake: Spirituality and the growth of a counterculture* (London: Abacus, 1976 [1973]).

Lincoln, B., 'Culture', in *Guide to the Study of Religion*, ed. by W. Braun and R. McCutcheon (London: Continuum, 2000), pp. 409-22.

Martin, W., *The Kingdom of the Cults* (Minneapolis, MN: Bethany House, 1965).

Martin, B., *A Sociology of Contemporary Cultural Change* (Oxford: Blackwell, 1983).

Marwick, A., *The Sixties: Cultural Revolution in Britain, France, Italy and the United States, c.1958-1974* (Oxford: Oxford University Press, 1998).

Masters, B., *The Swinging Sixties* (London: Constable, 1985).

Masuzawa, T., 'Culture', in *Critical Terms for Religious Studies*, ed. by M. Taylor (Chicago: Chicago University Press, 1998), pp. 70-93.

McCutcheon, R., *Manufacturing Religion: The discourse on sui generis religion and the politics of nostalgia* (New York: Oxford University Press, 1997).

Moore-Gilbert, B. and J. Seed, eds., *Cultural Revolution? The challenge of the arts in the 1960s* (London: Routledge, 1992).

Murray, J., 'Interview with Robin Hardy', in *The Quest for 'The Wicker Man': Historical, folklore and Pagan perspectives*, ed. by B. Franks, S. Harper, J. Murray and L. Stevenson (Edinburgh: Luath, 2005).

Musgrove, F., *Ecstasy and Holiness: Counterculture and the open society* (London: Methuen, 1974).

Neville, R., *Playpower* (St. Albans: Paladin/Granada, 1971).

Noyce, J., *The Directory of British Alternative Periodicals* (Hassocks, Sussex: Harvester Press, 1979).

Radway, J., *Reading the Romance* (London: Verso, 1987).

Robinson, J. A. T., *Honest to God* (London: SCM Press, 1963).

Robinson, J. A. T. and D. L. Edwards, *The Honest to God Debate* (London: SCM Press, 1963).

Rolph, C. H., ed., *The Trial of Lady Chatterley: Regina v. Penguin Books Limited* (Harmondsworth: Penguin, 1961).

Saunders, N., *Alternative London* (London: the Author, 1970).

_____, *Alternative England and Wales* (London: the Author, 1975).

Smith, J. Z., 'Religion, Religions, Religious', in *Critical Terms for Religious Studies*, ed. by M. Taylor (Chicago: Chicago University Press, 1998), pp. 269-84.

Summerfield, P., *Reconstructing Women's Wartime Lives: Discourse and subjectivity in oral histories of the Second World War* (Manchester: Manchester University Press, 1998).

Sutcliffe, S., *Children of the New Age: A history of spiritual practices* (London: Routledge, 2003).

Truzzi, M., 'The Occult Revival as Popular Culture: Some random observations on the old and the nouveau witch', *Sociological Quarterly*, 13 (1972), 16-36.

Webb, J., *The Occult Establishment* (La Salle, IL: Open Court, 1976).

Wicker Man, The – Special Edition Director's Cut, dir. R. Hardy. Canal ([1973] 2002).

Williams, R., *Keywords: A vocabulary of culture and society* (Glasgow: Fontana, 1976).

Wright, B. and C. Worsley, *Alternative Scotland* (Edinburgh: Edinburgh University Students Publishing Board, 1975).

Demotic Possession: The hierarchic and anarchic in *The Wicker Man*

Benjamin Franks

'Perhaps it is just as well you won't be here to be offended by the sight of our May Day celebrations'

Director, Robin Hardy, and (co-)writer, Anthony Shaffer, devised the film *The Wicker Man* (Hardy, 1973) as a critique of the New Age and Pagan cults that had become a noticeable part of the countercultural landscape of the late 1960s and early '70s.[1] The focus of Hardy and Shaffer's dissatisfaction was with what they saw as the incipient fascism of these movements. In separate interviews about the influences on their script, both refer explicitly to the horrors of National Socialism in connection to unorthodox religious activity. Shaffer, in discussion with the journalist Allan Brown, draws on the historic experience of Nazism in analysing the dangers of cultism. In this account, the Holocaust and Jonestown Massacre shared various central themes with Dark Age practices, especially the centrality of sacrifice as an 'articulation of power over weakness'.[2]

Hardy makes the same point more explicitly in an interview with David Bartholomew in the magazine *Cinefantastique*. He states that pre-Christian religious belief:

> [K]eeps people in the thrall of superstition. Maybe it's not too big a connection to make between the final scene of *The Wicker Man* and the Nuremberg rallies in Germany. It was no accident that Hitler brought back all those pagan feasts in his rise to power.[3]

---

[1] There was some dispute between Shaffer and Hardy as to who was responsible for the narrative. See Brown, *Inside 'The Wicker Man'*, p. 21, p. 26. Brown lists Shaffer as sole creator of the screenplay in his foreword to the 2000 Pan edition of the co-authored novel; see Brown, *Inside 'The Wicker Man'*, p. ix.
[2] Brown, *Inside 'The Wicker Man'*, pp. 21-22.
[3] Bartholomew, '*The Wicker Man*', p. 12. Note too that Hardy draws additional parallels between the Pagan Lord Summerisle and Hitler: see Bartholomew, '*The Wicker Man*', p. 34.

Even 30 years after the making of the film, Hardy still refers to the Jonestown Massacre and the Nuremburg Rally in connection with the final scene of *The Wicker Man*.[4]

Despite these explicitly stated authorial intentions, audiences have appropriated the film in a distinctly subversive manner. In terms of the politics, the creators' purpose and its reception are widely divergent, and this is partly due to the socially conservative, liberal theoretical account of authoritarianism that is presented in the film. The lacunae and contradictions in this type of interpretation of political oppression's causes have allowed for dissident readings of *The Wicker Man* from a wide variety of audiences, including those who identify with the 1960s counterculture.[5] Indeed, contemporary Pagans have been amongst the film's most avid supporters.[6] Political radicals from British anarchist movements have also utilised themes from *The Wicker Man*. The latter sections of this paper demonstrate how the film has been used in anti-capitalist propaganda to promote libertarian (and often libidinous) ends. These reconstructions of meaning, in conflict with the authors' stated intentions, could be termed a 'demotic possession' of the text.

The British Enlightenment tradition, personified by John Locke, stood opposed to superstition and the irrational use of power. From its beginnings, the use of reason became synonymous with governmental legitimacy. The origin of just rule lies in consent from rational sovereign subjects,[7] with government charged with the protection of private property, fairly distributed by consensual market arrangements.[8] Unjust authority, which arbitrarily enslaved, slaughtered or interfered with justly acquired property rights was the product of irrationality and

---

[4] Wojtas, 'A burning passion', p. 21.

[5] See, for instance, Knight, 'Between the Devil and the Deep Blue Uniform'.

[6] See, for example, Peg Aloi's 'Witch Cinema' on *The Witches' Voice* website, which states that the film is 'one of my favorite cult films of all time' and rates it at number one in Aloi's top ten favourite films. See also the *Wicca Net: The home of Wicca and Wiccans on the Web*.

[7] 'We are born Free, as we are born Rational'. Locke, *Two Treatises of Government*, p. 308.

[8] Locke, *Two Treatises of Government*, pp. 285-302.

defended by illogical claims such as traditional practice.[9] It is still a mainstay of liberal analysis to consider authoritarian regimes to be maintained through essentially non-rational means, whilst representative-democratic (and predominantly capitalist) societies are based on reason.

The categorisation of societies as 'authoritarian', 'totalitarian' or 'fascistic', is itself a contentious political activity. For instance, the changing interpretation of 'totalitarian' to exclude all but the old Communist states or those political systems hostile to American policy, by right-wing political scientists and senior American policy advisors, is indicative of how these political labels are used to influence public opinion and direct government policy.[10] James Molloy's overview of the use of these prescriptive as well as descriptive political labels by various academics, including the arch-conservative Jeanne Fitzpatrick (adviser to Ronald Reagan), begins with the father of political sociology, Max Weber.[11]

Weber argued that a society could only function if the power structure that supports it has the general acceptance of its populace. For Weber, different types of society function under three types of claim to legitimacy: traditional, charismatic and rational. Traditional authority rests 'on an established belief in the sanctity of immemorial traditions and the legitimacy of the status of those exercising authority'.[12] These beliefs that justify the structure of power are believed to 'have been handed down from the past [and] "have always existed"'.[13] Weber associates absolute monarchies and tribal patriarchy with this type of traditional authority.[14] Whilst the economy of traditional societies can be consistent with a free-market, more frequently the maintenance of traditional orthodoxies and other 'irrational factors', such as ancient practices, restrict the efficient operation of the marketplace.[15]

---

[9] Locke is particularly critical of Robert Filmer who advocated absolute monarchy based on primogeniture. See Locke, 'First treatise', *Two Treatises of Government*.

[10] Molloy 'Contemporary Authoritarian Regimes', p. 235.

[11] Molloy 'Contemporary Authoritarian Regimes', p. 229.

[12] Weber, *The Theory of Economic and Social Organization*, p. 301.

[13] Weber, *The Theory of Economic and Social Organization*, p. 313.

[14] Weber, *The Theory of Economic and Social Organization*, pp. 317-29.

[15] Weber, *The Theory of Economic and Social Organization*, p. 325.

The second form of legitimacy described by Weber is charismatic authority. This rests 'on devotion to the specific and exceptional sanctity, heroism or exemplary character of an individual person, and of the normative patterns or order revealed or ordained by him [*sic*].'[16] The person with charismatic authority is 'treated as endowed with supernatural [...] powers'.[17] The charismatic leader is associated with prophets and agents of revolutionary change. Control based on this charismatic form of authority can undermine traditional authority as the personal inspiration of the leader can break established norms. Such authority is considered the least rational.[18]

Economically rational structures, as Weber regards capitalism, require continuous routine. As a result, such an economy is antipathetic to the charismatic character. This makes charismatic leadership transitory and leads to its transformation into rational or traditional patterns of management.[19] The fear, which goes back to Plato's *Republic*, is that the exercise of freedoms wrought from breaking the restraints of traditional rules will inevitably degenerate into tyranny. In *Cinefantastique,* Shaffer directly links the sexual licence that characterises the Summerisle community to such societal decline.[20]

The final form of Weber's tripartite distinction is legal-rational authority. Here, rules and procedures are based not on the character of person holding the office but on governmental norms.[21] These laws, unlike those of traditional authority, are intellectually analysable,[22] and exist to support the smooth running of a capitalist economy. In legal-rational societies, officials are subject to the laws and not above them, and there is a strict hierarchy of powers. Appointment to higher positions is conducted by a fair and open scheme, not nepotism or primogeniture.[23] Offices are 'filled by a free contractual

---

[16] Weber, *The Theory of Economic and Social Organization*, p. 301.
[17] Weber, *The Theory of Economic and Social Organization*, p. 329.
[18] Weber, *The Theory of Economic and Social Organization*, p. 332.
[19] Weber, *The Theory of Economic and Social Organization*, pp. 332-34.
[20] Bartholomew, '*The Wicker Man*', p. 40.
[21] Weber, *The Theory of Economic and Social Organization*, p. 300.
[22] Weber, *The Theory of Economic and Social Organization*, p. 332.
[23] Weber, *The Theory of Economic and Social Organization*, pp. 306-7.

relationship'.[24] For Weber, legal-rational systems are the most efficient, and associated with 'capitalistic enterprise'.[25] Elsewhere in Weber's works, he associates the rise of capitalism with Protestant Christianity.[26]

Under Weber's tripartite division of forms of authority, traditional and legal-rational are considered permanent, and charismatic transitory. However, the 'irrational' forms of legitimacy are regarded as interconnected by liberal (especially conservative-liberal) commentators. This is because liberal-rational structures are thought by such critics to be able to generate change through the expansion of science and technology and the development of meritocratic institutions. Traditional authority acts as a constraint on necessary social developments, and as a result charismatic leadership is required to break the accepted social order and then reconstitute traditional authority.[27]

Whilst *The Wicker Man* concentrates on the clash of religious belief between Sergeant Neil Howie and the islanders, as David Bartholomew has suggested,[28] it also portrays a struggle between the types of authority Weber and others identify. The film's central conflict is one between legal-rational legitimacy associated with modern capitalism, as represented by Sergeant Howie, and authoritarian traditional authority infused with charismatic leadership as represented by Lord Summerisle. Lord Summerisle, as in the model for traditional leadership, appeals to ancient practice to maintain his rule: 'Here the old Gods aren't dead' he informs Howie at their first meeting at his castle. Along with a set of beliefs held to be fixed by long-established convention, the Summerisle community is regulated by a hierarchy which is similarly perceived to be set by long-standing custom. Summerisle's status is indebted to a pre-Christian practice that is maintained into the present day, that of primogeniture. Upon Howie's arrival on the island, the locals

---

[24] Weber, *The Theory of Economic and Social Organization*, p. 306.

[25] Weber, *The Theory of Economic and Social Organization*, p. 311.

[26] See Weber, *The Theory of Economic and Social Organization*, p. 197 and Weber, *The Protestant Ethic and the Spirit of Capitalism*. The novel makes clear Howie is an Episcopalian, part of the Anglican Communion. See Hardy and Shaffer, *The Wicker Man*, p. 5.

[27] Giddens, *Capitalism and Modern Social Theory*, p. 161.

[28] Bartholomew, '*The Wicker Man*', p. 33.

explain that all matters have to be reported to his Lordship, and continual reference is made to Summerisle's title at the apex of the pre-capitalist, feudal social structure. This deference is not simply honorific, as social hierarchies are much in force. For instance, on Howie's departure from the castle on the second occasion, Summerisle summons a minion, Broome, by ringing a small bell, and instructs his servant to take the policeman to his transport.

Whilst the Summerisle community is presented in the film as superficially idyllic – there is sexual licence, a strong sense of social solidarity and an approach to the natural world that fears neither death nor guilt – it is nonetheless governed by a rigid and unequal power structure. In keeping with the characterisation of the island being subject to traditional authority, there is an absence of critical thought from the islanders in opposition to patrimonial power. At no point in the film are any of Summerisle's subjects in dissent with the dominant ideology, nor are critical views expressed against his lordship. Those who held a contrary value system, like the church ministers, in Summerisle's words, 'fled the islands never to return'.

The distinctions foregrounded by the Weberian taxonomy of authority are implicitly recognised by *The Wicker Man*'s characters. With Summerisle's traditional practices under threat due to the failure of the crops, charismatic leadership is required in order to maintain them. Christopher Lee describes the persona of Summerisle as 'charming', a term with a myriad of magical connotations.[29] Summerisle's lead role in the ritual slaughter of Howie is indicative of the former's claim to magical ability over natural forces, to be able 'when necessary to appease' them. Through ritual sacrifice under Summerisle's control the crops, in his own words, 'will not fail'. Howie also recognises that Summerisle's authority is now based on charismatic claims, and seeks to undermine it. He attempts this first by stressing his opponent's own ordinary mortal status ('man' not 'lord'), then exaggerating Summerisle's social position (king). Second, and concordant with such an appeal to authority, if the sacrifice fails,

---

[29] Lee, 'A Letter from Lord Summerisle', p. 60.

Summerisle's own position is in direct threat; indeed, Howie's nemesis will be the next sacrifice:

> **Howie**: Killing me isn't going to bring back your apples Summerisle. You know it won't. Go on, man, tell them it won't.
> **Summerisle**: I know it will.
> **Howie**: Well don't you understand that if your crops fail this year, that next year you will need to have another blood sacrifice. And next year no one less than the King of Summerisle himself will do. With the crops' failure, Summerisle, your people will kill you on May Day.
> **Summerisle**: They will not fail. The sacrifice of the willing, king, virgin fool will be accepted.

This is consistent with Weber, who similarly identifies the dangerous instability of charismatic leadership:

> [T]he charismatic quality of the monarch, which was transmitted unchallenged by heredity, was upheld so rigidly that any misfortune whatever, not only defeat in war, but drought, floods or astronomical phenomena which were considered unlucky, forced him to do public penance and might even force abdication. If such things occurred, it was a sign that he did not possess the requisite charismatic virtue; he was thus not a legitimate 'Son of Heaven'.[30]

By contrast, Howie appears to be a straightforward incarnation of the legal-rational paradigm. Howie's commitment to the legal-rational approach imbues his character throughout the film, and informs his response to practices that are not based on

---

[30] Weber, *The Theory of Economic and Social Organization*, p. 330.

institutionalised norms. As he exclaims on leaving May Morrison's shop, 'You're all raving mad'. For Howie, the structures and beliefs that maintain the customs of Summerisle are not just wrong, but irrational.

In contrast to the Summerislanders' enthrallment by charismatic leadership, Howie is bound by the rules of his office. Howie owes allegiance to the charismatic leadership of Christ, but is able to repress it – at least partially – in the performance of his policing function. Even when he comes across transgression with which he agrees, such as in the opening scene of the longer 'Director's Cut' version, when he and a colleague (McTaggart) happen upon graffiti reading 'Jesus saves', Howie orders that the message be 'removed'. Despite his strong religious beliefs, Howie conducts himself in accordance with the office of the State, maintaining the distinction between his own deeply held spiritual values and his office, as required under bureaucratic rationality. As he tells Lord Summerisle at the end of the first meeting at the castle 'I am interested in only one thing – the law'.

Bureaucratic rationality requires respect for the legal hierarchy in which it operates. Howie's insistence on respecting such order includes seeking out his prime suspect's approval for the exhumation of Rowan's body, because of Summerisle's legal position as Justice of the Peace. Throughout his encounters on the island, Howie defines himself through his office, as he tells the schoolgirls, 'I am a police officer, here from the mainland'. His response to transgression is to report it to the appropriate agency. On his second meeting at Summerisle's castle he threatens that he shall 'report my suspicions to the Chief Constable of the West Highland Constabulary'. The islanders mock these bureaucratic-rational appeals to authority, with their corresponding division of duties. When Howie recounts the peculiar run of events, ending with the discovery of a hare in Rowan's supposed grave, Summerisle's rebuff is to remind him that 'you are supposed to be [the] detective here'. Under legal-rational authority, by which Howie claims to act, it is his duty to resolve the situation by virtue of his office.

Similarly, when the Sergeant threatens Miss Rose over her instruction on the 'Rites and Rituals of May-day', Howie's words perfectly encapsulates the legal-rational mentality: 'Miss, you can be quite sure that I shall report this to the proper authorities'. Miss Rose recognises the appeal to bureaucratic-rational authority that Howie is claiming. She undermines it by reminding him that under bureaucratic-rationality, legitimacy is tied to office and has 'a clearly defined sphere of competence in the legal sense.'[31] As she acerbically observes, 'I was unaware that police had any authority in matters of education'. Howie has no rebuttal to this reply.

The conflict between Howie and the islanders is thus apparently between two different forms of authority, one associated with liberalism, modernity and democracy and the other with tradition, pre-modernity and authoritarianism.[32] The brutal attack on a 'Christian copper' in which the whole community is complicit, was supposed (by the film's writer and director) to savagely indict the latter form of social organisation and the practices that underpin it. Shaffer refers to those interested in paganism and witchcraft as 'lunatics',[33] yet audiences have continually sided with the populace of Summerisle rather than with the virtues represented by Howie.

One grouping in particular, contemporary class-struggle anarchists, has embraced the imagery of *The Wicker Man,* utilising it in their anti-capitalist propaganda. There is insufficient space here to fully develop an account of a distinctive anarchist approach to 'reading' filmic and artistic texts, although some writers like Allan Antliff and Richard Porton have looked at specific anarchist themes in cinematic and other cultural forms, especially as promotional devices.[34] These, however, are not the only ways anarchists have used cultural products. Jude Davies and John Moore, to name but two, have explored the ways in which other popular cultural forms have been subverted (or détourned) by radicals, who unmask both the reactionary elements in mainstream media phenomena[35] but also their subversive potential.[36] This dissidence can lie in the properties of

---

[31] Weber, *The Theory of Economic and Social Organization*, p. 306.
[32] See also Weber *The Theory of Social and Economic Organization*, p. 389.
[33] Bartholomew, '*The Wicker Man*', p. 14.
[34] Antliff, 'Anarchy in Art'; Porton, *Film and the Anarchist Imagination*.
[35] Davies, 'Anarchy in the UK?', p. 76.
[36] Moore, 'Public Secret', p. 118.

the product (as in propaganda), the actions of the producer, the approach of the audience, and the interaction between these three, as well as in the reaction by existing authority.[37]

The example of such radical subversion I will draw on appeared in a free newspaper, *Hate Mail*, which was handed out in the run-up to the anti-capitalist May Day demonstrations in 2002. The paper's layout, displayed in Figure 1, pastiches the right-wing tabloid *The Daily Mail*. The article inside the paper (and trailed on the front page), like many others in *Hate Mail*, spoofs mainstream reporting of radical activities (see Figure 2). A characteristic feature of popular journalism is to seek out extraordinary origins for radical protest as a way of fixing the blame on the 'irrational' source of these disruptive movements, and damning both by association. These investigations often find that responsibility rests with 'outside agitators' or 'professional' revolutionaries inspired either by Soviet or Chinese Communism, and thus purportedly lie outside liberal rational societies.[38]

In this case the anarchists, emphasising their points by using stills from *The Wicker Man*, suggested that the 'inspiration' for their disorder lies in the film. In true tabloid style, they construct a collection of societal scapegoats supposedly lying behind the anti-capitalist disorders, composed of 'anarchists, football hooligans and pagans' as well as portraying anarchists as cider-quaffing vandals who receive instruction on destructive practices through the Internet.[39] By playing with the discourse used by socially conservative, economically liberal institutions such as the mainstream media, *Hate Mail* helps to illuminate how these operate, and hence undermines their effectiveness. Parody and

---

[37] Moore, 'Public Secret', p. 120.

[38] Following the anti-capitalist demonstrations of June 18th 1999, the mainstream press sought out the culprits, amongst squatter communities, 'crusties and New Age hippies, the anti-motorist groups and anarchists, and earth mothers': Nigel Hastilow of the *Birmingham Post*, cited in Anon., 'Column inches', p. 30. Paul of *The Daily Mail* blames 'anarchists' and 'eco-protestors' for the 'violence' at the May Day protests in 2000: Harris, 'Then the thugs came out to play', p. 4. For claims about Soviet Communism inspiring anti-capitalists see Heffer, 'This bestial behaviour is motivated by evil, not nobler concerns', p. 6 and for the association with Chinese socialism see Malone, 'The howling mob just bite the hands that feed them', p. 31.

[39]MacGregor, 'B-movie plot for Mayday mayhem', p. 5.

exaggeration demonstrate the underlying ideological assumptions in Weber's taxonomy of authority. The reductive subsumation of all anti-liberal democratic forces into either traditional or charismatic societies suggests that only capitalism provides a bulwark against tyranny. It is this highly questionable underlying assumption that *Hate Mail* lampoons, by claiming that *The Wicker Man* and its 'benevolent tyranny' is the inspiration and model for contemporary anti-capitalism.[40]

Fig.1: Front cover of the anti-capitalist *Hate Mail* using a still image from *The Wicker Man*.

This is not to say that there are not amusing parallels to be drawn between the activities of the Summerisle residents and subversive activists. The community has many attractive aspects, which have made audiences more sympathetic to the murderous Pagans than to the martyr. As Tanya Krzywinska points out in her analysis of the representation of the irrational in occult films,

---

[40] See Lee, 'A Letter from Lord Summerisle', p. 60.

Fig.2: 'B-movie plot for Mayday mayhem' in *Hate Mail*, p.5.

Howie's death fails to shock the audience out of their 'identification with Summerisle's anarchic paganism'.[41] The ludic, anarchic features of Summerisle are too beguiling for the audience to identify fully with the martyred 'Christian copper', and it is these seductive elements that radicals play with. These include sexual licence, the sense of community, rejection of the state religion and the mockery of oppressive legal authority.[42]

---

[41] Krzywinska, *A Skin for Dancing In*, p. 83.
[42] MacGregor, 'B-movie plot for Mayday mayhem', p. 5.

These subversive features of the Summerisle community are common also to anarchism. It is especially the latter, the assault on the judicial authority that maintains the structures of exploitation, that *Hate Mail* relishes. The article's pseudonymous writer, the archetypical tabloid reporter, has a 'top-secret plan' revealed to him by a suitably anonymous 'informant', which is 'to incinerate a top-level police figure. "The victim must represent the law of the land, he must come as a fool, he must come willingly and he must be a virgin. The first two can be arranged, the others I'm not sure about."'[43]

A further similarity that Summerisle residents (and modern Pagans) and anarchists share is a common commemoration of May Day (Beltane).[44] *Hate Mail* – created for the May Day protests – parodies the tone and style of its Northcliffe Publisher's near namesake, and draws direct analogies with the reclaiming of the streets of major cities on May 1st and the May Day celebrations of Summerisle:

> For example, the pagans have a procession where they are lead by a tuneless band – how similar to the racket of the evil 'Samba band' that urges modern day rioters on their Mayday mayhem! And in another telling scene, the officer requests that they remove the outlandish masks they wear to conceal their identity. They refuse to do so, in a scenario that has become all too familiar in the past couple of years.[45]

Yet there is much in the Summerisle community that is antipathetic to class struggle anarchists: the maintenance of patriarchal authority, the existence of a capitalist economy (although we only see it operating with Howie), and a rigid division of labour, with characters assigned roles by occupation ('doctor', 'fisherman', 'librarian' and 'school-teacher'), as well as the distinction between the governor and the governed. The

---

[43] MacGregor, 'B-movie plot for Mayday mayhem', p. 5.
[44] See, for instance, the demonstration on May 1st 2000 in San Francisco. Mahtin, 'Reclaim MayDay San Francisco'.
[45] MacGregor, 'B-movie plot for Mayday mayhem', p. 5.

original script also made clear that there was also a gendered
division of labour: May Morrison

> **Mrs Morrison**: My husband, like most of you
> men, leaves everything to be cleared up after
> him.[46]

The mocking tone of *Hate Mail* also draws attention to the
myriad weaknesses in Weberian analysis. First, as Herbert
Marcuse, a libertarian socialist and critic of Weber points out, the
'pent up aggression' produced by bureaucratically administered
capitalism legitimises for itself 'medieval cruelty' discharged
'scientifically'.[47] Capitalist bureaucracy produces impulses which
are suppressed, manifesting themselves in irrational, destructive
behaviour. Second, capitalism's claims to reason are not
adequately supported, for managerial constructions are often
based upon pre-existing theocratic institutions, just as Howie's
bureaucratic rationality is ultimately predicated on religious
faith.[48] Similarly, Summerisle's irrational religious superstructure
was constructed to maintain a rational entrepreneurial exercise.
As Lord Summerisle explains to Howie over a sample of one of
his cultivars, the 'joyous old Gods' were reconstituted to increase
economic efficiency and 'rouse them [the workers] from their
apathy'. Rather than being in conflict with technical reason,
traditional practices supported by charismatic leadership were
developed in order to maintain productive efficiency, based on
technological advance.

Third, *Hate Mail* derisively pastiches the socially conservative
liberal association of anti-capitalism with irreason and
consequently with tyranny. The hysterical tone of tabloids and
their mythic conspiracies (in which DIY stores selling wicker
garden furniture are negligent in selling anarchists the materials
for their diabolical plans)[49] show that the discourse supporting

---

[46] See Phillips, '*The Wicker Man*: Scenes filmed but never used'.

[47] Marcuse, *Negations*, p. 207.

[48] 'Knowing the law, in Christian Scotland, to be based on the teachings of Christ,
he saw his work in the police as an opportunity to give a practical expression to
his faith and convictions'. Hardy and Shaffer, *The Wicker Man*, p. 5.

[49] MacGregor, 'B-movie plot for Mayday mayhem', p. 5.

liberalism is partial and value-laden. Finally, bureaucratic reason's claims to superiority are unsupportable. Howie, who is wholly manipulated, falls victim to the mocking islanders and loses every argument, thereby questioning the consistency, and undermining the supremacy, of liberal 'rationality'. Similarly, *Hate Mail*'s ridicule of bureaucratic reason illustrates the superficiality, and the prejudices, that underwrite liberal-rational discourse.

Bibliography

Aloi, P., 'Witch Cinema'. *The Witches Voice*, <http://www.witchvox.com/media/cinema02.html> and <http://www.witchvox.com/media/cinema11.html> [Accessed 10 July 2003].

Anon., 'Column inches', *The Independent on Sunday*, 27 June 1999, p. 30.

Antliff, A., 'Anarchy in Art: Strategies of dissidence', *Anarchist Studies,* 11.1 (2003), 66-83.

Bartholomew, D., *'The Wicker Man'*, *Cinefantastique,* 6.3, Winter (1977), 4-18; 32-46.

Brown, A., *Inside 'The Wicker Man': The morbid ingenuities* (London: Sidgwick and Jackson, 2000).

Davies, J., 'Anarchy in the UK?: Anarchism and popular culture in 1990s Britain', in *Twenty First Century Anarchism: Unorthodox ideas for a new millennium*, ed. by J. Purkis and J. Bowen (London: Cassell, 1997), pp. 62-82.

Giddens, A., *Capitalism and Modern Social Theory* (Cambridge: Cambridge University Press, 1971).

Hardy, R. and A. Shaffer, *The Wicker Man* (London: Pan, 2000).

Harris, P., 'Then the thugs came out to play', *Daily Mail*, 2 May 2000, pp. 4-5.

Heffer, S., 'This bestial behaviour is motivated by evil, not nobler concerns', *Daily Mail*, 2 May 2000, p. 6.

Knight, R., 'Between the Devil and the Deep Blue Uniform', originally appeared in *Nuada,* 3 (2000), (personal copy provided by Gail Ashurst), 1-4.

Krzywinska, T., *A Skin For Dancing In: Possession, witchcraft and voodoo in film* (Trowbridge: Flicks Books, 2000).

Lee, C., 'A Letter from Lord Summerisle', *Cinefantastique*, 6.4-7.1, Spring (1978), 60.

Locke, J., *Two Treatises of Government* (Cambridge: Cambridge University Press, 1988).

MacGregor, W., 'B-movie plot for Mayday mayhem', *Hate Mail*, 1 May 2000, p. 6.

Mahtin, 'Reclaim MayDay San Francisco', Mid-Atlantic Infoshop, <http://www.infoshop.org/octo/m1_sf2.html> [Accessed 10 July 2003].

Malone, C., 'The howling mob just bite the hands that feed them', *Sunday Mirror*, 20 June 1999, p. 31.

Marcuse, H., *Negations*, trans. by J. Shapiro (London: Allen Lane, 1969).

Molloy, J. 'Contemporary Authoritarian Regimes', in *Encyclopedia of Government and Politics*, vol. 1, ed. by M. Hawkesworth and M. Kogan (London: Routledge), pp. 229-46.

Moore, J., 'Public Secret: Fredy Perlman and the literature of subversion', in *Twenty First Century Anarchism: Unorthodox ideas for a new millennium*, ed. by J. Purkis and J. Bowen (London: Cassell, 1997), pp. 117-31.

Phillips, S., 'The Wicker Man: Scenes filmed but never used', <http://www.steve-p.org/wm/script.htm> [Accessed 10 July 2003].

Porton, R., *Film and the Anarchist Imagination* (London: Verso, 1999).

Weber, M., *The Theory of Social and Economic Organization*, trans. by A. Henderson and T. Parsons (Glasgow: William Hodge and Company, 1949).

_____, *The Protestant Ethic and the Spirit of Capitalism,* trans. by T. Parsons (London: Routledge, 1992).

Wojtas, O., 'A burning passion that's close to worship', *The Times Higher Education Supplement,* 11 July 2003, pp. 20-21.

Wicca Net: The Home Of Wicca and Wiccans on the Web,
<http://wiccanet.tv/articles/01/11/25/008229.shtml>
[Accessed 10 July 2003].

Wicker Man, The, dir. R. Hardy. Canal+ (1973).

'Here On Official Business': Production, patriarchy and the hazards of policing a pre-industrial utopia

Belle Doyle

A Pastoral Paradise?

> The Wicker Man remains a truly remarkable film because it transcended its origins in the cheap, disposable world of 1970s British cinema and tapped into a well of fascination which sustains its reputation, indeed increases it, to this day. It is Janus-faced: it looked to the future, anticipating how our convictions would create new and novel social fragmentations. Yet it feasted on the most ancient of human archetypes, reformulating the oldest and most persistent of conundrums: how do we live with the difference of others? How do we construct systems to live by?[1]

Thus Allan Brown, in his fascinating account of *The Wicker Man*'s (Hardy, 1973) production and continuing popularity with contemporary audiences, identifies the film's central concerns. Certainly, the film's on-going cult status is attributable to more than its unusual narrative, rural setting and shock ending. While the film's *mise-en-scène* places it firmly in the early 1970s, its continuing relevance to contemporary audiences is precisely the 'Janus-faced' quality that Brown mentions. At the heart of *The Wicker Man* lies a complex analysis of the social anxieties that revolve around patriarchy and production, and this is undoubtedly an aspect of the film that the contemporary spectator recognises and finds rewarding. Current debates concerning food production, especially genetically modified crops, the declining standards of living in rural areas, the changing definitions of criminal behaviour and the consequences for policing, and the steady erosion of the influence of Christianity on people's everyday lives are all reflected in a film that, despite its flared trousers,

---

[1] Brown, *Inside 'The Wicker Man'*, p. 187.

paisley shirts and traditional music, reflects modern sensibilities to a marked degree.

'I'm here on official business' is the phrase Sergeant Howie uses in The Green Man Inn, to alert the rowdy pub crowd to his role as the investigating officer of Rowan Morrison's disappearance. It is this over-worked phrase that constantly draws attention to the ways in which *The Wicker Man* analyses the relationship between the precarious nature of food production and communal prosperity. The result of this investigation, personified by a figure who can truly be said to be the visible patriarchal representative of a triumvirate of Church, Law and State, opens up the complex system that co-operates between patriarchy and capitalism, and questions whether this system can effectively persuade us that it alone holds the monopoly on morality, family values, gender roles and social norms. 'Official business' is Howie's declaration of his own status and power, though it inevitably leads him to his death. It has to be said that some of the real cathartic pleasures in watching this film stem from the ease with which certain patriarchal institutions are destroyed and their lack of influence made palpable. And as a film that does not sit too comfortably within the horror genre, it nonetheless finds common ground with films like *Rosemary's Baby* (Polanski, 1968) and *The Omen* (Donner, 1976), where the figure of the child portends crisis and doom.

However, I would like to look first at the historical and cultural contexts of *The Wicker Man* before examining, specifically, its representations of patriarchy and production. While Allan Brown, in the introductory quotation to this chapter, was referring to the pre-historical aspects of the film – notably, its representation of Paganism, sun-worship and human sacrifice – the questions about rural life that the film highlights in terms of its policing, and its lack of moral and religious guidance, have been prevalent in British history since around 1600. Changeable weather conditions, poor harvests and a grossly unfair taxation system meant that, between 1550 and 1700, loss of farming land and migration from the countryside into cities and towns paved the way for the Industrial Revolution. These factors also led to a rejection, in many areas of the countryside, of allegiance to either the State or the national Church (to whom the peasantry were expected to pay tithes). The unpopularity of the established Church led to instances of horses and pigs being baptised as a protest.[2]

Furthermore, contemporary urban accounts viewed certain areas of the countryside – notably the poorer pastureland, heath land and forested areas where communities managed subsistence farming – as places that were virtually lawless, where locals harboured witches and their craft, and still believed in curses and charms.[3] Social changes at this time from a medieval society to a capitalist, industrial successor would have led to greater insecurities for rural dwellers. As Anne Llewellyn Barstow points out, the persecution of rural women for practising witchcraft became a national obsession in Scotland between 1590 and 1700.[4] She also notes the economic relationship between those accused of witchcraft and their accusers; the Courts, Church and State could seize the property and land of anyone found guilty, and would often give it to the accusers as compensation. This meant that older women who inherited property when their husbands died were especially vulnerable.[5] Witch hunts can be defined as institutionalised misogyny, in which the continuing economic control of financially independent women – who were denied access to legitimate trades and were often working on the margins of the male economy – played a significant role in their persecution. An additional catalyst for witch hunting was the suspicion that any activity not solely directed to the welfare of husband or children might in fact be 'anti-Christian'. The close relationship between the Church, the Court and the State was founded on an expedient *economic* basis rather than any moral association.

Three hundred years later in 2003, 30 years after *The Wicker Man* was released, the average farming income in the UK was only £11,000 per annum.[6] Less than 2% of the UK workforce is currently engaged in farming work, and in 60 years the number of farms in the UK has declined from nearly 500,000 in 1939 to

---

[2] Hill, *The World Turned Upside Down*, p. 29.
[3] Hill, *The World Turned Upside Down*, p. 47.
[4] Barstow, *Witchcraze*, p. 77.
[5] Barstow, *Witchcraze*, p. 102-07.
[6] Figure given by Blythman, *Shopped*, p. 135.

168,000 in 1999, and the figure is still falling.[7] Britain could now
be said to be struggling through a post-industrial phrase where the
ideologies of industrial production, with their emphasis on
uniformity, regulation and mass consumption, are applied to areas
such as 'the service industry', 'the tourist industry' and 'the
farming industry'. Food production, particularly the production of
fruit and vegetables, is now considered to be a *manufacturing*,
rather than a natural, process: in other words, farming is a
business, and a heavily policed and regulated one at that.
Contemporary issues, such as the over-use of agro-chemicals,
intensive farming methods, subsidies, soil erosion, animal welfare
and 'food miles', have become part of the continuing debate
about farming and food production: the idea of farming as a
traditional resource, a family-run practice in which generations
would occupy and work the same piece of land, is now outdated.[8]
One of the outcomes of the industrialisation and globalisation of
farming is that British consumers have come to expect fruit and
vegetables to be available 52 weeks of the year regardless of
whether the produce is in or out of season. As the five largest
supermarket chains sell almost four-fifths of all food consumed in
the UK, they have the economic clout to import fruit and
vegetables from anywhere in the world.[9] Friends of the Earth
have carried out a three-year survey into the retailing of apples
(co-incidentally enough, given the importance of the fruit to
Summerisle's economy), and found that 62% were imported, with
16% being imported from outside the EC. Only 38% of apples on
sale were from British orchards, and the number of apple
growers, unable to cope with growing competition from abroad,
has declined from 600 in 1990 to 400 in 2000.[10]

Set against the background of contemporary debates in
farming, *The Wicker Man* reflects an unusually radical

---

[7] Figures from Corporate Watch, 'Supermarkets'.
[8] There are a proliferation of websites on these subjects: two useful sites are
Friends   of   the   Earth   [www.foe.co.uk]   and   Transport   2000
[www.transport2000.org.uk].
[9] Figures collected by the Institute of Grocery and Distribution, *Grocery Retailing
2003*.
[10] Friends of the Earth Media Briefing, 'Home Grown Apples in Short Supply in
Big Supermarkets', p. 2.

politicisation of the rural economy. There are a variety of films which portray the countryside as an unruly and untamed space, ranging from *Psycho* (Hitchcock, 1960), *Deliverance* (Boorman, 1972), *The Texas Chainsaw Massacre* (Hooper, 1974), *An American Werewolf in London* (Landis, 1981) and the recent Scottish feature *The Last Great Wilderness* (Mackenzie, 2002); all show the countryside to be as dangerous and forbidding as the city. It is also the space where urban dwellers expect urban rules to apply, and this is often their downfall.

'Even These People Can't Be That Mad': Policing Summerisle

Policing, as the visible presence and embodiment of law and order in society, has a number of roles: the protection of individuals, property and goods; the recognition that a crime has been committed; and the pursuit of criminals and gathering of evidence to penalise criminal behaviour. Law and order underwrite an idealised notion of how individuals in a society should behave, while the police and justice system strive to maintain an on-going relationship with modern sensibilities: the decriminalisation of cannabis use and the criminalisation of domestic violence are two examples of a shift in policies in prosecution. To use as the main protagonist of *The Wicker Man* a policeman who sticks to the letter of the law in all circumstances means that while we might finally empathise with Howie as a victim, his interpretation of the law does not leave us room to find any sympathetic common ground with his investigation.

Whatever Howie's failings are as an investigator, he manages to police *himself* very effectively, and expects others to act in similar fashion. The revelation, very early in *The Wicker Man*, of Howie's religious beliefs serves to show that he does not represent straight, white masculinity unproblematically, and that the uniform which is the visible representation of his power is worn as a Lacanian parade of masculinity. He asks the islanders to defer to his uniform and the institution it represents: he reveals the stripes on his arm to the Harbourmaster in an effort to gain entry to the island; he foregrounds his status as a policeman during visits to the pub and the school ('As you can see, I am a

Police Officer'); at the Registrar's office, he shows the librarian his warrant card. In terms of narrative gender representation, the film prepares us for what appears to be a conventional mystery: a representative of masculinity as the active investigator, femininity as the passive recipient of investigation, as symbolised by the photograph of Rowan that Howie keeps in his pocket. To have such an overtly visual representation of masculinity inviting the gaze of other males without the reassuring counterbalance of heterosexuality, or a comparable female figure, confirms Steve Neale's view that the spectacle of masculinity always has to be confined to an action where a male protagonist will have to exert masculine control or be punished – hence the homoerotic subtext of the cowboy gunfight. As Neale says, 'where women are investigated, men are tested'.[11] Therefore, at the beginning of the film, gender roles seem easily recognisable, but Howie's reliance on his uniform, and his uneasy presence in the pub dealing with the locals, means that while he expects people to look to him as the visual representation of law and order, he constantly has to remind them (and himself) of his official powers.

From our first glance of the island, Summerisle looks – from the air at least – like a bustling centre of arable prosperity. The scene appears to be set for a crime that is easily identifiable, within a community that recognises the importance of law and order, and appreciates that a police officer should expect its support in order to carry out his or her duties. But the island is also marked as an unusual site, not only for its food production and fertility, but also, as Howie dourly points out, because it has 'no licensing laws' and permits 'singing and dancing on a Sunday'. The island, by the nature of its geography, is separate from the mainland, and potentially is difficult to police.[12] The most important roles of the policeman in society are those of crime's observation and definition. An individual police officer is expected to make a decision about whether a crime has taken place, and what laws have been broken. Howie's discomfort in

---

[11] Neale, 'Masculinity as Spectacle', p. 19.
[12] Discussions at 'The Wicker Man: Rituals, Readings and Reactions' conference, in July 2003 revealed that a screening of The Wicker Man was cancelled on BBC2 in the early 1990s because of the Orkney child abuse allegations.

witnessing the sexual displays outside The Green Man Inn is both
a narrative device to show his own sexual repression and also a
means of highlighting the difficulties of policing sexual
behaviour in what is to all intents and purposes a different
culture. Crime is not a fixed category but is identified and defined
by its cultural context.

It is the cultural differences of Summerisle that highlight how
much Howie's skills as an investigator are hampered by the
apparent complete disinterest of the islanders in co-operating with
him. The generic device of the detective means that we have
certain expectations of the text: an unravelling that will lead to a
body, a murderer, a motive. Howie's investigations on
Summerisle into the mystery of Rowan's absence – the 'red
herring' of the text – is meant in the beginning to reassure us, as
spectators, that there is a mystery to be solved, and that Howie
will solve it. It becomes apparent that Rowan Morrison may have
been burnt to death a few months earlier but Howie is hampered
by the fact that there is no physical evidence: there is no death
certificate and exhumation of her coffin reveals only the body of
a hare. If, as Howie argues with Miss Rose, the schoolteacher,
this is a culture that does not recognise death, then how is a
murder to be recognised as such, and solved as a crime? As he
says, 'she's either dead or she's not dead'. A similar semiotic
confusion arises over the naming of the churchyard – can it be
said to be a *church*yard when the Church is absent? As Howie's
efforts become increasingly undermined by the islanders, the
symbolic presence of the beetle tied to the nail in Rowan's school
desk becomes clear: as the beetle runs in circles, it eventually will
be pulled closer and closer to the nail and be unable ever to break
free.

The expectation that the narrative is a real mystery that must be
solved is undermined by the fact that Howie does *look*; he finds
an over-abundance of clues, and has no trouble in interpreting
them, but he cannot see the bigger picture. The original clue to
Rowan's identity – the photograph that was sent with the
anonymous letter – is Howie's (and the audience's) constant
reminder of her, but as an image it signifies an absence of Rowan
rather than a presence. In a photograph that looks like a studio
picture rather than a relaxed family snapshot, she stands with her

back to an apple tree full of blossom, smiling at the camera; the pose is unselfconscious and untroubled but to a policeman's eye, a missing girl on the verge of puberty is 'always trouble'. The apple blossom, which should enhance the visual image, becomes a reminder that time is running out, which becomes increasingly significant as Howie realises the importance of the harvest. He discovers another visual clue when he breaks into the chemist's shop and discovers the negative of the missing Harvest festival photograph. He makes himself a new print to discover that the harvest has failed in the previous year, and that the girl in the picture is none other than Rowan Morrison. Later, in the library, he discovers a book on traditional May Day celebrations and concludes that a human sacrifice will be made in order to maintain food production.

Howie's interpretation of events (strangely, yet also appropriately) rests on a Marxist analysis of crime being committed due to conflict arising from the pressures of existing in a capitalist system. The stresses arising from the competition to survive in a system that subjugates workers until they turn on their oppressors do eventually lead to violence, and Howie's conclusion, drawn from the clues left for him, is the logical explanation for the disappearance of Rowan – what else can the islanders do in the face of economic ruin? What he fails to appreciate, ironically for a Christian of strong belief, is the idea of a fundamental religious belief that would be powerful enough to impel its adherents to take another person's life. He cannot draw any analogies between his own Christianity and the islanders' religion; what he sees on Summerisle remains 'fake religion'. The clues about sacrifice and martyrdom are ever-present, however: an earlier scene in the film shows him giving a reading in church about the Last Supper, and taking Communion. Nonetheless, Howie's rigid belief system does not allow him to re-interpret Pagan practices in religious terms, but to understand them solely as a policeman whose duties are firmly tied to the protection of production and prosperity.

But he does strike a blow for modern criminology. While he might have believed at the start of the case that there was a person responsible on Summerisle for Rowan Morrison's murder – one bad apple, as it were – the result of his investigation is to come to the conclusion that the entire community has to bear responsibility. The letter sent to him bears witness to this: the writer argues 'I reckon it's all our business when a kid disappears'. Rather than relying on his 'Christian Copper' instincts to recognise evil when he sees it, Howie realises that policing is not necessarily about the removal of one inherently evil person from society, but that aspects of society might have a profound influence on behaviour: economic depression, unemployment, a rampantly consumerist society that excludes people. In this context, Howie's outrage in the girls' classroom at what he sees as inappropriate teaching resources, and his subsequent threats to take the matter further, are part of a recognition that the entire society of Summerisle, with all its 'degeneracy, brawling in bars, indecency in public places, corruption of the young', must collectively bear responsibility for Rowan's disappearance.

'Your Lordship Seems Strangely Unconcerned': Patriarchy and production on Summerisle

Howie selectively chooses to recognise only those aspects of island life that present a civilising veneer to Summerisle, and in spite of what he has witnessed – the orgy on the village green, Willow's deflowering of Ash Buchanan, and numerous fertility rites – he is aware that his role is to protect the social order. He recognises that there are families on Summerisle, as there are families on the mainland, and that Rowan Morrison is the product of a family. May Morrison sells strange sweets in the Post Office, she is vague about the whereabouts of one of her daughters, and she has odd ideas about family health, but she is still part of a family. This is really Howie's downfall – he is part of a policing system that upholds marriage as an ideal contract binding two people in a relationship recognised by the Church, the Law and the State. The family, therefore, is worth preserving because it is a measurable unit of moral stability, the basic unit of society itself; it is also a unit of both consumption and production. Though we never see Mr Morrison, Mrs Morrison maintains respectability through her role at the Post Office; she is middle-aged rather than young, and not blonde – in the film's codes of female sexual attractiveness, Mrs Morrison does not pass muster.

She is instead a touchstone for family values on Summerisle. But her role as mother is finally challenged by Howie on May Day as he asks, 'In the name of God, woman, what kind of mother are you?' He realises that motherhood is an unknown quantity on an island where women appear to function successfully outside the framework of a patriarchal capitalist production system. In patriarchal terms, good mothers are defined by their willingness to sacrifice themselves for their children; bad mothers are those who would sacrifice their children for the common good.

Howie's own readings of the business of Summerisle, and his notion of how that production should take place, are marked by his disgust at the tinned food, the sexually provocative women, the public displays of singing and dancing, and the far more sinister display of parthenogenesis – clearly, there is some sort of production going on but it is not anything he can recognise. Summerisle's fame as a site of apple production (which is heralded almost immediately at the start of *The Wicker Man* by the postmark on the anonymous letter) already marks it as a site of difference, a space in which fruit cultivation is local, instantly recognisable and part of a specific food culture. But we find frequent glimpses of an alternative economic system. While there appears to be no differentiation in gender roles, there is an absence of male productivity; even the men who appear to have a role – the laird in his castle, the publican, the baker, the doctor, the chemist, the gravedigger – do not appear to work too hard. Most male activity seems to revolve around singing, dancing and standing about (witness the group in the harbour watching the seaplane come in). In direct contrast to this, we have women that could possibly be read as over-productive. The post-mistress, the school-mistress, the registrar/librarian, and the landlord's daughter are all seen as taking their roles to extremes. The array of goods at Mrs Morrison's post office is similar to the display at the chemist's shop, but she also has plenty of customers. While the schoolboys do their maypole dance, the girls sit at their desks and study phallic symbolism under the watchful eye of Miss Rose. Willow's role is taken to extremes, so much so that her sexual favours are bestowed on every man she meets.

The most excessive displays of female productivity are saved for when Howie visits Lord Summerisle and witnesses both the group of pregnant women in the orchard and the girls attempting parthenogenic reproduction with fire. As Lord Summerisle explains to Howie, 'What girl would not prefer the child of a God to that of some acne-scarred artisan?' Howie's reaction – that this is 'fake biology' – is countered by Lord Summerisle's remark that Christ is 'himself the son of a virgin impregnated, I believe, by a ghost'. The urbane Lord Summerisle is another manifestation of patriarchy that, like Howie's role as a policeman, appears slightly out of place in the milieu of the island. The idea of the traditional laird – Summerisle wears a kilt when we see him for the first time – is undermined by the story of his grandfather who bought the island in 1868. This is therefore not a traditional family seat, held for generations: Lord Summerisle's grandfather was a Victorian scientist who needed land to grow crops and labour to harvest it. The presence of the original Lord Summerisle is therefore as a re-constructed Lord of the Manor. His argument for the return of the old religion to the island is purely pragmatic: it increased productivity. The triumph of the late Lord Summerisle's vision of an agricultural Eden, the success of his new strains of apples and his cultivation of 'joyous old Gods' now place the burden on his grandson to carry on the tradition. While Lord Summerisle's explanation confirms Howie's suspicions that Pagan worship is being carried out, it seems too neat an explanation for what is going on under the surface. The answer lies with the women of Summerisle.

On May Day, as Howie carries out his final, hysterical house-to-house search for Rowan, it is clearly noticeable that he intrudes mostly upon women's spaces, both private and public: the librarian in her bath, the masked women at the hairdresser, the young women ironing their costumes, the old woman dead in her coffin, as well the young girl who pretends to be dead and falls out of the wardrobe at his feet. There is only one space he refuses to invade and this is when he opens a door and finds a dark spiral staircase leading down to a cellar – the connotations with the dark mystery of femininity are all too clear. He looks but dares not enter. It is this final search of Summerisle that establishes Howie's position as a victim at a point when the film could be best described as 'male melodrama'. Neale, in his discussion of melodrama as a reflection of social anxieties, points out that the genre, always associated with female hysteria and paranoia, 'is a series of discourses about class, sexuality, property and family'.[13] The horror of *The Wicker Man* is not so much about the evidence of paganism, but the true horror of the end of patriarchal influence. One of the difficulties in defining *The Wicker Man* as a horror film has been the apparent absence of a 'monster'. The wicker man itself is terrifying but inanimate. So the real monster in the film is Rowan Morrison, who happily and helpfully leads a man to his death.

This aspect ties *The Wicker Man* to other American, rather than British, horror films of the 1970s.[14] *The Omen*, *The Exorcist* (Friedkin, 1973) and *Carrie* (De Palma, 1976) were all released in 1976 and the common elements between the three films point to a cultural and social crisis in the representation of the family, prevalent in the 1960s and 1970s. In each film 'normal' family relations collapse and the family home becomes a site of social and pathological dislocation, with the common result being a breakdown in parental responsibility for the child, who is re-defined as monstrous. Horror films therefore become a cathartic experience in which the stresses of living under a patriarchal system can be explored safely on screen. As Robin Wood points out in his essay on the American horror film, 'central to the effect and fascination of horror films is their fulfilment of our nightmare wish to smash the norms that oppress us and which our moral conditioning teaches us to revere'.[15] The family, as Wood observes, may not always be the site of the monster, but any family relations, tensions or repressions will trigger its arrival.

Therefore horror does not necessarily depend on a monstrous body – monstrosity is also symptomatic of a rift in the patriarchal system and is defined by the distance it has moved from the

---

[13] Neale, *Genre*, p. 29.

[14] *The Wicker Man* was released at cinemas as the B-feature with another outstanding British horror film, *Don't Look Now* (Roeg, 1973), which deals with the disturbing influence of second sight – traditionally a female trait – on a man grieving for his lost daughter. While both films could be said to deal with the dislocation of male activity and an impaired male gaze, and both end with the death of the male protagonist, the shattering denouement in *Don't Look Now* is a random act of violence rather than a planned destruction of patriarchal and paternal influence.

[15] Wood, 'An Introduction to the American Horror Film', p. 205.

patriarchal ideal. In *The Omen*, when the all-American family are unwittingly invaded by a devil-child and both parents are killed, Damien's presence as the hero of the narrative ensures that audiences can enjoy the destruction of traditional family values. The ending of *The Wicker Man* re-affirms our desire that all patriarchal control will be removed, as Howie, realising his fate at the top of the cliffs, argues desperately with the crowd, telling them they are about to commit murder. He points out that killing him will not bring back their apples: 'Crops are not meant to be grown on these islands – it's against nature.' But his exchange with Lord Summerisle shows Howie's brief induction in Pagan logic has been useful: Howie identifies Lord Summerisle, 'the king of the island', as the next sacrifice if the crops fail again. This gives another, deeper level to the text: for if Howie, an experienced police officer, could be hoodwinked into sacrificing himself, is it not credible that the islanders could have played the same deception with the original Lord Summerisle? The present Lord Summerisle's version of events, that paganism was imposed from above by the forces of patriarchal capitalism, is therefore undermined. If they have always worshipped the old gods, whether worshipping secretly behind closed doors, or openly under the gaze of the laird, the islanders have now enjoyed the benefits of over a hundred years of good harvests.

As Vivian Sobchack notes in her discussion of the marked familial crisis in a variety of film genres since the 1960s, 'there seems to be no viable way for patriarchy to symbolically envision a satisfying future for itself. All it can do is deny the future'.[16] *The Wicker Man*'s slow-burning but inexorable movement from patriarchal to potential matriarchal control shows a world where certain values – the dominant, patriarchal, capitalist imperatives that have embedded themselves into our culture by their very 'naturalness' – have become inverted. Thus the means of production are controlled by women: male virginity becomes more valued than female virginity. The success or failure of production now lies in the hands of the gods – surely no more random or arbitrary than the security of the global marketplace.

---

[16] Sobchack, 'Family Economy and Generic Exchange', p. 191.

There is no question that Lord Summerisle is next in line as the sacrifice for next year's harvest – and he is without a son and heir. The final presence of Rowan Morrison is undoubtedly a symbol of the island's future, where the tensions between patriarchal interests and matriarchal production will finally be resolved.

Bibliography

Barstow, A. L., *Witchcraze: A new history of the European witch hunts* (San Francisco: HarperCollins, 1997).

Blythman, J., *Shopped: The shocking power of British supermarkets* (London: Fourth Estate, 2004).

Brown, A., *Inside 'The Wicker Man': The morbid ingenuities* (London: Sidgwick and Jackson, 2000).

Corporate Watch, 'Supermarkets', <www.corporatewatch.org/pro files/food_supermarkets/supermarkets.html> [Accessed 9 July 2004].

Friends of the Earth, <www.foe.co.uk> [Accessed 6 July 2004].

Friends of the Earth Media Briefing, 'Home Grown Apples in Short Supply in Big Supermarkets', 18 November 2003, available from Friends of the Earth Press Office, 26-28 Underwood Street, London N1 7JQ, or for download at <www.foe.co.uk/resource/briefings/apples_short_supply.pd f>

Hill, C., *The World Turned Upside Down: Radical ideas during the English Revolution* (Harmondsworth: Peregrine, 1984).

Institute of Grocery and Distribution, The, <www.igd.com> [Accessed 9 July 2004].

_____, *Grocery Retailing 2003: The Market Report*, <www.corporatewatch.org/pages/whats_wrong_suprmkts.h tm> [Accessed 9 July 2004].

Neale, S., *Genre* (London: British Film Institute, 1987).

_____, 'Masculinity as Spectacle: Reflections on men and mainstream cinema', in *Screening the Male: Exploring masculinities in Hollywood cinema,* ed. by S. Cohan and I. R. Hark (London: Routledge, 1993), pp. 9-19.

Sobchack, V., 'Family Economy and Generic Exchange', in *American Horrors: Essays on the modern American horror film*, ed. by G. Waller (Urbana and Chicago: University of Illinois Press, 1987), pp. 175-94.

Transport 2000, <www.transport2000.org.uk> [Accessed 9 July 2004].

Wood, R., 'An Introduction to the American Horror Film', in *Movies and Methods Vol II,* ed. by B. Nichols (Berkeley: University of California Press, 1985), pp. 196-220.

'The Game's Over'. Breaking the Spell of Summerisle: Feminist discourse and *The Wicker Man*

Gail Ashurst

> *'Woman is the siren whose song lures sailors upon the rocks; she is Circe, who changes her lovers into beasts [...] the man captivated by her charms no longer has will-power, enterprise, future; he is no longer a citizen, but mere flesh enslaved to its desires...'*
> Simone de Beauvoir[1]

> *'I've always believed that the truth can be shown upside down'*
> Anthony Shaffer[2]

It is perhaps well known by now that the impetus for scripting *The Wicker Man* (Hardy, 1973) was to rework the well-worn conventions of the horror genre. As the late Anthony Shaffer once said, the aim was to create 'an intelligent picture' in which 'the Christian doesn't always come out on top'.[3] However, in its quest for a new language of horror, the film does not merely pose a challenge to the moral logic which typically organises the structure of the genre; it also disrupts the sexist ideology inherent in the conventional treatment of women therein, and thereby exposes some of patriarchy's most tenacious myths about the female sex.[4] Moreover, it challenges our own collective investment in a long history of female iconography, prompting the viewer to rethink conservative notions of sex and gender in patriarchal systems of representation.

Paradoxically, the film's progressive treatment of women nevertheless depicts them in a way which is, on the surface, both rigid and stereotypical; the 'Fallen Woman', in all her guises, is

---

[1] De Beauvoir, *The Second Sex*, p. 197.
[2] Cited in Bartholomew, '*The Wicker Man*', p. 14.
[3] Cited in Willsmer, 'The Wicker Men', p. 19.
[4] It should be noted that my use of the term 'myth' herein does not merely refer to a false story or a poeticised truth. Rather, it acknowledges the power myths hold over the human imagination, how they may uphold our perception of reality, and embody our most fundamental beliefs and values.

undoubtedly inscribed upon every inch of the film, and yet the film's women are explicitly iconoclastic. Such ambiguous representations have obvious implications for the viewer and so it is necessary to ask: how does the film serve to dismantle male-centred notions of femininity? In order to address this question I will discuss, in dialogue with a range of theoretical concepts drawn from feminist theory and gender studies, the ways in which the film manages to resist, even redress, rather than reinforce, the female stereotypes it self-consciously deploys.

My purpose, however, is twofold: while I suggest that *The Wicker Man* may be read as an exposé of male myths of femininity, it is also implicitly revealed in the film that 'femininity', as we tend to perceive it, is nothing more than a fictional construct pertaining to male discourses. My argument, in this instance, is largely mediated through the film's structuring metaphor: 'the game of the hunted leading the hunter'. Upon reaching the 'appointed place', it is revealed to Sergeant Howie that he has been the unwitting participant in a 'game' designed to manipulate his 'every thought and action'. Apart from the gendered connotations present in the opposition of hunter/hunted (which will be discussed in the subsequent section), this revelation, I argue, draws direct attention to the film's performativity, its artifice, and thereby calls for renewed questioning of its treatment of gender and sexuality. Furthermore, the film's innovative play with conventional narrative codes and visual pleasures serves to undermine both the traditional male-authored narrative structure within which it is working, and the voyeuristic male gaze. Thus, by implication, the film generates an empowering female mode of address.

'The game of the hunted leading the hunter'
In her seminal essay 'Sorties', Hélène Cixous posits the question 'Where is She?' in order to ascertain 'woman's position within the existing symbolic framework which gives rise to prevailing cultural notions of gender arrangements in the Western world'.[5] Gendered meaning, she concludes, derives from a series of binary oppositions, such as active/passive, culture/nature, light/dark, and

---

[5] Cixous, 'Sorties', p. 147.

so on. Cixous highlights the underlying pattern of sexual difference which is inherent in these binarisms and shows how woman is located in an inferior position to men: '[D]eath is always at work', she says, and here Cixous means that 'Woman', through a chain of symbolic binary oppositions, is 'forever excluded, negated, and deemed in terms of man's Other'.[6]

Representations of female 'Otherness' (that is, all that is non-male and so either vilified or idealised) in male discourses has been well documented.[7] By and large, the horror genre's moral logic operates around a Manichean struggle between good and evil; and the treatment of women therein serves to uphold dominant ideological configurations of the passive, notably desexualised, 'good woman', while the 'bad woman' is invariably one who ventures beyond the boundaries of her sexed identity as mapped out for her within male discourses. As Margaret Marshment states:

> While ideology claims that women cannot be powerful and independent, it also claims that when women are powerful and independent they are evil; from Medea to Lady Macbeth, from the fairytale stepmothers to film noir heroines, the history of female representation has a strong undercurrent of women who are bad and strong.[8]

The Wicker Man's moral framework is significantly less clear-cut and virtually obliterates the traditional usage of light and dark deployed within the genre to denote good and bad, since most of the action takes place against a glorious, brightly-lit backdrop. In turn, this serves to complicate the film's treatment of women: are the leading ladies truly monstrous? Or does the significant absence of stock stylistic devices usually deployed in constructing the 'bad woman' prompt the viewer to dig deeper into the function they may serve in the narrative? The film has

---

[6] Cixous, 'Sorties', p. 147.
[7] See, for example, De Beauvoir, *The Second Sex*; Creed, *The Monstrous-Feminine*.
[8] Gamman and Marshment, *The Female Gaze*, p. 27.

been described as '[A] brilliant example of the deceit practised by woman upon the unsuspecting male', although, sadly, the author in question does not pursue this point any further. [9] I suggest, however, that the film in no way posits a female who is deceitful by nature. In *The Wicker Man*'s own particular brand of horror, the women deliberately play up to the deceit which is traditionally levelled at the female sex, and are given free rein to exercise a critique of male authority from within the very stereotypes imposed upon women by patriarchy. This essentially cynical stance helps to consolidate a radical shift in the film's sex-gender dynamics, and marks a rare moment in the portrayal of gender in the horror genre more generally.

According to Peter Hutchings, however, the late 1960s and early 1970s witnessed a new direction in the portrayal of gender in British horror films, the cause of which he attributes to the rise of the women's movement and the general disillusionment with patriarchal institutions 'among the increasingly politicised and rebellious youth culture'.[10] As a result, a number of British horror films at this time 'were in their own way simultaneously drawn towards and repelled by figures of absolute male authority'.[11] Furthermore, the 'marginalisation' of the male figure, he claims, created a space in which to explore the 'possibility of a new female subjectivity'.[12] Michael Reeves' *The Sorcerers* (1967), for example, depicts a number of weak men in contrast to the domineering Estelle, who, Hutchings maintains, drives the film's action along.[13] Terence Fisher's *The Devil Rides Out* (1968) and Roy Ward Barker's *The Vampire Lovers* (1971), he states, 'both acknowledge a female desire that is, to an extent, independent of male control'.[14] Nonetheless, these films operate within a conventional narrative structure which ensures that any fleeting glimpse of female agency is ultimately subject to patriarchal recuperation. Moreover, the proliferation of sexually permissive and violent films in the early 1970s exhibited an increasing

---

[9] Hutchison, 'Horror and Fantasy in the Cinema', p. 215.
[10] Hutchings, *Hammer and Beyond*, p. 159.
[11] Hutchings, *Hammer and Beyond*, p. 135.
[12] Hutchings, *Hammer and Beyond*, p. 164.
[13] Hutchings, *Hammer and Beyond*, p. 143.
[14] Hutchings, *Hammer and Beyond*, p. 164.

obsession with the objectification of the female body. As Hutchings later notes, unlike *The Vampire Lovers*, the positing of a female desire in the subsequent two films in the Karnstein trilogy – *Lust For A Vampire* (Sangster, 1971) and *Twins of Evil* (Hough, 1971) – is completely eradicated.[15]

The Wicker Man, on the other hand, does not offer mere token images of powerful women. Rather, it penetrates and fractures the deep ideological structure of the horror genre, and indeed of classic narrative cinema. As Cixous notes: 'traditionally, the question of sexual difference is treated by coupling it with the opposition: activity/passivity'.[16] *The Wicker Man* overturns the logic of this stubborn dichotomy, for at the heart of the film there emerges an interesting reversal, one which is explicitly acknowledged in the phrase 'the game of the hunted leading the hunter'. The atrocities of the seventeenth- and eighteenth-century witch hunts are merely one historical reality conjured up by the phrase. The reference to the hunter/hunted opposition, towards the close of the film, cannot fail to chime with the oppression of women under a patriarchal regime. But in retrospect, this opposition provides an extended metaphor which resonates throughout the film as a whole. Typically, plot in narrative cinema is driven by an active male protagonist. Indeed, in the opening scenes of *The Wicker Man*, Sergeant Howie is quickly established in the role of active male – seeker of truth, knowledge and order – which suggests that he is to be the hero of the piece. Howie's quest to find the 'missing girl' and save the day, as it were, is hampered, not least, by the sudden and frequent interruption of song, dance, and elaborate ritual. Moreover, women orchestrate most of these narrative intrusions. Not only do these elements undermine male authority at the level of the plot, they also serve to poke fun at the overblown importance traditionally attributed to the role of the brave hunter in patriarchal narratives. It is possible, therefore, to read the film in terms of a mocking parody of the male quest. Interestingly, there is a scene preserved in the original shooting script which

---

[15] Hutchings, *Hammer and Beyond*, p. 183.
[16] Cixous, 'Sorties', p. 147.

explicitly compares Howie to Don Quixote, and so helps to consolidate this point:

> **Miss Rose:** May one know, without too much self-important mystery-making, what it is you have come here to investigate?
> **Howie:** I've come here to find a missing child – a child whom everyone says never existed.
> **Miss Rose:** How very quixotic of you.
> **Howie:** Quixotic?
> **Miss Rose:** From Don Quixote – an enthusiastic visionary, *a pursuer of lofty but impracticable ideals*. [My emphasis]
> **Howie**: Also a man of honour, I believe.
> **Miss Rose:** Which did not prevent him from continually making a fool of himself.

Moreover, just as Don Quixote's personal investment in medieval romance literature gives rise to his romanticised notions of women as hapless fair maidens, Howie's distorted fears of women are shown to have been shaped by both the restrictions of his puritanical system of belief, and the depiction of women therein. Hence, the root of Howie's ambivalence towards the female sex lies in that most fundamental of patriarchal myths: the Fall of Man, for which Woman, in the image of Eve, was held responsible. In its fleshing out of these ideas, the film undoubtedly invents a radical new role for the 'bad and strong' woman, as we shall see.   .

Wicker Women: Mad, bad, and dangerous to know?

Invariably, *The Wicker Man* is described in terms of a conflict specifically between paganism and Christianity. Tanya Krzywinska offers an alternative reading: 'the film might not be read as it was intended but it was meant to be an indictment of paganism'.[17] But is it not more accurate to say that the film merely selects at random those elements of a paganistic world-view which best serve to expose Howie's own world-view as

---

[17] Krzywinska, *A Skin for Dancing In*, p. 105.

narrow-minded and life-denying? Although Howie represents the church and the law, the overarching line of argument in the film purports that Howie's quest for salvation into the next world makes it impossible for him to live in this one. Moreover, the basis upon which the film endeavours forcibly to realise this premise is its depiction of Howie's reaction when confronted with woman. As Simone de Beauvoir claims, 'it is Christianity which invests Woman anew with frightening prestige [...] The Christian is divided within himself, the separation of body and soul, life and spirit, is complete; all ties of the flesh seem evil'.[18] This is a view *The Wicker Man* indubitably shares. Hence, the film stages a much broader conflict: that of Life versus Spirit, in which Howie's perception of women is shown to be symptomatic of his fraught struggle to reconcile his sexuality with his puritanical religious speculation. But it is the unique way in which the film dramatises its central themes that makes its treatment of women so prescient. The 'Seduction Scene', depicting Willow's erotic dance, is a case in point.

In terms of plot development, the scene sets out to test the moral convictions of Howie's faith, and further underlines his repression. And yet the execution of the scene is highly complex: Willow sports a knowing smile throughout, suggesting her knowledge of the power a beautiful woman has to beguile, bewitch, and thus control the male with her sexuality. Howie's puritanical fear of the sexually desiring woman, meantime, results in the invocation of that deadliest of alluring women, the Singing Siren – a role which Willow clearly knows she is playing to perfection. Feminist film theorists, such as Barbara Creed, Laura Mulvey and Molly Haskell, have long maintained that images of women in popular film merely reflect the myths and fantasies born out of the male imagination.[19] Part of their early project involved demonstrating the processes whereby seemingly normative representations of women are actually constructed upon male anxieties and/or desires. *The Wicker Man* repeatedly draws attention to these processes. Far from being gratuitously erotic or narcissistic, Willow's dance provides an example in the

---

[18] De Beauvoir, *The Second Sex*, p. 199.
[19] See Creed, *The Monstrous-Feminine;* Mulvey, 'Visual Pleasure and Narrative Cinema'; Haskell, *From Reverence to Rape.*

film where a knowing and cynical female stance is pushed to the fore. Howie is exposed as being merely one more in a long tradition of men who are ambivalent towards the female sex.

But what of the film's reception? Does *The Wicker Man*, in its radical deployment of the eroticised feminine spectacle, nevertheless underhandedly serve the voyeuristic male gaze? While it would be futile to deny the masochistic fantasies on offer in this scene, there are, nonetheless, a number of elements therein which pose a challenge to the male mode of address.

In her highly influential article 'Visual Pleasure and Narrative Cinema', Laura Mulvey argues that popular film constructs a mode of address which caters exclusively for the male spectator, since it is her contention that woman's sole function in film is that of the passive object of the masculine gaze. The 'male gaze', she argues, is mediated via a three-way process in which the male spectator is invited to be complicit with the male protagonist in his objectification of woman. Moreover, this is an operation which is almost always overseen by a male director.[20] In *The Wicker Man* this process is thwarted not least by virtue of the wall which denies Howie his gaze. Moreover, Willow appears to manipulate the audience as much as it would seek to manipulate her – most notably in her explicit attempt to make the viewer aware of his position as voyeur. Willow looks directly into the camera on more than one occasion, while her agitated movements, as she begins beating the window side-paneling, suggest a defiant, mocking stance towards the spectator, perhaps ridiculing him for his complicity in the very systems of gender representation which the film undermines. In fact, the film self-consciously highlights the cinematic spell at work whenever the women are looked at from the male protagonist's point of view. As most of the action is seen from Howie's perspective, the viewer is alerted to the exaggerated soft-focus which frames the women within his gaze. The overstated use of this classic stylistic device, then, does not only bespeak of Howie's ambivalence when confronted with women, it also works to expose the artifice inherent in the images of women we have grown accustomed to within patriarchal systems of representation.

---

[20] Mulvey, 'Visual Pleasure and Narrative Cinema', pp. 158-66.

If Willow's seductive dance provides a glaring insight into how female sexuality becomes monstrous in the eyes of the god-fearing patriarch, those scenes depicting Miss Rose as witch figure and powerful matriarch are even more confrontational. Howie, *en route* to Lord Summerisle's castle, is made to witness a pantomime, of sorts, in which excessive images of a powerful feminine principle are paraded before him (pregnant women transferring their life-force into the buds of apple trees, girls invoking the god of the flame in a bid to make them fruitful, while simultaneously jumping naked over bonfires, and so on). These scenes immediately precede the showdown between Howie and Lord Summerisle, in which the latter seizes the carefully crafted opportunity to challenge the logic of the Virgin Birth. When Howie dismisses the idea of parthenogenesis as nonsense, the Laird reminds him that his own god is 'Himself the son of a virgin, impregnated – I believe – by a ghost'. While reinforcing Lord Summerisle's aura of invulnerability, this scene raises important issues regarding the way in which the reality of female sexuality is denied in patriarchal religion. As Simone de Beauvoir claims, 'the archetypal image of the desexualised Madonna and child holds up before women an unrealistic ideal to which they can never aspire'.[21] Women, within this logic, are pre-ordained to a perpetually fallen state: the flip side of the Madonna is, of course, the Whore.

Many feminist theorists – Carol Christ, Luce Irigaray and Mary Daly, to name but a few – have pointed out how Christianity has helped to reinforce the oppression of women. Dissatisfaction with patriarchal religions has undoubtedly encouraged many women to seek alternative routes to spiritual fulfillment, which is evident in the growth of goddess-worship. However, in recent decades the figure of the goddess has been appropriated by some feminists for subversive ends. As Naomi Goldenberg states: 'worship of the goddess deliberately revalorises the connections of ancient goddesses with the earth and with the material, physical, sexual and bodily energies of human living that have been downgraded or devalued in the past'.[22] Although the paganism depicted in *The*

---

[21] De Beauvoir, *The Second Sex*, p. 186.
[22] Goldenberg, 'The Return of the Goddess', p. 263.

Wicker Man undoubtedly creates a matriarchal space (which may appeal to some female viewers, in particular), I suggest that the film's positing of a powerful female fecundity should not be taken at face value. If we read the aforementioned scenes depicting women carrying out fertility rituals as an uncritical celebration of woman's difference, we do so at the risk of closing down the possibility of seeing how they function as an exercise in the kind of 'strategic essentialism' described in Goldenberg's statement above.

In the next section I want to turn to that other seemingly innocuous medium pertaining to male discourses: the classic fairy tale.

No Rapunzel, She

The socialisation of gender arrangements begins early in life and is at its most seductive in the medium of the fairy tale. Moreover, 'the treatment of women in such tales depends largely upon her willingness to accept the male-defined script of femininity'.[23] The insidious message therein upholds the notion that when women are meek, mild and self-sacrificing there will come a reward, usually manifest in the shape of a handsome prince. *The Vampire Lovers* makes this dimension of the fairy tale explicit, though it seeks to exploit rather than redress the implications of its own insights. The film's narrative structure can be said to operate around the binary opposition of the 'traditional' and the 'subversive' woman. The precocious Laura (Pippa Steele), who is vampirised early on in the film, proves less of a challenge to Carmilla's (Ingrid Pitt) lesbian advances than Emma (Madeline Smith), whose whole-hearted investment in the belief that her prince will come is, arguably, by the end of the film the very thing which saves her. Emma pleads with Carmilla each night to read her bed-time stories from a book filled with chivalric accounts of men rescuing fair maidens. One night, Carmilla stops in mid-flow and announces: 'this is a silly book'. A similar dismissive attitude is demonstrated by the governess (Kate O'Mara), who, when comforting Emma after her nightmare, tells her 'the trouble with this part of the world is they have too many

---

[23] Ussher, *Fantasies of Femininity*, p. 61.

fairy tales'. Such outward displays of disregard for the conventional role of women as prescribed within the traditional fairy tale is, I would argue, a telling factor in the subsequent demise of both women.

Feminist novelist and critic Angela Carter perceived the narrative form of the fairy tale as being especially open to subversive reworking and is, perhaps, one of the best-known revisionists in this field. A frequent strategy in feminist appropriations of the fairy tale – and one which is often deployed in Carter's early work – has been to reverse the gendered binary opposition which conventionally operates along the lines of the active-male/passive-female dichotomy. Thus, Carter's appropriations, far from relying on the wit of the hero figure, often introduce a feminist twist in which a woman comes to the rescue of the 'damsel in distress', as is evident in *The Bloody Chamber* (1995). Moreover, the fairy tale's typically de-sexualised heroine, in Carter's hands, often undergoes a transformation whereby she becomes a sexually desiring subject.

The Wicker Man also provocatively reworks elements of the traditional fairy tale in a way that mirrors contemporary feminist revisions. For example, the 'Gently Johnny' scene, depicting Willow's fairness of face and cascading golden hair, as she gazes dreamily from her window at the handsome Ash Buchanan below, is encoded with many of the trappings of the Rapunzel tale; the film merely pushes back the very boundaries of the traditional version. Thus, the room-at-the-top-of-the-rose-wreathed-tower motif gives way to the upstairs window of The Green Man Inn, while Willow's transgression of the stereotypical 'damsel in distress' perpetuates the 'script of femininity', wherein passivity and sexual submissiveness are prescribed virtues of a proper code of female conduct. This scene also reveals a rare moment in the film in which Lord Summerisle's own male mythologies are challenged. 'Another sacrifice for Aphrodite', announces the laird, as Ash makes his way up to Willow's room. 'Surely you mean *to* Aphrodite?' she retorts, at which point Lord Summerisle makes an overblown remark in which he elevates her to the status of 'the goddess of love in human form'.

One of the main criticisms leveled at Carter's reworkings of the fairy tale hinges on the fact that, in merely reversing gendered power positions, she nonetheless leaves the logic of the binary in place. *The Wicker Man*, on the other hand, achieves much more than a simple reversal, since, in retrospect, this scene, like all the others, is merely one more manufactured facade in the islanders' repertoire of tricks staged in a bid to undermine Howie – to 'control his every thought and action', as it were. Thus, the game introduces a strategy which is sometimes absent from feminist appropriations of the fairy tale: it draws attention to its own performativity – its status as artifice.

'Woman' as Unstable Sign and the 'Performance of Gender'

The idea of 'gender as performance' is theorised within feminism and gender studies as a conceptual tool capable of exposing the social constructedness of gender categories. Within this theoretical framework, gender is not biologically fixed but rather an effect of culture.[24] Luce Irigaray was among the first to point out the subversive potential of theorising gender upon these terms. Basing her analysis of the construction of femininity on the concept of the 'feminine masquerade' (a term first coined by Joan Rivere who argued that professional women deliberately enact male-defined notions of femininity in order to be accepted in a male domain), Irigaray subsequently developed the masquerade in terms of a strategy of resistance, whereby women might 'mime the mimes of femininity in order to challenge patriarchal ideology.' This she describes as 'playing with mimesis'.[25]

In recent decades a number of feminist theorists have argued for the subversive potential of the feminine masquerade. As Mary Ann Doane states, the masquerade reveals that 'womanliness is a mask which can be worn and removed'.[26] However, for some feminist theorists, not all parody is subversive. As Paulina Palmer asserts: 'one of the problems with the concept of gender as performance is the difficulty in identifying instances where one is passively enacting a male-defined image of femininity' as

---

[24] See Palmer, 'Gender as Performance in the Fiction of Angela Carter and Margaret Atwood'.

[25] Irigaray, *The Sex Which Is Not One*, p. 133.

[26] Doane, 'Film and the masquerade', p. 253.

opposed to those where one 'is subversively "playing with mimesis"'.[27]

This brings us back to the overall device at the heart of *The Wicker Man*; within the context of the game, the women's various *performances* of female archetypes and stereotypes (assuming that some accept a difference in meaning) are actively foregrounded within a knowing manipulation of the feminine masquerade. In the context of my argument here, it is interesting to observe how the maypole scene, when compared with the fire leap dance (and the subsequent commentary on parthenogenesis), builds a fundamental contradiction into the film's logic. The supposed religious speculation on Summerisle has peculiar ramifications for its sexual politics: it simultaneously sees the penis as the 'regenerative force in nature', and something which can be dispensed with altogether in the business of reproduction. It is glaringly obvious, therefore, that, outside of the context of the game, these two scenes, in particular, do very little in the way of further establishing a believable or consistent account of the islanders' so-called religion. My point is that the film demands to be read in all its ambiguity, which, in my view, involves an appreciation of how the 'game' played on Howie simultaneously posits a powerful, politically aware, female voice.

'The Game's Over'

Fairy tales, Christian dogma, the genre film itself – these are all examples of patriarchy's most powerful socialising agents. What makes *The Wicker Man* all the more subversive is that it critiques of patriarchy from within a variety of the latter's own ideological forms. The film, I suggest, is not so much anti-pagan (or anti-Christian for that matter), as it is decidedly *anti-mythic*. As Cristina Bacchilega asserts, 'anti-myth is present in retellings since repetition reveals [myth] to be an artifice'.[28] The importance of the game, then, cannot be stated enough, since it is chiefly responsible for allowing a highly provocative portrayal of gender and sexuality to surface. The tactical way in which the women play the game, moreover, appears to anticipate some of the most

---

[27]Palmer, 'Gender as Performance in the Fiction of Angela Carter and Margaret Atwood', p. 79.

[28]Bacchilega, *Postmodern Fairy Tales*, p. 21.

current strategies developed within feminism and gender studies, strategies which are often deployed by feminist theorists in order to question and challenge the gendered logic of texts produced within a predominantly male sphere – mainstream film being a case in point.

The makers of *The Wicker Man* set out to turn the conventions of the horror picture on its head. In doing so, the film posits a powerful female agency which is not made subject to a male authority: despite their status as subjects of a paternal lineage, the women are in no way shown to be answerable to, or manipulated by, Lord Summerisle. It is also highly significant that our 'Wicker Women' do not meet with the grisly demise which traditionally awaits those insurgent women who actively choose not to ignore the terms and conditions of their sexed identity as set down for them within male ideologies. Rather, the women in the film serve to shatter a number of male myths which, by and large, are shown to be symptomatic of the double standard to be found in the archetypal opposition between Madonna and Whore. Moreover, it is this very same ambivalence towards the female sex which Simone de Beauvoir, and many other writers since, repeatedly uncover in a wealth of male-authored texts. Arguably, the film itself may act to seduce the viewer with the very fantasies it exposes. But when 'the game's over', and the spell of Summerisle is broken, the processes by which 'femininity' is constructed within male systems of representation are laid bare for those who have eyes to see.

Bibliography

Bacchilega, C., *Postmodern Fairy Tales: Gender and narrative strategies* (Philadelphia: University of Pennsylvania Press, 1997).

Bartholomew, D., '*The Wicker Man*', *Cinefantastique,* 6.3, Winter (1977), 4-18; 32-46.

De Beauvoir, S., *The Second Sex* (London: Vintage Press, 1949, 1997).

Cixous, H., 'Sorties' (1986), in *A Critical and Cultural Theory Reader*, ed. by A. Easthope and K. McGowan (Buckingham: Open University Press, 1992), pp. 146-57.

Creed, B., *The Monstrous-Feminine: Film, feminism and psychoanalysis* (London and New York: Routledge, 1993).

Doane, M. A., 'Film and the Masquerade: Theorizing the female spectator' (1982), in *The Film Studies Reader*, ed. by J. Hollows, P. Hutchings and M. Jancovich (London: Arnold, 2000), pp. 248-56.

Gamman, L. and M. Marshment, eds., *The Female Gaze* (London: The Women's Press, 1988).

Goldenberg, N., 'The Return of the Goddess: Psychoanalytic reflections on the shift from theology to thealogy' (1987), in *Religion and Gender*, ed. by U. King (London and New York: Routledge, 1995), pp. 145-63.

Haskell, M., *From Reverence to Rape: The treatment of women in the movies* (Chicago and London: University of Chicago Press, 1974).

Hutchings, P., *Hammer and Beyond: The British horror film*, (Manchester: Manchester University Press, 1993).

Hutchison, T., 'Horror and Fantasy in the Cinema' (1974), in A. Brown, *Inside 'The Wicker Man': The morbid ingenuities* (London: Sidgwick and Jackson, 2000), pp. 215-16.

Irigaray, L., *The Sex Which Is Not One,* trans. by C. Porter with C. Burke (New York: Cornell University Press, 1985).

Krzywinska, T., *A Skin For Dancing In: Possession, witchcraft and voodoo in film* (Trowbridge: Flicks Books, 2000).

Mulvey, L., 'Visual Pleasure and Narrative Cinema' (1975), in *A Critical and Cultural Theory Reader*, ed. by A. Easthope and K. McGowan (Toronto: University of Toronto Press, 1992), pp. 158-66.

Palmer, P., 'Gender as Performance in the Fiction of Angela Carter and Margaret Atwood', in *The Infernal Desires of Angela Carter: Fiction, femininity, feminism*, ed. by J. Bristow and T. L. Broughton (New York: Longman, 1997), pp. 24-42.

Ussher, J. M., *Fantasies of Femininity: Reframing the boundaries of sex* (Middlesex: Penguin, 1997).

Willsmer, T., 'The Wicker Men: The making of a cult classic', *Movie Collector*, 1.8 (1994), 16-23.

Sightseeing in Summerisle: Film tourism and *The Wicker Man*

Lesley Stevenson

Introduction

On November 25th 1972, an article entitled 'The Pleasure of their Company' appeared in a local newspaper, *The Galloway Gazette*. It announced the departure of *The Wicker Man* (Hardy, 1973) film crew from Galloway, and praised their behaviour while in the locality. Speaking of the particular material advantages generated by filming, the article claimed that:

> [...] the unit's stay in the area has brought unprecedented benefits to local hotels – who have virtually had a doubled tourist season. And there may be benefits yet to come in that respect. For when the film goes on release in early summer the attractions of our scenery will be shown to audiences throughout the world. Galloway will be mentioned in the film credits as the location in which the picture was shot.[1]

The article expresses anticipation that significant tourism benefits will accrue to Galloway because it served as the location for the filming of much of *The Wicker Man*. As the final sentence of this statement makes clear, Galloway served as the location, not the setting, for the film. The fictional Hebridean island of Summerisle was actually an amalgam of a number of sites throughout Scotland, including Plockton, Skye, Culzean Castle in Ayrshire, and several places in Galloway. Reading this statement over 30 years after the film's release raises questions about the extent to which its central expectation has been realised. Do fans of *The Wicker Man* really visit Galloway, simply on the basis that it is mentioned in the film credits as the location in which much of the film was shot? Or do they visit the Western Isles, in search of the fictional 'Summerisle'? In an attempt to answer such questions, this paper will outline the role that *The Wicker Man*

---

[1] Anon., 'The Pleasure of their Company', p. 6.

has played in generating tourism to Galloway in particular, and Scotland more generally. It will investigate how the film has been used for tourism purposes and the extent to which the tourism activity generated by *The Wicker Man* conforms to conventional film tourism trends.

Film Tourism

There is a small but significant body of evidence within the relevant academic literature supporting the contention that feature films play a substantial role in generating tourism to the areas in which they are shot. Roger Riley and Carlton Van Doren, for example, point to the impact which several motion pictures have had on visitor numbers to sites which they portray, or simply display.[2] John Boorman's 1972 film *Deliverance*, they observe, has acted as the catalyst for the development of a thriving white-water rafting company in Rayburn County, Georgia. Similar observations are made in respect of the films *Steel Magnolias* (Ross, 1989), *Field of Dreams* (Robinson, 1989) and *Thelma and Louise* (Scott, 1991), all of which are credited with increasing visitor numbers to their respective settings shortly after being released. Riley and Van Doren conclude that it is the thematic content, rather than scenic attractions, portrayed in films which induce tourists to visit their respective locations.

This thesis was further developed by Riley, Michael Baker and Van Doren in a 1998 study, which termed travel to sites in which films are shot, or ostensibly set, 'movie-induced tourism'.[3] This particular study gathered data relating to 12 US film locations, all of which experienced substantial increases in visitor numbers in the years immediately following the release of the films with which they were respectively associated. The authors attributed this increased visitation not only to these films' depictions of attractive scenery, but also to their thematic content, dramatic sequences, and portrayals of human relationships.

Such an interpretation is essentially allied to John Urry's notion of the 'tourist gaze'.[4] Urry argues that the manner in which tourists view, or 'gaze' upon, destinations is socially conditioned

---

[2] Riley and Van Doren, 'Movies as Tourism Promotion'.
[3] Riley, Baker and Van Doren, 'Movie Induced Tourism'.
[4] Urry, *The Tourist Gaze*.

and systematised, and as such differs according to the society, social group and historical period in question. Tourists elect to gaze upon particular places because their expectations regarding them are positive, and they anticipate that they will offer pleasurable experiences. Urry argues that film can be instrumental in forging such preconceptions:

> Places are chosen to be gazed upon because there is an anticipation [...] Such anticipation is constructed and sustained through a variety of non-tourist practices such as film, TV, literature, magazines, records, and videos which construct and reinforce that gaze.[5]

According to this logic, films are influential in creating awareness of, and constructing visitors' perceptions of, destinations. Indeed, Richard Butler argues that the destination images which are portrayed by film and TV are increasingly becoming more influential than those portrayed in print media in terms of raising awareness of, and stimulating tourism to, sites in question.[6] Developing this theme, Nigel Morgan and Annette Pritchard argue that destination images constructed by filmic media tend to be so potent as to dominate any sense of objective reality.[7] As a result, one's subjective feelings regarding a destination tend to govern in the process of tourism decision-making. The implication is that is it is not the objective reality of places which attract tourists to particular destinations; rather, it is the meaning represented by destinations which renders them symbolically important to the visitor.

This is illustrated by research carried out by the Scottish Tourist Board in 1997, which concluded that almost 60% of respondents were influenced in their decision to visit the Stirling area by the film *Braveheart* (Gibson, 1995). Much of the film was shot in Ireland, however, indicating that for these visitors it was the meaning which the film represented, rather than its actual

---

[5] Urry, *The Tourist Gaze*, p. 3.
[6] Butler, 'The Influence of Media in Shaping International Tourist Patterns'.
[7] Morgan and Pritchard, *Tourism Promotion and Power*.

location, that was the attraction.[8] Nicola Tooke and Michael Baker similarly note that Shrewsbury, the purported setting for the TV drama *Cadfael*, benefited from a sudden increase in visitor numbers after the screening of the series, although it was actually filmed in Hungary.[9] Contrary to the hopes expressed by *The Galloway Gazette*, such findings suggest that when a film's location differs from its setting, it is generally the latter which is more successful in terms of generating tourism activity. The implication, therefore, is that tourists will reject the place mentioned 'in the film credits as the location in which the picture was shot' in favour of the destination which the film represents. As will become evident, however, such findings cannot be easily applied to *The Wicker Man*, for when the place portrayed is fictional, visitation trends become far more complex.

It is also important to acknowledge that all studies of 'movie-induced tourism' have focused upon films which were commercial successes, a description which can hardly be applied to *The Wicker Man*'s initial theatrical outing. Thus, a further important implication emerging from these studies concerns the life-cycle of film tourism. Without exception, the literature demonstrates that locations experience a sudden increase in visitor numbers shortly after the release of the film in question, followed by a gradual decline. As Tooke and Baker observe, however: 'awareness, appeal and profitability of film diminishes over time', a factor which apparently impacts on the nature of tourism generated.[10] Unless a given film is the object of repeated viewings and re-releases, its commercial and cultural profiles are likely to diminish over time, as is its potency as a tourist attraction. Riley, et al., state that on average movie-induced tourism enjoys a lifespan of 'at least four years' after the film's release.[11]

---

[8] Seaton and Hay, 'The Marketing of Scotland as a Tourist Destination, 1985-96', p. 230.
[9] Tooke and Baker, 'Seeing is Believing'.
[10] Tooke and Baker, 'Seeing is Believing', p. 88.
[11] Riley, et al., 'Movie Induced Tourism', p. 932.

The Wicker Man and Tourism Promotion

Given the conclusions reached by such studies, it is unsurprising that tourism authorities have begun to capitalise upon the impact of feature films in terms of visitor generation. Notable in this regard is the British Tourist Authority's 'Movie Map', a guide released in 1995 and designed to introduce potential visitors to places in the UK which have served as film locations. Targeted at international visitors, the map features some 200 locations throughout England, Scotland and Wales. *The Wicker Man* locations are absent from the map, a fact that can be attributed to its status as a cult film, and its consequently limited appeal for the mass tourism market.

It is somewhat more surprising, however, that sites associated with *The Wicker Man* are absent from tourism promotion literature at the regional level. Dumfries and Galloway Tourist Board's website and *Visitors Guide*, for example, both neglect to advertise the various film locations in the region. These appear somewhat singular omissions when one considers that a readers' poll in *Empire* magazine in 1996 named *The Wicker Man* the greatest British film of all time.[12]

The absence of reference to the film at the local level of tourism promotion can perhaps be attributed not only to the perceived limited commercial appeal of such a cult text but also to the contentious nature of its subject matter. The filming of *The Wicker Man* in 1972 was the subject of some controversy amongst the local population, not least because Britt Ekland famously christened Newton Stewart 'the most dismal place in all creation'.[13] For a small but vocal minority, it was the film's subject matter which proved controversial, however, with some local residents expressing disquiet at the themes of Paganism, human sacrifice and sexual liberation portrayed in the film. The prevalence of this attitude was noted by Allan Brown in 1998: amongst the locals, he argued, 'the older set regard it much as Howie did the islanders: as a slightly seedy, somewhat unnecessary entity that gives decent folk a bad name'.[14] Indeed, opposition to *The Wicker Man* remained so virulent in some

---

[12] Brown, 'Pagan's Progress', np.
[13] Dearden, 'Ekland issues a belated apology', p. 1.
[14] Brown, 'Pagan's Progress', np.

quarters, that it was still generating controversy on the letters page of *The Galloway Gazette* some 25 years after its initial release. On 18 December 1998, Jean Patterson of Wigtown wrote:

> This production should be a matter of shame, not pride. In the film evil triumphs, and evil will triumph in the Machars [the name of the area in Galloway in which the film was largely shot] as long as it is given place. There can be no lasting good from something so inherently evil.[15]

Continuing local discontent surrounding the film's portrayal of a Pagan society renders *The Wicker Man* a particularly contentious tourism promotion tool, a fact evinced by the controversy which accompanied the development of the first Wickerman Festival in 2002. As reported in *The Scotsman*, the inaugural staging of this music event was 'dogged by complaints from residents worried about noise, pollution, and pagan undertones'.[16]

Given the opposition of this small but vocal minority it is unsurprising that *The Wicker Man*'s association with Dumfries and Galloway rarely features in the region's self-produced tourism literature. As Anthony Seaton and Brian Hay note, 'the message of a feature film will not always conform to the strategic objectives set by a destination'.[17] This observation is certainly of relevance to *The Wicker Man*, for a film which depicts a Pagan community indulging in human sacrifice is unlikely to accord with officially sanctioned promotional objectives. This is particularly the case in Dumfries and Galloway, for the region is frequently promoted as the home of Christianity in Scotland. Tourist brochures direct visitors to St. Ninian's Cave in Wigtown Bay (see Figure 1), the site at which St. Ninian is reputed to have sheltered after bringing Christianity to Scotland in the mid-fifth century. (Indeed, as Figure 2 illustrates, the cave has become a

---

[15] Patterson, 'Letter', p. 6.
[16] Jamieson, 'Wicker man organisers deny pagan undertones', p. 3.
[17] Seaton and Hay, 'The Marketing of Scotland as a Tourist Destination, 1985-96', p. 231.

site of pilgrimage, with many visitors leaving makeshift crosses inside it). In the final scenes of *The Wicker Man*, by contrast, Rowan Morrison stands at the entrance of St. Ninian's Cave, enticing Sergeant Howie to follow her into the cave complex, from where he is lured unwittingly towards his death. Given the evident contradiction between the diegetic depiction of the site and that promoted within the official tourism agenda, it is entirely predictable that *The Wicker Man* locations in Galloway have enjoyed little marketing support at the institutional level.

Independent Promotion
Despite this lack of official ratification, the development of the Internet has allowed entrepreneurs and fans to publicise, and access, information about *The Wicker Man* locations. In recent years a number of websites have appeared which direct potential visitors to the various sites which served as locations for the filming of *The Wicker Man*. The Creetown village website, for example, offers readers an introduction to the film itself as well as directions to its various locations. Fans of the film can therefore take what is essentially a 'virtual tour' of Summerisle. They can, moreover, discover information regarding the film locations in books including *The Movie Traveller* and *Scotland the Movie*.[18]

The increased levels of awareness which such publications have afforded *The Wicker Man*'s locations have allowed a number of local businesses to capitalise upon their connections to the film. The heritage centre in Creetown, for example, has developed an exhibit devoted to *The Wicker Man*, while a holiday cottage in the village regularly invites fans of the film in to see its bakers' ovens, in which the bread-men in the film were baked.[19]

The local business which has benefited most from the increased promotional opportunities afforded by the development of the Internet is the Ellangowan Hotel in Creetown. For most *Wicker Man* fans, this is the high point of the tour of 'Wicker Country', for the interior of the Ellangowan Hotel doubled as that of Summerisle's The Green Man Inn. The hotel proprietor, Bill

---

[18] Foster, *The Movie Traveller*; Bruce, *Scotland the Movie*.
[19] Christie, telephone interview.

Fig.1: St. Ninian's Cave. (Courtesy of © South West Scotland Screen
Commission)

Fig.2: Interior of St. Ninian's Cave. (Courtesy of © South West Scotland Screen
Commission)

Christie, confirms that the hotel has benefited significantly from the trade created by travellers in search of this key film location: 'There is now a constant stream of *Wicker Man* enthusiasts [...] People from around the United Kingdom come here and we also have a great deal of interest from the United States'.[20] Whilst *The Wicker Man* market offers Christie regular custom, he estimates that it constitutes no more than 5% of his overall business today.[21]

Nevertheless, it is only since 1998 that *Wicker Man*-induced tourism has reached even this level. Christie attributes this recent upsurge to two factors, the first of which is the increased publicity and TV screenings the film has received in recent years. After a terrestrial broadcast of the film in 1988 there was a notable increase in visitors who were in search of the original shooting locations, although this amounted to no more than a small but 'fairly steady trickle'. According to Christie, however, 'When it seemed to take off again was when BBC Scotland did a documentary [...] to celebrate the 25th anniversary of the release of the film'.[22] Screened in 1998, the BBC documentary raised awareness of the Ellangowan amongst the film's fans, and was consequently followed by an increase in visitor numbers.

Christie also attributes the development of *Wicker Man*-related tourism to the development of the hotel's website: this features a page devoted to *The Wicker Man* which receives more hits than any of the other pages featured on the site. The development of its own website has allowed the Ellangowan to make contacts with hundreds of *Wicker Man* fans and as a result the hotel has been able to organise a fan gathering, Wicker Man Week, which takes place annually around May Day. Attending one such gathering in the year 2000, the *Guardian* journalist Elisabeth Mahoney reported being shocked to find that attendees were 'mainly bright, intelligent and – well, it has to be said – normal people'.[23]

For Christie, the types of visitors attracted by the film are so diverse in terms of demographics as to evade any kind of

---

[20] Khan and MacMillan, 'Cult of Wicker Man sets tourism on fire', p. 12.
[21] Christie, telephone interview.
[22] Christie, telephone interview.
[23] Mahoney, 'End of the world', p. 17.

definitive categorisation. They vary, too, in terms of their
fascination with the film, ranging from those who simply have a
'passing interest' in the movie, to others who are more devout in
their following of *The Wicker Man*. With regard to the latter,
Christie observes that, 'some of the people come back on a
number of occasions and it's almost like a real pilgrimage, to
come back up to the area and go round the same locations time
after time'.[24] The locations to which Christie refers includes sites
such as the ruined kirk at Anwoth, the remains of the Wicker
Man figure at Burrowhead and St. Ninian's Cave.

   In the West Highlands, Plockton served as the location for the
opening shots of Summerisle's harbour. Mary Gollan, the
proprietor of The Plockton Inn, confirms that the town trades
little on its *Wicker Man* connections:

> The reason that *The Wicker Man* is mentioned
> on our web page is that some [*Wicker Man*]
> fans were in the bar and couldn't believe that
> no mention was made anywhere in Plockton of
> the [*Wicker Man*] connection, so we put it on
> the web page![25]

Whilst reference to the film was placed on the business's website
specifically at the behest of enthusiasts, this is not to suggest that
Wicker Man induced visits to Plockton are commonplace. Rather,
according to Gollan, only a handful of the most devoted fans have
made the pilgrimage to Plockton.

Searching for Summerisle
Indeed, the desire to find Summerisle has taken some particularly
dedicated fans somewhat further afield, into the realm of the
fictional. Mahoney recounts meeting two enthusiasts at Wicker
Man Week who had previously travelled 'to the Summer Isles
thinking the place really existed, only to find a barren, craggy
place'.[26] For these two travellers, the fact that Galloway is
mentioned in the film credits as the place where the film was

---

[24] Christie, telephone interview.
[25] Mary Gollan, personal communication, 12 July 2003.
[26] Mahoney, 'End of the world', p. 17.

shot, certainly did not induce them to visit, initially at least. Rather, they sought out the Summer Isles, an archipelago of islands which lie off the northwest coast of Scotland. Upon arrival, however, they were disappointed not to find a sub-tropical island in which apples and palm trees flourish.

Such confusion is perhaps unsurprising given that it was only with the development of the Internet that the film's various locations came to be widely publicised. The corollary of this development is, of course, the ease with which spurious accounts of the film's origins have been publicised. A feature that appeared in *The Oban Times* in December 2002, for example, made an explicit connection between the film and the Summer Isles:

> The name Summer Isles will be etched forever in the minds of some as home of *The Wicker Man*, a dark film about paganism, supposedly based in the islands. However, none of the scenes were filmed on the Summer Isles but many people have been thrilled to find out that these islands do exist in the remote north-west of Scotland.[27]

Even a BBC website provides erroneous information, claiming that *The Wicker Man* 'was filmed in some 25 locations all over the Scottish Highlands'.[28] Moreover, the film's opening credits, in which the producer thanks 'Lord Summerisle and the people of his island off the West Coast of Scotland for this privileged insight into their religious practices and for their generous co-operation in the making of this film', is utterly spurious, but serves for many fans to confirm that Summerisle is indeed an actual destination. In this respect it is unsurprising that, for some fans, the identities of the actual Summer Isles and the fictional 'Summerisle' of the film have become conflated.

Perhaps, however, the trip which these two fans made to the Summer Isles is indicative of something less prosaic: namely, a

---

[27] Anon., 'The Summer Isles - wild Scotland at its best'. p. 14.
[28] BBC website, *'The Wicker Man' - the Film*.

desire to encounter the 'actual' Hebridean islands which, while
not the setting for *The Wicker Man*, at least gave the imagined
Summerisle its plausibly realistic name. The largest and only
inhabited island in the Summer Isles archipelago is Tanera Mhor.
The island's postmaster Bill Wilder is the main point of contact
for potential visitors who are seeking tourist information. Wilder
confirms that he regularly receives enquiries from Wicker Man
fans, seeking confirmation that Summerisle and the Summer Isles
are indeed one and the same place. As Wilder states:

> [...] we do get queries about the *Wicker Man*,
> people believing that the film is based here. It
> seems there is quite a cult following. Those
> who accept that the film is not actually about
> here still have trouble accepting that it was not
> filmed here (and the other way round). Yes,
> some do actually get here.[29]

Even in this age of increased ease of access to information
regarding the various locations in which *The Wicker Man* was
filmed, some fans of the film prefer to search for the real
'Summerisle'. As Wilder stresses, some even actually visit the
island, believing it to be either the setting or the location for the
film. Indeed, for one visitor the image constructed by *The Wicker
Man* was so potent as to cloud any sense of objectivity: as Wilder
recounts, 'One enthusiast would not accept that I was not Lord
Summerisle'.[30] Wilder's attempts to offer a 'convincing denial'
apparently had no impact whatsoever, indicating that it is not
only the presence of misinformation which causes some *Wicker
Man* fans to seek out or visit the Summer Isles. Rather, this
particular visitor practised a selective interpretation of the
available evidence. The manner in which she/he gazed upon the
Summer Isles was wholly informed and determined by *The
Wicker Man*.

---

[29] Bill Wilder, personal communication, 16 June 2003.
[30] Bill Wilder, personal communication, 16 June 2003.

Conclusion

To return to the quotation which opened this paper, it is evident that the tourist activity which *The Galloway Gazette* anticipated *The Wicker Man* would generate did not materialise, initially at least. After making little initial impact at the box-office and having been the subject of some controversy, the film did not enjoy any marketing support from local tourism authorities. As a result, its impact in terms of visitor generation was minimal. However, the proliferation of Internet sites in the past five years dedicated to the film's locations has permitted fans to find those sites with ease. Conversely, it has permitted the dissemination of misinformation and the marketing of erroneous *Wicker Man* connections. Thus, it is not only the film itself which constructs the tourist gaze: the way in which that film is harnessed for tourism purposes also contributes to the structuring of the gaze.

Moreover, it has become evident that the theories which have emerged regarding 'movie-induced tourism' are specific to those films which attain box-office success at a very specific point in the chain of consumption, namely, initial cinema release. In particular, the life-cycle routinely associated with movie-induced tourism cannot be extrapolated to films such as *The Wicker Man* which enjoy a cult following. Rather than experiencing a sudden increase in visitor numbers followed by a gradual decline, *The Wicker Man* locations only began to attract a significant amount of film-inspired tourism some 25 years after the film's original cinema release. As *The Wicker Man* has been, in recent years, the object of two documentaries, repeated TV screenings and a recent DVD 'special edition' release, awareness of the film itself and its various locations has increased steadily every year, as has tourism to those sites. As events such as the Wickerman Festival keep the film in the public eye, it appears that *The Wicker Man* will continue to confound conventional film tourism trends.

Bibliography

Anon., 'The Pleasure of their Company', *The Galloway Gazette,* 25 November 1972, p. 6.

Anon., 'The Summer Isles – wild Scotland at its best', *The Oban Times,* 5 December 2002, p. 14.

BBC website, *'The Wicker Man'* – *the Film* <http://www.bbc.co.uk/dna/h2g2/A660232> [Accessed 21 June 2003].

British Tourist Authority, *Movie Map*, 1995 <http://campaigns.visitbritain.com/moviemap/index.htm> [Accessed 19 June 2003].

Brown, A., 'Pagan's Progress', *The Sunday Times*, 6 December 1998   <www.compulsiononline.com/wicker.htm> [Accessed 29 May 2003].

Bruce, D., *Scotland the Movie* (Edinburgh: Polygon, 1996).

Butler, R. 'The Influence of Media in Shaping International Tourist Patterns', *Tourism Recreation Research*, 15 (1990), 46-53.

Christie, B., Telephone interview, 21 June 2003.

Creetown village website, <http://dalbeattie.com/scotland-creetown/thewickerman/> [Accessed 21 June 2003].

Dearden, K., 'Ekland issues a belated apology', *The Galloway Gazette,* 11 June 1999, p. 1.

Dumfries and Galloway Tourist Board website, <http://www.dumfriesandgalloway.co.uk/> [Accessed 29 May 2003].

Dumfries and Galloway Tourist Board, *Visitors Guide 2002* (Dumfries: DGTB, 2002).

Foster, A., *The Movie Traveller* (Edinburgh: Polygon, 2000).

Jamieson, A. 'Wicker man organisers deny pagan undertones', *The Scotsman*, 20 July 2002, p. 3

Khan, S. and A. MacMillan, 'Cult of Wicker Man sets tourism on fire', *The Observer*, 14 July 2002, p. 12.

Mahoney, E., 'End of the world', *The Guardian*, 3 May 2000, p. 17.

Morgan, N. and A. Pritchard, *Tourism Promotion and Power: Creating images, creating identities* (Chichester: Wiley, 1998).

Patterson, J., 'Letter', *The Galloway Gazette*, 18 December 1998, p. 6.

Riley, R., Baker, D. and C. Van Doren, 'Movie Induced Tourism', *Annals of Tourism Research*, 25 (1998), 919-35.

Riley, R. and C. Van Doren, 'Movies as Tourism Promotion: A 'pull' factor in a 'push' location', *Tourism Management* 13 (1992), 267-74.

Seaton, A. V. and B. Hay, 'The Marketing of Scotland as a Tourist Destination, 1985-96', in *Tourism in Scotland*, ed. by L. R. MacLellan and R. Smith (London: International Thomson Business Press, 1998), pp. 209-40.

Tooke, N. and M. Baker, 'Seeing is Believing: The effect of film on visitor numbers to screened locations', *Tourism Management*, 17 (1996), 87-94.

Urry, J., *The Tourist Gaze* (London: Sage, 2002).

Things that go Clunk in the Cult Film Text: Nodes and interstices in *The Wicker Man*

Justin Smith

Introduction

One of the dilemmas facing the cult film scholar involves establishing the textual qualities that contribute to a film's accretion of cult status amongst fans and critics. In approaching the relationships between film texts and fan practices, critics of the phenomenon of 'cult' have been divided between those (like Umberto Eco) who argue for a corpus of cult attributes embedded in the film text which signify its particular status, and others (like Timothy Corrigan) who contend that 'no film [...] is naturally a cult film; all cult films are adopted children'.[1] In truth, there is something to be said for both attitudes. Certainly, while one might almost despair at the diversity of production-side attribution – 'There are cult movies, cult directors, cult actors, and even cult film composers [...] there are also cult posters and cult stills'[2] – some solace may be found in the notion that all this depends upon the accordance of a certain status which is in the gift not of the producer, but the consumer.

I make no apology then for prefacing this reading of Robin Hardy's 1973 British cult classic *The Wicker Man*, with the disclaimer that cult film practices (the creative work and rehearsed competences of cult fandom) may share more common characteristics than the films they idolise. Indeed, in the introduction to a recent contribution to the field, Jancovich, et al., claim that '"cult" is largely a matter of the ways in which films are classified in consumption', though the authors concede that filmmakers often share 'the same "subcultural ideology" as fans and have set out to make self-consciously "cult" materials'.[3] While this much may be true of sub-genres (slasher movies, shlock horror and the like) that trade on repeated formulas, the same cannot be said of those filmic oddities whose cult status has accrued (often to the surprise of their producers) long after their

---

[1] Eco, 'Casablanca'; Corrigan, 'Film and the Culture of the Cult', p. 26.
[2] French and French, *Cult Movies*, p. 8.
[3] Jancovich, Lázaro Reboll, Stringer and Willis, eds., *Defining Cult Movies*, p. 1.

original release. The subcultural appeal of such 'one-offs' resides as much in their production and exhibition histories, as in the secret pleasures of their unique texts.

In order to explain the cult status of *The Wicker Man* it will be necessary both to highlight certain aspects of its production and post-production history which have contributed to its popular critical mythology, and also to consider how incidents in that history have marked the film itself. For, as Eco suggests, a cult film must firstly 'provide a completely furnished world so that its fans can quote characters and episodes as if they were aspects of the fan's private sectarian world'. But furthermore, in order for a fan to engage with it, it must be possible 'to break, dislocate, unhinge it'. In short, 'it must live on, and because of, its glorious ricketiness'.[4] The aim here shall be to identify in the film the particular pleasures of such unevenness, but first to try to locate the origins of this quality in the circumstances of the production.

Production and Exhibition History
From the outset, *The Wicker Man* was dogged by conflict, as extensively documented in Allan Brown's recent study.[5] By the early 1970s, its production company, British Lion, was struggling financially in a domestic production sector sewn up by Rank and ABC, whose exhibition interests guaranteed them the major share of new British products. With the general decline in cinema-going already set in, the future for once vigorous independents seemed bleak. In April 1972 British Lion was sold by Star Associated (a conglomerate owning theatres, bingo halls and discos) who had run the ailing studio for less than a year (retaining John Boulting as Managing Director). The new buyer was tycoon John (Pretty Boy) Bentley whose operation Barclay Securities invested £7.5m, apparently on the strength of the development potential of British Lion's Shepperton Studios site.[6] However, partly to appease union fears of peremptory asset-stripping, it was necessary for the new management quickly to produce some films. Bentley appointed Canadian independent producer Peter Snell in July 1972, quickly promoting him from Head of Production to

---

[4] Eco, 'Casablanca', p. 198.
[5] Brown, *Inside 'The Wicker Man'*
[6] Brown, *Inside 'The Wicker Man'*, p. 3, p. 28.

Managing Director; Snell brought with him the script of *The Wicker Man* and Bentley approved the proposal virtually on the spot. British Lion's board, however, had its doubts. When they read the script they considered the project unviable, especially in America – a vital market if production costs were to be recouped. But Bentley backed the film, according it a modest £420,000 budget and an on-location shoot that would not trouble the financiers unduly or take up any studio space at Shepperton. This appeased union fears and underlined that British Lion was making films again. But Bentley's backing rested on one condition: filming had to begin immediately – tricky in late summer 1972 for a film set in a blossoming Scottish Maytime.[7] So, according to Brown, a mixture of ulterior motives and unseemly haste set the pre-production climate.[8]

If the now-legendary tales of organised chaos, fractious starlets and whisky-fuelled artistic egos that have grown up around the story of *The Wicker Man* shoot are to be believed, it is a wonder the film was made at all. In truth, most location-shot productions trail their own caravans of tittle-tattle and embroidered anecdotes: put any bunch of film people, actors and eager locals together and the stuff of myth inevitably accrues. Certainly the 1977 special issue of *Cinefantastique* devoted to the film, and the more recent research conducted by Brown, have woven a compelling mythology from the established facts. It would be as easy to play down the seven week shoot in scattered locations across Dumfries and Galloway as a workmanlike job: first-timer Robin Hardy directing Anthony Shaffer's sharp script with economy and style, supported by veteran cinematographer Harry Waxman and experienced art director Seamus Flannery, and fronting acting talents and star appeal in the forms of Christopher Lee, Edward Woodward, Britt Ekland, Ingrid Pitt and Diane Cilento. However, what the catalogues of conflicts and upsets recorded by David Bartholomew and Allan Brown demonstrate (beyond their contribution to the film's cult notoriety) is how creative tensions in the collaborative process of film-making produce certain kinds

---

[7] Brown, *Inside 'The Wicker Man'*, p. 29.

[8] 'John Bentley [...] commissioned the film only to placate fermentation within the British film unions, with little thought for *The Wicker Man*'s commercial or creative future', Brown, *Inside 'The Wicker Man'*, pp. 38-39.

of results on screen. A few brief examples (derived from these sources) will suffice to illustrate this point.

To begin with the relationship between the screenwriter (Shaffer) and the director (Hardy), it is difficult not to see this in the light of the former advertising partners' later estrangement.[9] But, as Brown reports, 'their relationship wasn't always so fractious' as it subsequently became.[10] Whether they saw eye to eye on the shoot, it is difficult to say, in the light of their different assessments of the film.[11] Certainly they collaborated over the script,[12] but according to Brown's interviews with Shaffer, the writer also had some influence on casting,[13] and seems to have been present on set throughout the shoot,[14] an unusually active and prolonged involvement from a screenwriter.

Additionally, Hardy fell out with art director Flannery (whose responsibility it was not only to design and build three wicker man effigies for the film's climactic scenes but to produce orchards of (fake) apple blossom in autumn). Flannery, who accompanied Hardy on the location tour, was initially dismayed at the lack of preparation and haste to get the film into production.[15] Once shooting had begun, he describes Hardy's direction thus: 'He couldn't communicate with the crew he had assembled. There was no vision and no organization'. In Flannery's words, this showed on screen: 'You had a melodrama which the director shot as a musical, then, when the film is released, it's become a fantasy movie!'[16]

---

[9] Brown, *Inside 'The Wicker Man'*, p. 59.

[10] Brown, *Inside 'The Wicker Man'*, p. 20.

[11] 'He's quite a tortured man, arrogant and often silly. I only wish he'd made a better job of directing *The Wicker Man'*, Shaffer later recalls. See Brown, *Inside 'The Wicker Man'*, p. 60.

[12] Brown, *Inside 'The Wicker Man'*, pp. 22-24.

[13] Especially the female members of the cast, according to Brown: 'The choice of Britt Ekland didn't please Anthony Shaffer [...] He also had misgivings about Ingrid Pitt', while Diane Cilento was literally wooed by the writer. See Brown, *Inside 'The Wicker Man'*, pp. 41-43.

[14] 'As shooting progressed, I found he was becoming intemperate. You couldn't talk to him and that's why he produced something less than first rate'. Shaffer interviewed by Brown, *Inside 'The Wicker Man'*, p. 62.

[15] Brown, *Inside 'The Wicker Man'*, p. 36.

[16] Cited in Brown, *Inside 'The Wicker Man'*, pp. 31-32.

Again, unusually for a location film, the producer, Peter Snell, commuted between London and Scotland during the shoot and thus was frequently absent from the set. According to Flannery, 'Jake Wright, the assistant director, effectively became the line producer, he was doing all the jobs a producer needed to do'.[17]

Yet Snell was present to persuade Hardy on two occasions not to sack cinematographer Waxman, who irritated the director throughout with his unwelcome creative interventions. He was there, Hardy recalls, on 'a condition made by Film Finance' to ensure the final shot of the burning Wicker Man was properly realised: 'It was a crucial shot but a difficult one to accomplish, so we had Waxman there in case it went wrong [...] I can't say I enjoyed working with him. He never understood the script, I think it offended him'. Hardy concedes, however, that 'he lit the Willow's dance sequence beautifully'.[18]

Someone else whose contribution to the picture is allegedly explained (or excused) by his lack of understanding, or moral sensibilities, was the film editor, Eric Boyd-Perkins. The composer Paul Giovanni told *Cinefantastique*: '*The Wicker Man* was an original and he [Boyd-Perkins] never understood what it was about or how it should work, *as an accumulation of details*' (my emphasis).[19]

Perhaps what such instances demonstrate is a culture clash between industry professionals of an established order working on material and in conditions to which they were unused, and new-age, subversive ideas in the hands of inexperienced creative agencies. Arguably, such tensions did nothing to inhibit some of the finest features of the film: Shaffer's memorable script, Waxman's photography, fine performances from Woodward and Lee, Flannery's imaginative set designs, Paul Giovanni's lyrical score, Stewart Hopps' choreography, Sue Yelland's costumes. But what the results seem to show (as I shall illustrate below) is an assemblage of individual creative contributions not properly synthesised or integrated by a singular vision (and in some instances actually working against one another, pulling the film in

---

[17] Cited in Brown, *Inside 'The Wicker Man'*, p. 60.
[18] Cited in Brown, *Inside 'The Wicker Man'*, p. 61.
[19] Cited in Bartholomew, '*The Wicker Man*', p. 36.

different directions). If this last point is a tendency noted by early reviewers of the film (see below), it is partly a product also of the editing process.

As Brown relates, post-production work began at Shepperton in February 1973 against a backdrop of change within British Lion. The company appointed two new men – Michael Deeley as Managing Director and Barry Spikings as his deputy – and a sell-out to EMI was mooted. In March, Peter Snell was told he was to be replaced. By November, though a print had been made, *The Wicker Man* remained unreleased.[20] Then took place the celebrated private screening for Mr and Mrs Christopher Lee, after which Lee allegedly told Deeley that he had enjoyed the film very much but there was lots missing and Deeley branded it one of the ten worst films he'd ever seen.[21]

Before it was available for preview, and prior to his departure from British Lion, Snell had set up a promotion at the Marché at Cannes, utilising the remaining wicker effigy in a stunt which drew enough attention to attract the interest of Roger Corman, veteran American independent producer.[22] He offered Deeley $50,000 for the rights to distribute the film in America and cut it to his specification.[23] A print of the original 102-minute cut was duly shipped to Corman in the States. Corman returned a letter to British Lion suggesting how the film might be slimmed down because it lacked pace. Eric Boyd-Perkins, following instructions, completed the edit overnight removing some 15 minutes from the running time, significantly cutting the film's opening scenes on the mainland, removing the initiation of Ash Buchanan and reducing the narrative time from two nights to one.[24] This 84-minute cut was released to British audiences with *Don't Look Now* (Roeg, 1973), previewing in London's Victoria Metropole in December 1973, before its official opening on 21 January 1974 at the Odeon Haymarket.[25] As I shall argue below, the truncated version of the film, known as the original theatrical release, only

---

[20] Brown, *Inside 'The Wicker Man'*, p. 104.
[21] Christopher Lee, cited in Brown, *Inside 'The Wicker Man'*, p. 104.
[22] Brown, *Inside 'The Wicker Man'*, p. 105.
[23] Brown, *Inside 'The Wicker Man'*, p. 106.
[24] Brown, *Inside 'The Wicker Man'*, p. 107.
[25] Brown, *Inside 'The Wicker Man'*, pp. 113-14.

compounded the narrative incongruities which were in part the results of the difficulties of the shoot. This disunity was a weakness which contemporary critics noted.

Most reviewers recognised the film's concept and damned its execution, praised the script and the calibre of the actors, but deemed the whole less than the sum of its parts. *The Financial Times* was not alone in its claim that the film's 'fascinating ingredients do not quite blend'.[26] Dilys Powell in *The Sunday Times* conceded: 'one must admire the playing and the distinction with which Robin Hardy has directed [...]'.[27] *The Sunday Telegraph* said the film lacked the balanced 'inter-relation of the ordinary and the extraordinary that marks the best fantasy fiction'.[28] When it was previewed at Burbank Studios in Hollywood on 3 May 1974, Alan Howard in *The Hollywood Reporter* complained, 'Hardy completely botches the scenes in which villagers sing and dance more like music hall professionals than the cosmic worshippers they're supposed to be'.[29] Such negative reactions not only reflect the common difficulty in locating the movie within established generic conventions, they also point to the very narrative incohesion which, I want to suggest, gives the film cult appeal. British Lion's own press pack declared (not without a hint of despair) that the film 'defies conventional classification. If one had to give it a label perhaps "a black thriller" would be a fair description, for, if comedy can be black why not thrills?'[30]

Arguably, *The Wicker Man* would have remained a minor curiosity in British film history had it not been for two sequences of events which have subsequently cemented its cult stature. First was the determination of a partnership of American film buffs who, with the assistance of Hardy, Shaffer and Lee, eventually succeeded in producing and releasing a restored version from the Corman print, which finally saw the light of day in 1977, aided by a celebratory issue of *Cinefantastique* devoted to *The Wicker Man*

---

[26] Andrews, 'Holiday Fodder', p. 3.
[27] Powell, 'Just Men', p. 37.
[28] Hinxman, 'Sting in the Tail of the Year', p.10.
[29] Howard, 'The Wicker Man', p. 3.
[30] British Lion Press Book, 1974, p. 3.

saga.[31] Second was the steady growth of a cult following (first in America and later in Britain) inspired partly by the story of the film's chequered history, partly by college campus screenings and partly through cable TV, video and BBC Moviedrome re-releases. Since the early 1980s an active and dedicated fan culture has emerged, initially around print fanzines such as *Summerisle News* and *Nuada*,[32] location tourism and television documentaries, and latterly on the Internet with newsgroups debating releases of soundtrack and DVD, literature and collectables.[33] I have tried to suggest that one reason for the film's cult status is the mythology surrounding its production history. I now want to consider how elements of that (often turbulent) history have marked the text in ways which make it particularly conducive to cult appreciation.

The Cult Text

The complicated history of the film's different versions begged a definitive 'Director's Cut' that Hardy was only too pleased to endorse. Such flamboyant marketing ploys are designed to appeal to the film buff, the cultist and the collector – to rebrand a past product with classic status. It is significant therefore that the new DVD edition of *The Wicker Man* (released in 2002) offers both the 84-minute and the 102-minute edits. Important to cult fans is the existence, side-by-side, of different versions that can be compared, replayed, debated and dissected. Like the record collectors' world of limited editions, coloured vinyls, alternative sleeves and misprinted labels, the cult film fan thrives in a fundamental sense on *difference*. So what of the differences? And wherein does *The Wicker Man*'s originality lie?

The purpose of the opening mainland scenes (102-minute cut) is surely to establish Sergeant Howie's dour, spotless Christian copper (Edward Woodward) and to ridicule him, using his 'long-haired' subordinate McTaggart (John Hallam) and the saucy postman (Tony Roper) as representatives of normality. Shaffer's

---

[31] See Bartholomew, '*The Wicker Man*', pp. 38-46, and Brown, *Inside 'The Wicker Man'*, pp. 126-44. For additional details of the American resurrection of *The Wicker Man*, see also Byron, 'Something Wicker This Way Comes' and Byron, 'Back Talk'.
[32] See Brown, *Inside 'The Wicker Man'*, pp. 169-71.
[33] See for example, 'wickerman@yahoogroups.com'.

script extended this pre-Summerisle sequence to include Howie's evening patrol of the local taverns, witnessing with undisguised disgust the debauchery of drinking and whoring amidst squalid backstreets. While the script's opening descriptions of the 'scum and effluent that floats on the disturbed surface of the water in the harbour'[34] is metaphor enough for the 'Fallen' world Howie polices alone, Shaffer endorses the cut, concluding that, 'It's better the way it is, just with Howie walking past the 'Jesus Saves' graffiti. You play against the grain from the off, you don't give the story to the audience'.[35] That said, the differences point up subtle, but significant shifts of emphasis in these various narrative beginnings. If the mainland appears to be as debased and un-Christian as the Summerisle we discover, then corruption is universal (not either simply urban, or remote). Similarly, this scenario condemns Howie from the start. It seems to me the chief argument in favour of the truncated opening (84-minute cut) is that Howie is an unknown quantity *until* he reaches Summerisle. We have no pre-judgments about his character except (crucially) the assumptions we might have about a policeman (whether that be as an agent of reactionary state authority or, more likely, a reassuring embodiment of sober reason). It is important that, at least to start with, we are *with* Howie; we discover this strange island through his eyes. If Howie is damned from the outset, his entrapment is surely less beguiling.

The other major narrative change in the shorter version of the film is the conflation of the two nights Howie spends on Summerisle into one, and the excision of the initiation rite of Ash Buchanan (Richard Wren). The three-day term Howie endures under the influence of the islanders' Pagan practices, which builds towards his May Day sacrifice, carries a weight of religious symbolism the shorter version loses. And the ritual offering of the virgin youth to the landlord's daughter Willow MacGregor (Britt Ekland) establishes her (over and above the bawdy barroom celebration of her sexual charms) as the siren Howie must resist in the second night's encounter. Furthermore, we are denied the introduction of Lord Summerisle (Christopher Lee) who brings

---

[34] Shaffer, cited in Brown, *Inside 'The Wicker Man'*, p. 149.
[35] Cited in Brown, *Inside 'The Wicker Man'*, p. 151.

the boy to her window, with his elegy to fecundity and the promise of tomorrow's 'somewhat more serious offering' – an intimation that the capture of Howie (body and soul) is not merely planned in advance, but, more sinisterly, pre-destined.

The remainder of the reduction from 102 to 84 minutes' running time amounts to the trimming of Howie's exchanges at Lord Summerisle's home (shedding some of what Lee considered to be his best lines on the relative merits of different varieties of apple) and the perhaps more significant loss of some ritual iconography from the build up to the May Day procession leading to the film's cliff-top climax. The dramatisation of Pagan practices, with their rich, symbolic suggestiveness and colourful carnival spirit, is arguably the most celebrated and successful ingredient in this curate's egg of a movie. Not only were these elements painstakingly researched in the planning stage by both Hardy and Shaffer (drawing heavily on J. G. Frazer's Victorian study of comparative religion, *The Golden Bough* [1890-1922]), they are also among the best dressed, best staged and imaginatively shot scenes in the whole film.[36]   True, the difference that one more phallic symbol might make could be considered marginal in a film already replete with totemic charms. However, in my view, the shorter version hurries the final build-up, sacrificing the self-conscious lingering upon ritual elements that constitutes Robin Hardy's signature. Certainly, Shaffer and Hardy agreed that while often outrageous and sometimes shocking, it is crucial to the film's credibility that the Pagan world of Summerisle be believable. If Howie is duped by this alien culture, then an audience surely must be complicit in the elaborate fooling. Herein lies the moral balance of the film, between our identification with Howie as a representative of reason (despite his narrow creed) and our sympathy with his sacrificial humanity, and the seductive religious rhetoric of this alternative community which must continue to intrigue even as it appals. In short, it commands a certain devotion on the part of the audience.

I want to highlight now some of those self-conscious elements in the narrative which seem at first sight to jar, but (particularly on repeated viewing) have a resonance that propels them into cult

---

[36] See Brown, *Inside 'The Wicker Man'*, pp. 24-26.

appeal. These are moments in the text I have dubbed 'nodes' and 'interstices': elements which seem either to stand out in bold (sometimes incongruous) relief from the narrative texture or to reveal the cracks in its surface. These manifest themselves in several ways: in symbolic reference, in acting styles and body language, in the use of music and in the juxtaposition of certain camera shots. But together they conjure a sort of dissonance which might be termed *the spirit of play*.

This playful subterfuge begins the moment Howie sets foot on the island and is met with denial by the harbour-master's inscrutable cronies, and continues with postmistress May Morrison's (Irene Sunters) resistance to the idea that her own daughter is missing – she has a daughter, not Rowan, but Myrtle, whom she introduces. When Mrs Morrison intervenes in his questioning of the girl to offer him tea, though he accepts, the scene ends and we cut to The Green Man Inn later that evening.

The barroom drinking song disrupts the impetus of Howie's investigation just as he has intruded upon their bawdy entertainment. There is a distinctive slap-stick style about this musical interlude, involving as it does the whole company in an obviously rehearsed set-piece which impinges radically, if playfully, in the diegesis, wresting power from Howie's serious purpose. Indeed, the incongruity of the film's musical set pieces (pared down from the demands of the original script which freely plunders Cecil Sharp's Victorian folk-song anthology)[37] was endorsed by the composer of the film score. Paul Giovanni said he 'felt right from the beginning that what I was doing was not stylistically in keeping with the screenplay'.[38]

In this scene the rational disruption is compounded further by the camera's dwelling upon the missing harvest festival photograph and Willow's pointed retort that 'some things in their natural state have the most vivid colour', after Howie complains about the unappetising appearance of the tinned food he is served for supper. Later, as the hapless Sergeant takes the air before retiring, he witnesses couples openly engaged in sex on the village green. This sequence is shot in a stylised slow motion which

---

[37] Brown, *Inside 'The Wicker Man'*, p. 45.
[38] Cited in Bartholomew, '*The Wicker Man*', p. 36.

conveys the drowsy, hypnotic sexual power which has descended upon the villagers with nightfall. They are undisturbed by his incredulous observation.

The initiation of Ash Buchanan introduces Christopher Lee's Lord Summerisle whose body language is curiously stiff throughout, as if he were wearing a corset (see Figure 1). There is something strange about the way he holds himself: the lower back, neck and shoulders. He is, we might say, a living totem: his physical power (and thus his political status amongst the islanders) is expressed symbolically (rather than actively) in this rigid, muscular, constrained posture. There is something sensually alluring and gratifying in his physical symmetry and command.

Summerisle's controlled posture contrasts markedly with Howie's increasingly frenetic physical activity. Howie's waning authority is echoed in the literal stripping of his body: first, as a sexually tormented figure sweating in his pyjamas at Willow's potent dance, then the donning of the Fool's costume stolen from Alder MacGregor (Lindsay Kemp), and finally in being attired in a plain, messianic shift at the moment of sacrifice.

Fig. 1: Christopher Lee's Lord Summerisle, whose body language is curiously stiff throughout, as if he were wearing a corset (Courtesy of © Canal+ Image UK Ltd.)

From his fruitless discussion with Summerisle, Howie receives permission to exhume the body of the missing girl Rowan

Morrison (Geraldine Cowper). The sequences in the ruined churchyard at Anwoth are arguably among the most successful, but highlight two important features typical of the film. In the first sequence Howie discovers a young mother breast-feeding, an egg held in her palm, and clears the stone altar, fashioning a crude cross from apple box wood – a moment redolent with a symbolic strangeness. The second features an encounter with Aubrey Morris's gravedigger whose playing (like that of Russell Waters' harbourmaster and Lindsay Kemp's innkeeper) is wonderfully and irreverently camp. In terms of acting styles the supporting roles are almost uniformly overplayed. Yet what comes across as coquettish in the females' dealings with Howie (Britt Ekland's Willow, Diane Cilento's schoolmistress and Ingrid Pitt's librarian) is played as high camp when it comes to the men. This playful, mocking tendency is borne out in Christopher Lee's own urbane, charismatic charm: there is a mesmeric quality in his low, rather throaty, delivery.

The discovery of a hare in the coffin of Rowan Morrison is captured in close-up with an accompanying musical twang from the Celtic harp. This is another repeated technique in narrative italicising – almost cartoon style – which is overdone throughout. Similarly, there are visual gags, such as the lingering close up on the organ stop 'flute d'amour' at Lord Summerisle's castle, which confound narrative verisimilitude (see Figure 2). Yet, I would argue, it is precisely such jarring discords (in camera work and sound) which the cultist adores, and, on repeated viewing, one anticipates such self-conscious moments with relish.

In terms of codes of realism, such dissonance is disruptive and (at least in part) deliberately so, as the ineluctable process of Howie's ridicule and entrapment builds to its climactic moment. Yet unlike mainstream horror, which relies for its effects on the accretion of suspense and the corresponding release of genuine shock which are contained within the rhythm of narrative discourse, *The Wicker Man* seems riven with cracks in its narrative structure. This disharmony, which has confounded critics who have sought to place it within the horror genre is, it

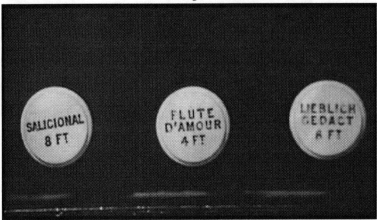

Fig. 2: Visual gags such as the lingering close-up on the organ stop 'flute d'amour' confound narrative verisimilitude (Courtesy of © Canal+ Image UK Ltd.)

seems to me, what makes the film unique. At one level, the persistent undermining of Howie's sober narrative of police investigation through the emergence of the discourse of Pagan ritual practices, dramatises a clash of cultural values and religious power which remains appealing (not least to cult fans). It is no accident that this remote community's reincarnation of the old religion also draws on the contemporary counterculture of the hippy era. At least theoretically, there is a coherent, perhaps radical, thesis underpinning the film's objectives. However, in the manner of its execution and its aesthetic, the film's sinister purpose and tone is continually disrupted by the elements of play which intervene, often comically, always self-consciously, to delimit our psychological and emotional involvement, upon which the success of horror, as of other genres, depends. As Shaffer told *Cinefantastique*:

> Our intent was to do an unusual picture in the horror vein, one that hopefully works on the accumulation of details. To a certain extent, you are meant to put it together for yourself. I feel you *must* leave something for your audience to do, you have to [emphasis retained].[39]

---

[39] Cited in Bartholomew, '*The Wicker Man*', p. 16.

Some, if not all, cult films tread these cracks in the paths of narrative engagement in the way they subvert codes of cinematic realism. In so doing, they become celebrated and cherished, as much for their hyperbolic flaws as their visual excesses. Such textual incongruities open up narrative spaces for fan intervention peculiar to cult films. They rehearse playful rituals which fans appropriate, re-enact and invest with meaningful pleasures beyond the realm of the text itself. *The Wicker Man*, then, offers the believer the raw materials of religious, sexual and political transgression within the safe, fairytale world of vicarious play. The textual imbalance, the 'glorious ricketiness'[40] of these ingredients, constitutes a large part of the film's cult appeal. Howie's tragic fate is pre-ordained in the working out of an elaborate human charade, or more prosaically, the telling of a terrible joke.

Bibliography

Andrews, N., 'Holiday Fodder' (Film Review), *The Financial Times*, 14 December 1973, p. 3.

Anon., 'Britt...and the Fury of Provost Plunkett', *Daily Record*, 18 December 1972, p. 3.

Bartholomew, D., '*The Wicker Man*', *Cinefantastique*, 6.3, Winter (1977), 4-18; 32-46.

British Lion Press Book, 1974.

Brown, A., *Inside 'The Wicker Man': The morbid ingenuities* (London: Sidgwick and Jackson, 2000).

Byron, S., 'Something Wicker This Way Comes', *Film Comment*, 13.6, November/December (1977), 29-31.

Byron, S., 'Back Talk', *Film Comment*, 14.2, March/April (1978), 78.

Corrigan, T., 'Film and the Culture of the Cult', in *The Cult Film Experience: Beyond all reason*, ed. by J. P. Telotte (Austin: University of Texas Press, 1991), pp. 122-37.

---

[40] Eco, '*Casablanca*', p. 198.

Eco, U., 'Casablanca: Cult movies and intertextual collage', in Faith in Fakes: Essays, ed. by U. Eco, trans. by W. Weaver (London: Secker and Warburg, 1987), pp. 197-212.

French, K. and P. French, Cult Movies (London: Pavilion, 1999).

Hinxman, M., 'Sting in the Tail of the Year' (Film Review), The Sunday Telegraph, 23 December 1973, p. 10.

Howard, A., The Hollywood Reporter, 231.18, 9 May 1974, p. 3.

Jancovich, M., A. Lázaro Reboll, J. Stringer and A. Willis, eds., Defining Cult Movies: The cultural politics of oppositional taste (Manchester: Manchester University Press, 2003).

Powell, D., 'Just Men' (Film Review), The Sunday Times, 16 December 1973, p. 37.

Now a Major Motion Picture? *The Wicker Man* Novelisation

Mark Jones

It is a given of commentary surrounding *The Wicker Man* (Hardy, 1973) that the film was effectively 'dead' for many years, before an astonishing if gradual rediscovery, culminating in the UK release of the sumptuous 'director's cut' double-disc DVD in 2002. While the film's obscurity was probably no greater than that of any other British horror feature of the early seventies, it was clearly a text that, other than for a handful of reproduced stills in genre books and magazines, barely had a public presence, at least in Britain. With no marketing campaign, and a low-key release, little material remained to remind the audience of the cinematic experience. Even that sole staple of pre-*Star Wars* (Lucas, 1997) marketing campaigns, the movie tie-in book, was notable by its absence. This should not necessarily be seen as a marker of condescension over the film's generic identity or production qualities – such horror non-entities from the early 1970s as *Captain Kronos: Vampire Hunter* (Clemens, 1974) and *The Vault of Horror* (Baker, 1973) were supported by novelisations.[1] The lack of any related publications is, though, a signal of British Lion's failure to properly market and exploit their property.

Generally seen as the most disposable items of printed culture, novelisations usually appear more or less concurrently with the theatrical release of a film, and tend to be out of print by the time the video is issued. It is highly unusual, although not unknown given the belated novelisation of some 1930s Universal horror classics, for a novelisation to appear subsequent to a film's departure from the big screen. This was, though, apparently the case with *The Wicker Man*, published in Britain six years after the film's limited theatrical release.[2] But the first edition of Robin Hardy and Anthony Shaffer's 'novelisation' was published in the US in 1978, during its extended trawl through American cinemas,

---

[1] Novelisation by Enfield, *Kronos*; novelisation by Oleck, *The Vault of Horror*. See Pringle, 'SF, Fantasy and Horror Movie Novelisations', pp. 38-52 for an incomplete list of genre tie-ins.
[2] Hardy and Shaffer, *The Wicker Man*, 1979.

and could be seen as a concurrent marketing device.[3] However, again unusually, *The Wicker Man* was not at the time the object of a national multi-screen release, with the usual marketing fanfare. As a result, it is more useful to see the publication of the novel as a reflection of the response engendered by the film, rather than a promotional tool for it. As with the belated publication of Jane Campion's collaborative explication of *The Piano*, Hardy and Shaffer's *The Wicker Man* seems to have served a demand for a more expansive and expository version of the film.[4] It was thus a marker of a variety of fans' interests in the film, from the commemorative to the analytical, and a signal that the film was becoming a significant cinematic text.

For British readers and audiences, the period of the novel's original availability coincided with *The Wicker Man*'s greatest obscurity. The effective existence of a novelisation without a cinematic source ascribed a variety of significations to the novel. Firstly, it stood as a 'replacement' for the little-seen and rare film, as a marker of the space in which the film should have been, but which could, due to the modes of distribution generally available at the time, only be occupied by a novelisation. Secondly, though, even for those UK cinemagoers who had seen the film on its original release, the book supplied a 'supplement' to the text, the only reproduction of the excised material from the original cut of the film, or even, perhaps, from the supposed full version, or the original screenplay. Thirdly, the novelisation marks a 'recognition' of the film. The film is deemed important enough to require some kind of material and commercial existence and also to contain sufficient artistic merit to have its missing segments restored. The book thus indicates the film's status as both a potential classic and a cult object. The first UK paperback edition makes explicit claims for *The Wicker Man*'s classic status – 'The film of *The Wicker Man* has been called the best horror movie to come out of England in thirty years'.[5] While the differentiation between 'classic' and 'cult' is difficult to define and maintain, a securely placed classic would probably not require such a recommendation. The emergence of the book at its specific point

---

[3] Hardy and Shaffer, *The Wicker Man*, 1978.
[4] Campion and Pullinger, *The Piano*.
[5] Hardy and Shaffer, *The Wicker Man*, 1979, back cover.

in time is an indication of the complex web of creation, production, distribution, contractualisation, reproduction and consumption that marks the formation of both classic and cult reputations.

The Wicker Man's claim to cult status is formed partly by its exceedingly troubled and somewhat obscure production and distribution history. The novelisation also has a contribution of its own to make to this contextual background. Its genesis has been open to some dispute; credited on covers and title pages to Robin Hardy and Anthony Shaffer, it has no further indications of indebtedness, adaptation or ownership. This is highly unusual in the publishing of novelisations which, more than most cultural products, tend to be mired in, and then display the complexity of, their contractual obligations. Shaffer claimed that the book was written from his screenplay, though it is unclear as to when this was undertaken. Hardy, on the other hand, has stated that his novel – at least in draft form – actually came first, and that the screenplay was adapted from it by Shaffer.[6] The acknowledgement of Shaffer as co-author on the novel seems to undermine Hardy's version that Shaffer made no real contribution.

The packaging of the original US and UK editions indicates that the novel has a separate identity to, and perhaps even a kind of primacy over, the film. The only allusion to the film on the front covers of the early editions is iconographic, and the mention on the back cover of the first UK paperback of 'The film of *The Wicker Man...*' leaves open the possibility that it is the film that is the adapted text. Taking these aspects of production and presentation together with the unavailability of the film in Britain throughout most of the 1970s and 1980s, it might have been expected that Hardy's novel, the only easily obtainable version of the text, might have more effectively influenced public awareness and knowledge of the film. However, the cultural marginalisation of the novelisation as a form, together with its usual subservient position within the process of creative production, generally precludes it from being seriously considered to contribute towards an understanding of the cinematic original. With the case

---

[6] Brown, *Inside 'The Wicker Man'*, p. 160.

of *The Wicker Man* novel, though, its special circumstances position it as more of a parallel text than a novelisation. It is in some of these terms – as a possible interpretation, a retelling, or even a series of expansive footnotes to the film – that the novel will be addressed in what follows.

The main purpose here is to make the material of the novel more readily available in interpretations of the film, rather than to perform a close analysis of the novel itself, notwithstanding the book's qualities. There are several contributions the novel can make towards the illumination of various aspects of the film; these fall into three major categories – addition, expansion, and interpretation. There is a substantial amount of material present in the book that is not in any extant version of the film. Much that is in the film is expanded upon in the book and there are clear interpretative gestures within the book that are largely absent from the film. Additionally, there are a handful of direct contradictions between the two texts, and some minor deletions from film to novel. These differences between film and novel percolate through the various areas of narration and representation, and will be considered in terms of events and characters, narration and point-of-view, and ideology and politics, including the representation of sexuality. For all purposes of comparison the 'director's cut' will be taken as the authoritative film text, which lessens the differences between the book and the film as first shown.

There are several substantial deviations between the narratives of film and novel texts. A fairly lengthy section at the opening of the book is missing from the film completely. The novel opens with Sergeant Neil Howie off duty, though still considering himself to be on police business, bird-watching for golden eagles with his fiancée on an isolated island, but also on the look-out for an egg stealer. A shotgun-wielding poacher kills one of the pair of eagles and Howie dramatically struggles with and arrests the malefactor. The scene following this, in which Howie is given the letter from a 'child lover', occurs on the same Saturday evening, and is followed by an encounter with Jewish-American and English tourists who have missed the last ferry before the Sabbath to St Ninian's Isle. Howie takes Mary home, but they, for apparently the first time, indulge in some fairly physical petting

in the parked car. Prematurely halted, Mary expresses her
frustration, and they suddenly decide to marry in two weeks.
Howie leaves for Summerisle the next day, after attending
church.[7]

Other differences in the ordering or occurrence of events are
more substantial than would ordinarily be expected in the
novelisation of a film (although these differences are fewer than
in the typical *novel-to-film* adaptation). They amount to the
following:

- A mysterious figure in 'American style
sneakers' spies on Howie and Mary. It is
intimated later that this is Lord Summerisle[8]
- Howie encounters T. H. Lennox, the
chemist and photographer, earlier, just before
meeting Dr Ewan[9]
- The island has no Public Records Office, so
Howie radios McTaggart on the mainland for
the information. Ingrid Pitt's registrar character
is missing[10]
- The visit to the library occurs earlier –
immediately after the meetings with the
chemist and doctor[11]
- Lord Summerisle's gillie ('attendant for
hunting or fishing [...] from Scottish Gaelic
gille boy, servant') who is a woman called
Sorrel, and her brother Beech, are absent from
the film[12]
- Certain expansive elements of Howie's
encounter with Lord Summerisle are missing
from the film, including most particularly the
following: Summerisle's family have preserved
and protected perhaps the last colony of great

---

[7] Hardy and Shaffer, *The Wicker Man*, 1979, pp. 1-24.
[8] Hardy and Shaffer, *The Wicker Man*, 1979, pp. 21-22.
[9] Hardy and Shaffer, *The Wicker Man*, 1979, pp. 77-81.
[10] Hardy and Shaffer, *The Wicker Man*, 1979, pp. 81-83.
[11] Hardy and Shaffer, *The Wicker Man*, 1979, pp. 84-87.
[12] Hardy and Shaffer, *The Wicker Man*, 1979, pp. 88-93.

auks in the world; Summerisle is a close friend
of Howie's Chief Constable; Summerisle and
Howie visit the experimental apple orchard[13]
- The book features a sacred grove guarded
  by Beech, whom the islanders consider to be
  mad[14]
- Howie several times 'borrows' Dr Ewan's
  motorbike for his night-time explorations[15]
- Before Willow's dance she speaks to Howie
  and he sees her naked[16]
- Following her dance Howie has a relatively
  detailed dream in which he finds Rowan in the
  sacred grove and, armed with a claymore, he
  attempts to save her from the villagers[17]
- The hobbyhorse chase is much reduced[18]
- An RAF bomber flies over the island to
  check the location of the police seaplane, and
  one of the crew catches a glimpse of 'a huge
  man standing on a cliff'[19]
- Beech 'blasphemes' (according to the
  beliefs of Summerisle) just before Howie enters
  the wicker man[20]
- Howie's last act while the wicker man is
  burning is to free several of the birds that have
  been caged within it.[21]

There are a number of other differences between the two texts,
which are not so much events as distinctions in the
communication of facts. Rather than having Lord Summerisle
address his doggerel to the snails, Howie finds a scroll containing

[13] Hardy and Shaffer, *The Wicker Man*, 1979, pp. 94-111.
[14] Hardy and Shaffer, *The Wicker Man*, 1979, pp. 113-14.
[15] Hardy and Shaffer, *The Wicker Man*, 1979, p. 120, p. 144.
[16] Hardy and Shaffer, *The Wicker Man*, 1979, pp. 129-32.
[17] Hardy and Shaffer, *The Wicker Man*, 1979, pp. 140-42.
[18] Hardy and Shaffer, *The Wicker Man*, 1979, pp. 156-57.
[19] Hardy and Shaffer, *The Wicker Man*, 1979, pp. 177-78.
[20] Hardy and Shaffer, *The Wicker Man*, 1979, pp. 207-08.
[21] Hardy and Shaffer, *The Wicker Man*, 1979, pp. 211-12.

the same passage on his bedside table.[22] Dr Ewan reports Rowan's death as 'metamorphosis' whereas May Morrison supplies the information that 'She was so hot, burning... poor love!'[23]

Although many of the purely plot-based differences between the two texts are simple additions and expansions that might not necessarily alter our reading of *The Wicker Man*, several might be seen as significant. Aside from Mary Bannock, Howie's fiancée, the most important difference in characters between the texts is the presence of Sorrel and Beech, Lord Summerisle's gillie and her mentally unstable brother. Both of them have their functions within the novel, which provide distinctive differences from the film, and have some effect on the development of the plot.

Sorrel is seen by Howie as a potential ally, especially as she is openly critical of Miss Rose, the school teacher, who Sorrel calls 'a preachy bitch'. Trained in forestry and veterinary studies, Sorrel insists that she is as qualified to be the teacher as Miss Rose, who got the job only because, as Sorrel declares, 'She and Lord S ... are very close',[24] and whose qualifications are in comparative theology and pre-medieval music – 'a bit artsy-craftsy for my taste'.[25]

The gillie's importance is multivalent and economical. She signifies a practical rationality, the continuation on the island of the scientific attitude towards the cultivation of flora and fauna, which was initiated by Summerisle's grandfather, along with the pantheistic religion. In her gossipy familiarity she also functions as apparently the most normatively socialised of the inhabitants of the island encountered by Howie.

She is straightforward and friendly, and though she features only relatively briefly, Howie continues to factor her into his plans for locating and retrieving Rowan. However, at the conclusion, she appears only very briefly; 'Lord Summerisle's exultant look was exactly mirrored by that of Rowan and Sorrel and Miss Rose and May Morrison and Cuckoo and Lark and Swallow and the rosy-cheeked girl who had so prophetically

---

[22] Hardy and Shaffer, *The Wicker Man*, 1979, p. 56.

[23] Hardy and Shaffer, *The Wicker Man*, 1979, p. 80, p. 76.

[24] Hardy and Shaffer, *The Wicker Man*, 1979, p. 92.

[25] Hardy and Shaffer, *The Wicker Man*, 1979, p. 93.

called "alive – alive – Oooooooh!"".[26] It is thus emphasised that
neither rationality nor apparent sociability are of any assistance to
Howie – the sacrificial ritual of the Wicker Man is predicated on
a different understanding of humanity's social existence and
interdependency, indeed in its relationship to the physical world
per se.

Sorrel's brother, Beech, also marks a divergence from the
otherwise united front of the island. His deviation, though, is in
matters of religious belief and practice. According to Sorrel,
Beech 'believes that he is the king that guards a sacred grove....
For a time, Beech thought he was the rightful Lord Summerisle'.
Howie questions her on the specifics of this: 'Lord Summerisle
and the rest of you don't believe that there is anything for Beech
to guard, is that right? Maypoles are *in*, and sacred groves, as it
were, are *out?*' Sorrel replies:

> 'Well, of course, there are always
> *Protestants*... That's what we call people here
> who don't understand the truth. They protest
> that the sacred grove is at the heart of our
> religion. Lord Summerisle is very patient with
> them. He uses reasoned argument and logic and
> they *always* see the light'.[27]

Beech seems to symbolise a genuine and self-discovered nature
religion, and allows the reader to figure Lord Summerisle's
Paganism as, in fact, a Victorian construct, a manipulative
imposition on the islanders. The further significance of this
emerges at the end of the novel, when Beech perceives Howie
just before his sacrifice as 'the real King'. '"The real king's name
is Jesus. Go and read about Him!", said Howie quietly to Beech,
planting the seed of a new faith in the man'.[28] In this way, the
novel marks a potential repeat of the eventual triumph of
Christianity over Celtic religions. Alternatively, perhaps, it may
signal some deeper identification in Frazerian terms of
Christianity with a genuine Druidical belief system, again casting

[26] Hardy and Shaffer, *The Wicker Man*, 1979, p. 210.
[27] Hardy and Shaffer, *The Wicker Man*, 1979, pp. 115-16.
[28] Hardy and Shaffer, *The Wicker Man*, 1979, p. 208.

Summerisle's Paganism as fundamentally artificial and an expression of ideology rather than spirituality.

The most important distinction between the film and the novel, though, comes generally in the area of narrational method; its significance extends into all other aspects of the text. This distinction is partly a result of the differing narrative techniques that are available to prose and film, but it is not an inevitable outcome. Though not in first person, the novel is almost entirely focalised through Howie. There are only two very brief scenes – each no more than a page long, and neither in the film – in which the events are not perceived through Howie's point of view. This method of narration, as well as its particular features, introduces some issues of quite fundamental significance in the interpretation of *The Wicker Man* generally.

Firstly, in terms of the filmed narrative, it demonstrates perhaps more explicitly than even the film does just how tied we are to Howie during the course of the story. In general, apart from Willow's dance and Summerisle's address to the snails – both of which stand outside the otherwise generally realistic film narrative mode – we see and know only what Howie sees and knows. This extreme limit on our knowledge is not unknown in film, but it is perhaps somewhat unusual. Strong narrative parallels can perhaps be drawn with two other early 1970s films – *Chinatown* (Polanski, 1974), in which again we only know exactly what Jake Gittes knows as he investigates a case involving a missing child, before discovering the final, awful truth; and *Don't Look Now* (Roeg, 1973) in which, again, apart from a handful of uninformative – in fact, misleading – scenes, we are continually in the presence of a 'partially-sighted' central protagonist, John Baxter, meeting a gruesome end as he pursues what is apparently a child in danger. A consideration of this narrational approach might have something to contribute to a discussion of the generic identity of *The Wicker Man*, perhaps locating it as a detective thriller, rather than a horror film. The novel's foregrounding of Howie's policing methods, in particular his scrupulous compiling of case notes each evening, certainly leads us closer to this view.

As well as emphasising Howie's continual presence, the focalisation of the story through him significantly expands our

understanding of his character. In some places, in fact, the added
information on attitude, method and motivation might serve to
contradict the readings easily obtainable from the film. For
instance, in the scene where Howie confronts Miss Rose in her
classroom, he appears bombastic and inflexible: 'Everywhere I
go on this island I find degeneracy [...] and now I know where it
all stems from – the filth taught here in this schoolroom'. The
book, however, continues with a note on Howie's self reflection:
He was aware of how pompous he must sound, even as he spoke,
but he didn't care. The phrases might be clichés but they gave
vent to his feelings quickly and succinctly'.[29] A recurring feature
of the novel is the reporting of Howie's consciousness of his
methods as a working copper, which at least balances out his self-
identification as a Christian. From the novel we get a sense of
Howie's dogged professionalism, rather than his dour
Presbyterianism. This is, of course, unsurprising, as one of the
crucial pieces of information imparted explicitly by the book is
that Howie is, in fact, an Episcopalian. This is implicitly revealed
in the film, where Howie attends an Anglican service, though
several details are incorrect. An important gloss is provided on
the exchange that occurs early in both the book and the film
between Howie and McTaggart:

> 'The whole place [Summerisle] is a bit strange
> by all accounts. No licensing laws. Dancing on
> a Sunday. Oh, that'd appeal to a heathen like
> you, McTaggart'. Sergeant Howie laughed as
> he said this for it was a joke between them that
> Hugh McTaggart resented all the Presbyterian-
> inspired Scottish laws relating to the Sabbath,
> mostly for the extra work it involved policing
> them. Privately, Howie agreed with the older
> man, but for different reasons. He could not
> think of the small-minded, mean-spirited
> horrors of the Scottish Sabbath as God-given.

---

[29] Hardy and Shaffer, *The Wicker Man*, 1979, p. 63.

> But to him the law was the law, however he felt
> about it.[30]

The picture of Howie, which emerges from the novel, is of a resourceful and responsible police officer, an honest man doing a difficult job and a legitimate representative of the social order.

This character discourse might still be seen as somewhat repressive, patriarchal and paternalistic. But it is – again – at least partially offset by Howie's attitudes to politics and race, and perhaps also to sexuality, as they are gradually revealed through the course of the novel. The early encounter with a Jewish American couple leads to Mary's comment that:

> 'Jewish people fascinate you, don't they, Neil?'
> 'Aye. They do,' he acknowledged. 'Imagine believing you're God's chosen people and there being quite a lot of evidence to support the idea: Abraham, Noah, Moses, Jesus, Saint Paul, Karl Marx, Freud, Einstein to name but a few'.[31]

Howie's list of figures which he believes important firmly locates him within the liberal Enlightenment tradition. In fact, Howie turns out to be a committed socialist.

> As he followed Broom down a labyrinthine passage, Howie reflected bitterly what an unfair advantage Lord Summerisle had over any ordinary citizen who was due to be interviewed by the police. A man who could only be approached by his personal gillie and his very own bagpiper, living in a castle large enough to rehouse half a Glasgow slum. It was right, he thought, that people like Lord Summerisle should be taxed until the pips squeaked.[32]

---

[30] Hardy and Shaffer, *The Wicker Man*, 1979, p. 11.
[31] Hardy and Shaffer, *The Wicker Man*, 1979, p. 14.
[32] Hardy and Shaffer, *The Wicker Man*, 1979, p. 95.

Howie is also clearly identified as anti-racist and generally tolerant of religious difference. Although he appears to draw the line at the Pagan rites of Summerisle, it should be noted that, although it is not excessively foregrounded in either book or film, much of the activity which most offends Howie involves the combining of children and sex. The book makes it clear that one of his chief theories as to the fate of Rowan Morrison is that she has been or will be the victim of a sexual assault or ritual murder. When Howie 'rescues' Rowan, and they are ascending through the tunnel, she tells him that the grotto they are in is symbolic of the womb:

> 'Miss Rose says our female magic comes from there. It's why I've always looked forward to becoming a woman. So that I'll have my own magic. In a few months it would have been too late to sacrifice me'. Howie [...] wondered whether she meant that by then she would have reached her maturity, or lost her virginity. On this island the two events were probably almost concurrent, he thought bitterly.[33]

Just how that might occur is perhaps indicated by hints that the *droit du seigneur* remains in operation on the island, at least in some symbolic form.[34]

Howie's attitude to sex is, in fact, one of the most fully explored aspects of the novel, which interrogates quite thoroughly the reasons for, and implication of, the particular expression of his spiritual beliefs in relation to sexuality. An early acknowledgement of the behavioural effects of sexual repression comes through one of the few paragraphs in the book to be focalised through a character other than Howie – Mary:

> [She] had explained to Neil that she loved his enthusiasms, that they excited her. She had hardly dared to say to herself, let alone to him,

---

[33] Hardy and Shaffer, *The Wicker Man*, 1979, p. 197.
[34] Hardy and Shaffer, *The Wicker*, 1979, pp. 168-69.

> that she, as a woman, waited with increasing
> impatience for some of his passion to be
> channelled into loving her physically.[35]

A page later, and back with Howie, 'He realised that it was he who was afraid of being inadequate'.[36] Several subsequent key scenes, which will be familiar from the film, together with some additionally supplied information, complete the picture of Howie's self-reflective, self-admittedly confused, and evolving attitude towards sex. On arriving at the village Howie is aware of the vegetative beauty, which is explicitly linked to sensuality:

> [T]his town was, for him, uncomfortably,
> extravagantly beautiful! There was something
> sensual about the way the flowers and the
> buildings seemed to lavish their felicities on the
> visitor's senses. It was unScottish. Howie
> found that disturbing and, in a way that he put
> down to the events of the night before, exciting.
> Perhaps, he thought, my love for Mary has
> heightened my senses. He blessed her for that.[37]

Later, as in the film but in more detail, Howie is sexually disturbed and excited by Willow. There are several gratuitous references to her 'lovely arse', which may be an in-joke on Hardy's part, given the refusal by Britt Ekland to allow herself to be photographed naked from the rear, and thus would also contribute to the argument that the novel was written substantially after the completion of filming.

The material around Willow's dance is more serious, though. Firstly, 'she did something so sexy with her luscious lower lip that Howie had to frantically reprove his all too responsive flesh'. Immediately after, he is fantasising a scene of sadistic sexuality – 'To his horror, he found that the idea excited him. Was almost every male, he wondered, afflicted with this atavistic desire to

---

[35] Hardy and Shaffer, *The Wicker Man*, 1979, p. 17.
[36] Hardy and Shaffer, *The Wicker Man*, 1979, p. 18.
[37] Hardy and Shaffer, *The Wicker Man*, 1979, p. 31.

master a woman?'[38] Shortly after Howie sees Willow naked, the
vision initiates a complex interplay of the sensual and the
spiritual. 'The lighting of her body reminded him of a religious
postcard that he had always held dear since the day his Mary had
sent it to him, after their first date. It was called *The Education of
the Virgin*'.[39] The passage continues, 'it showed the Blessed
Virgin Mary as a child, holding her hand close to a candle, to stop
it guttering, so that the light of the flame showed through the very
flesh of the little girl who would become the Mother of God'.[40]
The parallel with the still virginal Howie's subsequent
experiences should not be lost.

When Willow's dance is in progress Howie suddenly sees that
in her unsatisfied desire she is:

> [I]n a kind of pain that only he could assuage
> [....] He knew of the pain Willow felt because
> he remembered that Mary Bannock had felt it
> too [....] He'd sensed her pain when he had
> taken his hand from inside her thigh [..... I]t
> had been unnatural of him not to marry her far
> sooner and take away the pain of waiting.[41]

Howie is clearly not simply a prude. He is, in fact, and quite
appropriately for a relatively young, well-educated man of his
time, a thorough Lawrentian. This is spelt out by a reference to
the *Lady Chatterley's Lover* trial:

> The defence had triumphed partly because an
> Anglican bishop [...] had answered the
> prosecution's question, 'Can you imagine a
> decent woman worshipping a man's balls?'
> with the reply 'Yes indeed'. And yet Howie
> knew the bishop had meant his answer in the
> context of what 'a wonderful thing' (as a

---

[38] Hardy and Shaffer, *The Wicker Man*, 1979, p. 130.
[39] Georges de la Tour (attributed), *The Education of the Virgin*, c.1650, The Frick
Collection.
[40] Hardy and Shaffer, *The Wicker Man*, 1979, p. 132.
[41] Hardy and Shaffer, *The Wicker Man*, 1979, p. 136.

creation of God) 'is a man'. In that context, of course, his balls, custodians of new life, were indeed wonderful. But something told Howie that when the school mistress said venerate the penis she meant it in the sense that he, Howie, venerated the host.[42]

On the green earlier, Howie had been brought face to face with the actuality of sexual intercourse for the first time: 'He longed to roar, "Stop it. It looks ugly to me. And I was so sure it would be beautiful!"' But then he sees on a girl's face 'a fleeting image of what he imagined as the love of God expressed in the sexual act. To see that look on Mary Bannock's face, to know that he had put it there, would surely be wonderful'.[43]

The licentious sexuality of the island is only one aspect of its ideological make-up, and in combination with other factors it is perhaps more likely to be seen as a means of control, rather than as unsubjugated libidinal expression. The reading of the island as, in fact, a fascistic cult, is promoted by the reference to Howie, in the burning wicker man:

> [R]eminded of having seen, one night on BBC television, the replaying of a famous documentary about the Nuremberg Rally. It had been called the *Triumph of the Will* [Riefenstahl, 1934]. Lots of well-scrubbed blond people with expressions just like this congregation. Of course, they hadn't burned anyone there, as far as he could remember. That had come later. He realized he still didn't know if he was the first of their human sacrifices, but he knew, looking at their faces as they sang, that he wouldn't be the last.[44]

Though not explicitly referenced earlier, this invocation of Nazism as explanatory of the ideological operations of

---

[42] Hardy and Shaffer, *The Wicker Man*, 1979, p. 62.
[43] Hardy and Shaffer, *The Wicker Man*, 1979, p. 47.
[44] Hardy and Shaffer, *The Wicker Man*, 1979, p. 210.

Summerisle serves to combine much that has gone previously. From the early identification of Howie as philo-semitic, through the various mystically geometric symbols encountered on the island, to Lord Summerisle's simultaneous exploitation of a rationalist scientism and 'Aryan' mythology, the story of *The Wicker Man* is retrospectively refigured as analogous to the historical and social processes which gave rise to the Holocaust. For instance, there are many references in the novel to the Celtic race and its myths; crude racialist historicism typically locates the Celts as Aryans, or Indo-European.

Although there is little in the novel of thematic substance that is not indicated somewhere in the film, the former does prioritise its themes in a distinctive manner. There is a significant expansion of the available political interpretations, together with a more complex attitude to sexuality. The horror – and whatever *The Wicker Man*'s generic identity, it does, of course, end as a horror film – of Howie's burning becomes much more experiential and considered than observational and spectacular. The location of Howie as a sympathetic centre of the text, is, of course, a problem for some. Several amateur reviewers and fans have expressed reservations about the novel, including a reader who wrote on Amazon, 'I was not as keen on the book as the others who have reviewed it, principally I suspect because I didn't want to be made to like Sergeant Howie!'[45] Most of the potential pro-Pagan readings frequently obtained from Anthony Shaffer's *The Wicker Man* are proscribed by a consideration of Hardy's book. Though more textually complex in many ways than the film, the novel is, finally, much less ambiguous.

Bibliography
alexandria1121, 'Interesting addition to the film', 25 February 2002, <http://www.amazon.co.uk/exec/obidos/ASIN/033039018 X/qid=1076053330/sr=1-1/ref=sr_1_11_1/202-1355312- 7399809> [Accessed 6 February 2004].

---

[45] alexandria1121, 'Interesting addition to the film'.

Brown, A. *Inside 'The Wicker Man': The morbid ingenuities* (London: Sidgwick and Jackson, 2000).

Campion, J. and K. Pullinger, *The Piano* (London: Bloomsbury, 1994).

Enfield, H., *Kronos* (London: Fontana, 1972).

Hardy, R. and A. Shaffer, *The Wicker Man* (New York: Crown, 1978).

Hardy, R. and A. Shaffer, *The Wicker Man* (Feltham: Hamlyn, 1979).

Oleck, J., *The Vault of Horror* (New York: Bantam Books, 1973).

Pringle, D., 'SF, Fantasy and Horror Movie Novelisations', *Interzone*, 80, February (1994), 38-52.

Wicker Man, The – Special Edition Director's Cut. Dir. R. Hardy. Canal+ ([1973] 2002).

Mister Punch as Sacrificial Victim in *The Wicker Man*

Melissa Smith

Why does Sergeant Howie end up dressed as Punch before he is ritually sacrificed in *The Wicker Man* (Hardy, 1973)? The use of Punch as sacrificial victim in the film seems to bear little resemblance to the figure's traditional role as the homicidal stick-wielding menace of Punch and Judy fame. The first recorded script of the hand puppet show, *The Tragical Comedy or Comical Tragedy of Punch and Judy*, based on an 1827 performance by Giovanni Piccini, features a Punch who beheads his neighbour, beats and murders his baby and Judy, murders the doctor who tries to help him after a fall from a horse, beats to death a servant, kills a beggar, assaults the constable who comes to arrest him, hangs the hangman who tries to execute him, and finally slays the Devil himself.[1] One of Punch's traditional final speeches after the Devil's defeat is reproduced in Neil Gaiman and Dave McKean's graphic novel, *The Comical Tragedy or Tragical Comedy of Mr. Punch* (1995), a fictional account of a man's encounters with the violence in his own family history, and with the staged violence of the Punch and Judy show. Here Punch proclaims, 'Hooray! Hooray! The Devil is dead! Now everybody is free to do whatever they wish!'[2] The benefits of this situation are unclear, however. One might argue that Punch has singlehandedly demonstrated the dangers of everybody being allowed to do whatever they wish.

Howie's role in *The Wicker Man* seems directly opposed to Punch's, as the sergeant's finger-pointing and moralising ways suggest someone much more invested in maintaining social controls. The film's depiction of Punch is further complicated by his symbolic position in the May Day festival. In Howie's researches at the Summerisle library, we learn with him that Punch's role in the 'fertility dramas' makes him 'the most complex of all the symbolic figures. [He is] a privileged simpleton, and king for a day.' Later, as Howie is about to be sacrificed, Miss Rose explains some of the further implications of the Punch costume he is wearing:

---

[1] Cited in Leach, *The Punch and Judy Show*, pp. 9-13.

[2] Gaiman and McKean, *The Comical Tragedy*, p. 78.

> You are the fool, Mr. Howie, Punch. One of the
> great fool victims of history. For you have
> accepted the role of king for a day, and who but
> a fool would do that?

The film's use of Punch seems related primarily to its investments in a carnivalesque role-reversal, whereby Howie as fool becomes the focal point of the May Day celebrations, and the key figure in Summerisle's appeasement of its gods.

An examination of the origins of the Punch of puppet theatre suggests the complex roots of this character's behaviour, and provides further insight into the theatrical nature of *The Wicker Man*'s use of the Punch costume. As theatre historians have argued, Punch's origins are traceable to the *Commedia* figure Pulcinella. Pulcinella shares Punch's hooked nose, and is sometimes depicted with a hunchback. Pulcinella was the basis for popular characters in both the marionette and the hand-puppet theatres. A possible key to understanding Howie's misfortunes on Summerisle may be found in the contrast between these two derivations of Pulcinella. Michael Byrom describes 'Pulcinella's dual personality [...] his character as a glove-puppet [is] cunning, witty, lewd, but essentially homicidal.' However, 'as a marionette [...] his nature was basically [...] that of a half-witted buffoon although including an element of peasant guile.'[3] The human mask of the *Commedia* 'is submissive, cowardly, greedy and lazy, but good humoured; like the circus clown, he gets all the kicks'.[4] A potential key to Howie's fate in *The Wicker Man* may be found in one of the more popular Pulcinella *Commedia* plots, in which Pulcinella is 'the ill-bred country bumpkin who [comes] to town with disastrous results'.[5] As he investigates the disappearance of Rowan Morrison, Howie stumbles through Summerisle, surprised and disgusted by everything he sees, and repeatedly revealing his limited imagination.

Further complicating the use of Punch in *The Wicker Man* is the idea of the scapegoat derived from one of the film's sources,

---

[3] Byrom, *Punch in the Italian Puppet Theatre*, p. 124.
[4] Byrom, *Punch in the Italian Puppet Theatre*, p. 124.
[5] Byrom, *Punch in the Italian Puppet Theatre*, p. 133.

James Frazer's *The Golden Bough* (1890-1922). Although there are many examples of scapegoating discussed in Frazer's study, of particular interest is a custom practised by the Greeks of Asia Minor in the sixth century BCE:

> When a city suffered from plague, famine, or other public calamity, an ugly or deformed person was chosen to take upon himself all the evils which afflicted the community [...] he was beaten seven times upon his genital organs with squills and branches of the wild fig and other wild trees, while the flutes played a particular tune. Afterwards he was burned on a pyre built of the wood of forest trees; and his ashes were cast into the sea.[6]

The use of a physically deformed individual as scapegoat offers a partial explanation for the use of the Punch costume in *The Wicker Man*, since its twisted facial features and hunchback give Howie the deformed appearance of this type of sacrificial victim. In his keynote address at the July 2003 *The Wicker Man* Conference, held at the University of Glasgow's Crichton Campus in Dumfries, Robin Hardy made a further connection between Punch's hunchback and the use of the costume in the film, arguing that Punch's physical deformity is an integral part of the figure's position as human sacrifice. In his account, the hunchback is the target of the whips used to scourge the scapegoat.[7] Presumably, when the costume is employed, this hunchback provides a cushion to render the scapegoat's punishment more symbolic than actual. However, in the case of *The Wicker Man*'s ultimate ending, the sacrifice becomes real enough.

The use of the Punch costume in *The Wicker Man* engages with the origins of the character Punch in a number of ways, but it is in the theatrical impact of the Punch and Judy hand-puppet shows that the film most fascinatingly engages with traditional

---

[6] Frazer, *The Golden Bough*, p. 579.
[7] Hardy, 'Keynote Address'.

uses of Punch. An examination of the similarities between Howie's adventures on Summerisle and Punch and Judy exposes some of the ways in which *The Wicker Man* exploits and subverts notions of role-playing, theatricality, and narrative. In accordance with Punch's mixed origins, the residents of Summerisle blend ritual and drama in a manner that renders the two indistinguishable from each other. Howie himself is in turns the bumbling Pulcinella, struggling with cultural standards that are completely foreign to him, and the belligerent Punch who allows his belief in his home culture's values to fuel his desire to heap abuse on Lord Summerisle and his followers.

On a meta-theatrical level, Howie's experiences on Summerisle reciprocate the Punch and Judy show's use of audience interaction. As John Harries notes in his discussion of a contemporary Punch and Judy performance, 'it is seemingly the children who control the fate of the actors [...] through the giving and withholding of information, [they appear] to be orchestrating the entire sequence of dramatic action'.[8] Harries notes the artificial nature of this empowerment, however, arguing that:

> Finally [...] the Punch and Judy world, where children are little gods directing the fate of wooden mortals, is simply play [...]. The whole situation in which the children are allowed to play at power is tightly controlled by the performers: they tell the children what to say, when to say it, when to believe and when to doubt.[9]

As we shall see, Howie's sense of authority and control is not only limited by the Summerisle residents; it is regulated by them in accordance with their plan to ritually sacrifice him. The use of Punch in *The Wicker Man* suggests a number of issues at work in the film: the idea of identity as something that is 'put on'; the blurring of the lines between audience and performer, between

---

[8] Harries, '"Come See a Traditional Punch and Judy"', p. 73.
[9] Harries, '"Come See a Traditional Punch and Judy"', p. 74.

role and player; and the idea that the story being told is in some sense pre-determined.

Performing Punch has traditionally entailed a long course of training and engagement with tradition that results in the show forming part of the performer's identity. Robert Leach discusses the inheritance of Punch and Judy through a family line in Blackpool. Joe Green, the Punch and Judy man on whom he focuses, grew up observing the performances of his father. The Punch and Judy show has been a part of his life since childhood.[10] The physical requirements of performing Punch, and the traditions by which the techniques for doing so are handed down, require the performer to view Punch and Judy as part of his or her identity. On another level, some studies suggest the physical characteristics of Punch himself are the result of the combination of the hand puppet with the human hand that wears it. Leach suggests that Punch's aggressive tendencies stem from the hand puppet's ability to hold and wield the stick that proves so damaging to the other characters in the show, a trait not shared by the marionette.[11] Leslie Katz and Kenneth Gross observe that hand and puppet work together to create the character of Punch:

> The range of [Punch's] actions equals and interprets the range of movements and actions available to a human puppeteer's hands, wrists, and upper arms [....] Punch's delight in grabbing and tossing – both tiny objects and other puppets – might even suggest a sense of the puppet's willingness to let a human hand act as its animating 'soul,' the hand *cum* puppet's delight in becoming, though only a part of a body, still magically, sufficiently whole.[12]

---

[10] Leach, 'Punch and Judy and Oral Tradition', p. 76. Fascinatingly in this context, Leach notes that when one of Joe Green's Punch figures 'becomes too battered or worn down to continue using, he adapts it so it becomes Judy or Joey or another character. When he has finished with it, he burns it, for he cannot bear the idea of someone else using one of his puppets', p. 76.

[11] Leach, *The Punch and Judy Show*, p. 18.

[12] Katz and Gross, 'The Puppet's Calling', pp. 4-5.

In his use of Punch to create a work of fiction, Neil Gaiman uses
the idea of Punch's tendency to absorb the wearer's identity to
explore the possibility of gaining new insight. In Gaiman's *Mr.
Punch*, the narrator describes a childhood experience of putting
on the crocodile puppet:

> I slid the puppet onto my left hand; and it came
> to life. I'm not talking about anything
> fantastical here. You can try it yourself – find a
> hand-puppet, slide it on your arm, flex your
> hand, move your fingers. And somehow, in the
> cold space between one moment and the next,
> the puppet becomes alive.[13]

This experience is empowering for the narrator: he fantasises
about taking the crocodile to school with him and frightening his
teachers, and taking it home to eat his sister.[14] Later, however, he
fears the prospect of putting on the Punch puppet, ultimately
refusing to do so when offered the opportunity: 'I almost put it
on. It would have whispered its secrets to me, explained my
childhood, explained my life.' He imagines being a part of the
Punch drama, 'walking from town to town with my burden on my
back, teaching the children, and those with an eye and a mind to
see with, the lessons of death that went back to the dawn times,'[15]
but he cannot. The mysteries he has repeatedly confronted
throughout his life remain unexplained. It seems that he finds the
prospect of truly sharing Punch's perspective too chilling.

The blending of the characteristics of costume and wearer
associated with dressing as Punch occurs in *The Wicker Man*
perhaps most obviously as the putting on of the Punch costume is
the final step Howie takes before losing his life. On more than
one level, this change in costume costs Howie his identity. Prior
to this, Howie definitely equates his identity with his uniform, as
he repeatedly reminds those with whom he speaks that he is a
police officer. 'I am a police officer' he shouts at the harbour

---

[13] Gaiman and McKean, *The Comical Tragedy*, p. 40.
[14] Gaiman and McKean, *The Comical Tragedy*, p.40.
[15] Gaiman and McKean, *The Comical Tragedy*, p. 74, p. 76.

master through a loud speaker. In The Green Man, he interrupts the patrons' performance of the song 'The Landlord's Daughter' to announce, 'I think you all ought to know that I am here on official business'. In the schoolhouse, he tells the female students, 'I am a police officer, as you can see', making reference to his own uniform as a signifier of his identity. This identity proves ultimately as superficial as the uniform itself, however.

In knocking Alder MacGregor over the head and stealing his Punch costume — a distinctly Punch-like act — Howie makes the gesture that eventually results in his death. This action may be read as a sort of sly glance at the Punch and Judy show's use of the policeman who tries to arrest Punch and is killed by him. In putting on the Punch costume, Howie re-enacts the violence done by Punch to the policeman in the traditional Punch and Judy shows. Here Howie effectively 'kills' one identity and allows Punch to take over. Additionally, the costume makes explicit Howie's completion of at least one of the conditions of his appropriateness as a sacrifice: that he should come as a fool. In playing Punch, Howie goes beyond mere play, combining his own identity with that of the character of Punch to become the ideal sacrifice.

Howie's deadly costume change thus becomes a key point of the blurring between his identity and the role he is lured into adopting. This confusion is part of the film's larger scheme of topsy-turvy theatricality, by which it blurs the line between audience and performer, observer and observed. While Howie comes to the island to investigate the disappearance of Rowan Morrison, essentially to observe, he is frequently subjected to the blank stares of the Summerislanders as he attempts to interrogate them. The eye that decorates the prow of the harbourmaster's boat that rows Howie ashore becomes an ambiguous signifier, inviting the question of whose eye is on whom. The film's ostensible plot encourages the impression that Howie is observing the strange rites and rituals of Summerisle's heathen culture, and invites the viewer to observe along with him. However, *The Wicker Man*'s ending reveals that the gaze has in fact been directed at Howie since before the action of the film began, and that he has been deliberately drawn to the island and into the ritual itself.

The question of who performs and who watches in the film is increasingly complicated as Howie is led by the Summerislanders through a drama of their devising – in this sense, he is the sole audience member in the play they are constantly creating around him. Indeed, the islanders actively obscure their true agenda by supporting Howie's delusion that he is on Summerisle as an investigator. When he demands to know where Rowan is, Lord Summerisle responds, 'Sergeant Howie, I think that you are supposed to be the detective here'. This prompt evokes Howie's most exemplary behaviour as detective, as he is inspired to renew the investigation, and he breaks into the photographer's shop, develops the photograph that reveals the picture of Rowan as queen of the harvest festival, and pieces together a provisional solution to the mystery of her disappearance. A flashback reminds us that Lord Summerisle has already hinted at the possibility of an impending ritual sacrifice. In addition to telling Howie that he honours the rituals of the old gods, he has planted the seeds of suspicion by commenting, 'perhaps it's just as well that you won't be here tomorrow to be offended by the sight of our May Day celebrations'. If Howie were uncertain about the significance of May Day, the calendar in the photographer's shop has the day circled in red, a further reminder of the day's importance and potential dangers. Convinced by this evidence that Rowan is still alive, Howie's prejudices with regard to Pagan society lead him directly to the conclusion that Rowan is going to be sacrificed, which is precisely the conclusion Lord Summerisle has desired him to reach.

The performative nature of the Summerisle residents' plot is perhaps exemplified in the sequence in which Howie attempts to find Rowan by searching the village. As Howie invades houses and storms into businesses, the villagers continue to play with his expectation that he will discover the truth, refusing to remove their masks, showing him the costumes they plan to wear in the festivities, and in the case of the woman in the bathtub, allowing him to stare frankly. One of the more vicious flirtations with fulfilling Howie's desire to discover the truth involves the young girl who falls out of the cupboard with a trace of blood at the corner of her mouth, apparently dead – a parody of the corpse of Rowan that Howie might expect to find.

The villagers' performances become increasingly theatrical as they require that Howie move to the place of sacrifice. Howie is apparently so engaged in his role as investigator that he does not question why the hobby-horse seems to deliberately invite him to follow, pausing in doorways and snapping his jaws so that Howie can find him. Having been led to the place where the villagers are gathering prior to the procession, Howie listens from behind a wall as Lord Summerisle announces the starting point and route the villagers will follow. He also gathers the information about MacGregor's use of the Punch costume. Back at the inn, Willow and her father engage in a sort of stage-whispered conversation outside of Howie's room, obviously planning that Howie will hear what they say and preparing the way for his appropriation of the Punch costume. As the sole audience member for the Summerisle residents' performances as Pagans with sinister motives, Howie is compelled to perform the conditions of the ritual sacrifice in which he becomes the key figure.

The Wicker Man thus evokes the idea that life and drama are inseparable: the Summerislanders appear to prepare for a mock ritual in order to enact the ritual that they believe will actually save their crops and secure their livelihoods. This notion is present in traditional Punch performances as well. Although Punch performances do vary from one another, many of them contain, as Harries notes, an emphasis on Punch's tradition of violence. The Punch and Judy performer he interviews maintains that this violence is not only integral to the idea of Punch and Judy, but that the physical capabilities involved in performing these actions are a part of his identity as a Punch and Judy man. Keeping Punch in frenetic action for fifteen minutes as he kills victim after victim is physically challenging:

> Yet again in his claim to skill, in his ability to do what others cannot, Professor Wotsit is maintaining a sense that his performance is traditional, for he previously argued that one element of the real Punch and Judy is that Punch is never bested [...]. To let Punch die is

to allow the puppeteer's lack of endurance to compromise history.[16]

In *Mr. Punch*, the human characters behave increasingly like the violent figures from the show. In one especially disconcerting episode, the young narrator witnesses his grandfather beating his mistress with a wooden plank. Drama and life almost literally bleed into one another in a manner that is especially disturbing given the nature of Punch's story.

On Summerisle, the distinction between life and drama breaks down, as does the distinction between the residents' performances as a form of entertainment and as ritual. Lord Summerisle tells Howie that his father 'brought me up [...] to reverence the music and the drama and the rituals of the old Gods'. For Summerisle society, drama and ritual are virtually indistinguishable, both taking on additional purpose beyond entertainment, and beyond even such cultural significance possessed by something like Punch's twisted morality play.

In order to position Howie as the focal point of this ritual, Lord Summerisle and his followers participate in the tradition of verbal insurrection that is part of the Punch and Judy show. As Katz and Gross note, Punch combines 'violence and coercive misnaming [...] like speech intentionally mishandled by its speaker, [this technique] undermines the assumption of a natural connection between language and intention'.[17] In the show, Punch thus convinces the servant to rename the bell as a different instrument each time he strikes him with it, finally killing him with a succession of blows: 'This is my bell [*hits*], this is my organ [*hits*], this is my fiddle [*hits*], this is my drum [*hits*], and this is my trumpet [*hits*]—there! a whole concert for you.'[18] This form of verbal confusion is practised throughout the film by many of the Summerislanders, but Miss Rose in particular.

When Howie confronts Lord Summerisle and Miss Rose with the corpse of the hare he has found in Rowan's purported grave, he tells them, 'I found that in Rowan Morrison's grave [...] a sacrilege.' Miss Rose responds, 'Only if the ground is

---

[16] Harries, '"Come See a Traditional Punch and Judy"', p. 70.
[17] Katz and Gross, 'The Puppet's Calling', p. 9.
[18] Cited in Katz and Gross, 'The Puppet's Calling', p. 8.

consecrated to the Christian belief.' This distinction is among the many Miss Rose makes as she plays at educating Howie in the ways of Summerisle. To most of his questions, including that of whether or not Rowan is dead, she responds, 'you would say so', or 'after a manner of speaking', appearing to comply with his interrogation while ultimately providing no answer at all. Howie tells her, 'Miss, I hope you don't think I can be made a fool of indefinitely'. Unfortunately for him, this is exactly her intention. In rendering Howie a fool long before he actually puts on the Punch costume, Miss Rose and the other Summerisle residents fashion an identity for him that fits the costume itself.

The lack of distinction between ritual and drama becomes especially clear in the final scene of *The Wicker Man*, in which the story Howie (and, arguably, the first-time viewer of the film) believes he has been dealing with gives way to the ritual that has propelled it all along. The revelation of the covert Pagan agenda thus exposes the double nature of the plot of *The Wicker Man*, as Howie's investigation is subsumed by the ritual intended to renew Summerisle's crops. Although Howie has been pursuing his investigation, the Summerisle residents have brought him to the island in order to test his appropriateness as a ritual sacrifice. As Lord Summerisle tells him, he is uniquely suited to his new role. He is:

> The most acceptable sacrifice that lies in our power. Animals are fine, but their acceptability is limited. A little child is even better, but not nearly as effective as the right kind of adult [...].You, Sergeant, are the right kind of adult.

Howie's king-like authority, established through his representation of the law, his arrival on Summerisle of his own free will, and his virginity all make him precisely the figure Summerisle requires for its sacrifice. The final component, that he is a fool, is one that the residents have created through their plot against him.

The Wicker Man's double plot has some implications for different models of narrative at work in the film, with radically different ideas of the role of free will and human decision-making in the determination of the ultimate fate of the characters. This is an issue at work in *Mr. Punch*, particularly in a scene in which a seaside puppet show must continue, despite the lack of a performer and the presence of only one audience member. As the child narrator watches, Judy explains, 'Even if there's only one of them, it's started now, and it can't be stopped, not even if the Devil and all his crocodiles came up from hell to stop it.' Punch's immediate question, 'Where's the baby?' suggests that he's all too eager for the show to go on.[19] In this scene, Gaiman exaggerates an aspect of Punch and Judy performance that is implied in its structure.

Leach maintains that the structure of the Punch and Judy show is not consciously formed by the performer, but is inherited. The Punch and Judy performer he examines, Joe Green:

> Has never sat down and consciously planned the structure of the show, never, as it were, formulated a script in any abstract manner. On the contrary, the ability to combine and structure episodes in this way by 'folk' artists is almost always unconscious, born of a lifetime passed in the milieu of the genre, learned by imitating a closely related older practitioner. This is what Lord has called the 'poetic grammar of oral composition,' and it is assimilated in listening and watching, and then developed in performing.[20]

In *The Wicker Man,* the model used by the people of Summerisle absorbs the narrative model within which Howie operates – which depends upon the idea that he determines his own fate. Once the true nature of the plot is revealed at the end of the film, it is immediately evident that Howie's capacity to affect his environment is neutralised. He will not, as he had planned, save Rowan Morrison and fulfil his role as detective-hero. In addition to being physically prevented from escaping, it is revealed that

---

[19] Gaiman and McKean, *The Comical Tragedy*, p. 5.
[20] Leach, 'Punch and Judy and Oral Tradition', p. 84.

his actions have not been free since his arrival on the island. Indeed, his ability to act autonomously is subsumed under the aegis of the ritual, as the residents inform him that his coming to Summerisle of his own free will is one of the conditions of the sacrifice. In the final sequence, the narrative of the ritual expands to retroactively subsume the entire plot of the film. Lord Summerisle explains this in language that is significantly play-oriented. 'The game's over,' he tells Howie:

> The game of the hunted leading the hunter. You came here to find Rowan Morrison, but it is we who have found you and brought you here. And controlled your every thought and action since you arrived [...] as our painstaking researches have revealed, you, uniquely, were the one we needed.

Like Punch's actions in *The Tragical Comedy*, Howie's behaviour is part of a larger cyclical narrative, determined by traditions beyond the control of the individual. In *The Wicker Man*, Howie's identity serves to fulfil the needs of the cycle rather than to determine the action of the plot.

There is a final similarity between Howie and Punch. Punch's relationship to his audience is often hostile, as the children who typically view the Punch and Judy show do not share his moral codes, and are often called upon during the performance to tattle on Punch as he misbehaves. In *Mr. Punch*, Punch defends himself against the audience's accusations that he has killed the baby, crying, 'O! You wicked storytellers!'[21] Although Howie's motivations are generally quite different, Punch's hostility here is reminiscent of Howie's reaction to the schoolchildren when he finds the record of Rowan Morrison in the attendance book. 'Liars! Despicable little liars!' he shouts at them. Howie's experiences in Summerisle as a whole cause him to view its people as 'wicked storytellers'. This conflict is in part attributable to the fact that their narrative codes operate in a different manner than those Howie embraces.

---

[21] Gaiman and McKean, *The Comical Tragedy*, p. 18.

Howie's Christian culture has conditioned him to view his identity as of singular importance. In the final scene, he tells Lord Summerisle, 'as a Christian, I hold for resurrection, and even if you kill me now, it is I who will live again, not your damned apples'. For the Summerisle residents, however, individual identity is transformed through the cycle of life into other forms, and thus becomes less central within the narrative they follow. The temporary – if not ultimate – triumph of this cyclical narrative over Howie's is suggested by Lord Summerisle's comment that while Summerisle will have its ritual sacrifice, Howie's personal narrative might still be accommodated, 'for believing as you do, we confer upon you a rare gift these days: a martyr's death'. Like Punch, then, Howie persists in attempting to achieve autonomy and complete freedom of action. And also like Punch, Howie is essentially a puppet, operating within a cyclical narrative that ultimately determines his fate.

Bibliography

Byrom, M., *Punch in the Italian Puppet Theatre* (London: Centaur Press, 1983).

Frazer, J., *The Golden Bough: A study in magic and religion* (Hertfordshire: Wordsworth Reference, 1993).

Gaiman, N. and D. McKean (illustrator), *The Comical Tragedy or Tragical Comedy of Mr Punch* (New York: DC Comics, 1995).

Hardy, R., 'Keynote Address', *'The Wicker Man': Rituals, Readings and Reactions*, University of Glasgow, Crichton Campus, Dumfries, Scotland, 14-15 July, 2003. An edited version of the text of this address is available in Franks, Harper, Murray and Stevenson, eds., *The Quest for 'The Wicker Man': Historical, folklore and Pagan perspectives* (Edinburgh: Luath, 2005).

Harries, J. A., '"Come See a Traditional Punch and Judy": Meaning and history according to a London puppeteer', *Culture and Tradition*, 12 (1988), 60-75.

Katz, L. and K. Gross, 'The Puppet's Calling', *Raritan, A Quarterly Review*, 15, no. 1 (Summer 1995), 1-28.

Leach, R., 'Punch and Judy and Oral Tradition', *Folklore*, 94.1 (1983), 78-85.

_____ *The Punch and Judy Show: History, tradition and meaning* (London: Batsford Academic and Educational, 1985).

Wicker Man, The, Dir. R. Hardy. Canal+ ([1973] 2002).

'The Other Coppers': Uncanniness, identity and *The Wicker Man* audience

Stephen Harper

> As I was walking, one hot summer afternoon, through the deserted streets of some provincial town in Italy which was unknown to me, I found myself in a quarter of whose character I could not long remain in doubt. Nothing but painted women were to be seen at the windows of the small houses, and I hastened to leave the narrow street at the next turning. But after having wandered around for a time without enquiring my way, I suddenly found myself back at the same street, where my presence was now beginning to excite attention. I hurried away once more only to arrive by another *détour* at the same place yet a third time. Now, however, a feeling overcame me which I can only describe as uncanny, and I was glad enough to find myself back at the piazza I had left a short while before, without any further voyages of discovery.[1]

In his foundational essay on the subject ('The Uncanny', 1919), Freud offers this coy yet dreamlike anecdote as his own exemplary experience of uncanniness. Freud is travelling nervously in an unfamiliar geographical, social and moral milieu. The place is unnatural ('painted') and the protagonist is threatened on all sides by the 'narrow streets' and 'small houses', frequently surprised by the 'sudden[ness]' of events. Freud's euphemistic superciliousness ('further voyages of discovery') as he describes being sucked into this disreputable quarter is a defence against his uneasiness. Despite its passive verbs and tight narrative structure, there is in this passage an eerie and claustrophobic atmosphere.[2] Although Freud's adventure is that

---

[1] Freud, 'The Uncanny', p. 237.
[2] For a fuller analysis and a discussion of the passage from Freud quoted above, see Lyndenberg, 'Freud's Uncanny Narratives', 1072-86.

of a scandalised bourgeois *flaneur*, its strange and disorientating atmosphere is also evoked in Robin Hardy's pastoral horror film, *The Wicker Man* (1973). In that film, a Christian policeman investigates the disappearance of a young girl on a remote Scottish island, whose inhabitants espouse Pagan beliefs and practices. Just as Freud seeks to overcome his nervousness with irony, so, throughout *The Wicker Man*, Sergeant Howie (Edward Woodward) masks his disorientation with irascible sarcasm. But the sarcasm is insufficient to quell Howie's – or the audience's – feelings of uncanniness as he encounters this alien culture. This comparison between Howie's psychological state and elements of Freud's 'The Uncanny' is fruitful, since *The Wicker Man*, as I shall show, seems to borrow from the essay frequently, directly and (seemingly) consciously; indeed, 'The Uncanny', like Frazer's *The Golden Bough*, might even be regarded as one of the film's sources.

The strong influence of Freud on the makers of *The Wicker Man* is beyond doubt. As Rowan leads Howie through the tunnel at the end of the novel of *The Wicker Man*, for example, she indicates to the policeman that she believes the cave they are in represents a womb: 'Miss Rose says our female magic comes from there. It's why I've always looked forward to becoming a woman. So that I'll have my own magic. In a few months it would have been too late to sacrifice me'.[3] Indeed, Freudian symbolism is prevalent in both the book and the film. In this paper I shall focus specifically, however, on the significance of uncanny visual elements in the film version of *The Wicker Man*, drawing on Freud's essay. In doing so I am sensitive to the fact that psychoanalysis is currently under question as an analytical method. In fact, I share the concerns of many critics, scientists and philosophers who have questioned the scientific basis and explanatory reach of psychoanalysis. While there is no space in this chapter to explore such issues in detail, I agree with Mark Jancovich that 'psychoanalysis has a built-in tendency to produce interpretations which […] have little or no relation to one's actual

---

[3] Hardy and Shaffer, *The Wicker Man*, p. 197.

experiences of a text'.[4]

These concerns aside, certain film texts very strikingly resonate with aspects of psychoanalytic theories and in ways which do not necessarily demand our subscription to psychoanalysis; I shall argue that *The Wicker Man* is one of them. The uncanny – whose study Freud himself averred is not properly within the scope of psychoanalysis – has long slipped its psychoanalytic moorings and has been mobilised in the discourses of postcolonialism, nationalism and deconstruction.[5] My own interest is in Shaffer and Hardy's apparently conscious use of the theme of uncanniness to give a sense of hermeneutic depth to the film – and in the response of the film's countercultural audience to this manoeuvre.

Initial reactions to *The Wicker Man* vary enormously, but most often the film is described as 'weird', 'strange' and, indeed, 'uncanny'.[6] Despite the problematic and incomplete nature of Freud's essay 'The Uncanny', the high degree of fit between these audience responses to *The Wicker Man* and Freud's original concept is clear, whatever reservations one might have about the legitimacy of psychoanalytic theory. The uncanniness of *The Wicker Man* is reinforced by the film's setting – the remote Scottish island of Summerisle. As Nicholas Royle notes, the word 'uncanny' is first used in the poems of the seventeenth-century poet Robert Fergusson, so that 'the "uncanny" comes from Scotland, from that "auld country" that has so often been represented as "beyond the borders", liminal, an English foreign body'.[7]

The Wicker Man also conforms to Tzvetan Todorov's definition of the uncanny fantastic text. Todorov famously discerned three forms of fantastic text: the uncanny, the marvellous and the fantastic. The marvellous text consists of irrational spectacles that can only be accounted for if the audience

---

[4] Jancovich, *Horror*, p. 12. It might be noted, however, that the phrase 'actual experiences' is problematic, insofar as it implies the possibility of a 'pure' or prediscursive textual apprehension prior to the business of critical interpretation.
[5] See, for example Bhabha, *Nation and Narration*; Ziarek, 'The Uncanny Style of Kristeva's Critique of Nationalism'; Royle, *The Uncanny*.
[6] See Petric, *Screening Scotland*, p. 53.
[7] Royle, *The Uncanny*, p. 12.

accepts, at least for the duration of the text, the existence of another plane of reality. The fantastic text, on the other hand, leads the audience to hesitate or oscillate between supernatural and rational explanation. In the uncanny text, according to Todorov, 'events are related which may be readily accounted for by the laws of reason, but which are [...] incredible, extraordinary, shocking, singular, disturbing, or unexpected'.[8] The uncanny is also linked, Todorov adds, to the sentiments of the characters in the text rather than to a reason-defying (or marvellous) event. As a text about disturbing but *not* supernatural events, *The Wicker Man* fulfils the first of Todorov's criteria of uncanniness, while the dominance of the hero's reactions and perspectives in the film – we do, after all, see Summerisle through his eyes – fulfils the second. This latter point usefully reminds us of the film's emphasis on the psychology of its hero, a point to which I shall return at the end of this paper. Nevertheless, general taxonomies such as Todorov's will not take us very far in the analysis of the individual text. Freud's famous description of the uncanny, I shall suggest, resonates in far more direct and interesting ways within the narrative of *The Wicker Man*.

As is widely known among students of horror, Freud's intriguing and incomplete writings on the uncanny (*das Unheimliche*) are contained in a 1919 essay on what Freud regarded as a 'remote province' of aesthetics.[9] Freud saw the uncanny as an experience or irruption of the 'strangely familiar'. His etymological musings on the terms *heimlich* and *unheimlich* led him to argue that the meaning of *heimlich* 'develops in the direction of ambivalence' so that, in the end, *heimlich* signifies not only the 'homely', but also its apparent semantic opposite. Thus the uncanny is precisely *not* that which is entirely unknown or unfamiliar, but is a frightening experience of strangeness, which directs the subject back to the *heimlich*, 'to what is known of old and long familiar'.[10] The uncanny, says Freud, borrowing a phrase from Schelling, is the irruption of 'that which ought to have remained hidden but which has come to light'.[11]

[8] Todorov, *The Fantastic*, p. 46.
[9] Freud, 'The Uncanny', p. 219.
[10] Freud, 'The Uncanny', p. 220.
[11] Freud, 'The Uncanny', p. 225.

Experiences of uncanniness, Freud argues, are prompted by symbols and motifs which reinvoke repressed infantile or primitive beliefs. 'An uncanny experience occurs', he writes, 'either when infantile complexes which have been repressed are once more revived by some impression, or when primitive beliefs which have been surmounted seem once more to be confirmed'.[12] As an enigmatic subjective experience beyond language, the uncanny is resistant to rationalisation or indeed to rationality itself. The uncanny is experienced only by 'split', or fully acculturated subjects (such as Howie). For Freud and (with modifications) Jacques Lacan, experiences of uncanniness are symptoms of castration anxiety, although post-Freudian psychoanalysis has proffered other explanations.[13]

Numerous objections can be made to Freud's theory. My own view, for example, is that the theory (if that is an appropriate term for what is really a collection of observations and suggestions) is underdeveloped, over-assimilated and, like so much psychoanalytical writing, pays insufficient attention to the aesthetic surface of the texts it discusses. Other critics may take issue with the notion of repression that underpins the theory. Michel Foucault, for example, notoriously argued that 'repression' is a tendentious and mythical construction.[14] However that may be, I shall argue here that irrespective of its psychoanalytical import and theoretical validity, uncanniness as described in Freud's essay is a recurring trope within *The Wicker Man*. I shall also argue that for a certain section of the film's audience, at least, the film's self-conscious moments of uncanniness serve as an index of Howie's increasing 'alienation', 'repression' and self-doubt.

In *The Wicker Man*, frequent irruptions of uncanniness disturb the otherwise imperturbable Sergeant Howie, as he attempts to 'bring to light' the secret of a young girl's disappearance. In the course of his investigations, Howie discovers that the islanders, under the influence of Lord Summerisle (Christopher Lee) live according to a Pagan belief system that has been long repressed by Christianity. Much of the uncanniness in this encounter is

---

[12] Freud, 'The Uncanny', p. 249.
[13] See, for example, Weber, *The Legend of Freud*.
[14] Foucault, *The History of Sexuality Vol I*.

generated by the music, as scenes of Pagan weirdness are punctuated by startling and disorientating sound effects and haunting folk songs. I shall concentrate on the film's visual details here, however, many of which are identical to those discussed in Freud's essay.

For example, Freud cites the severed hand as one of many possibly uncanny motifs. The motif appears towards the end of the film when Howie is duped by the landlord and his daughter into believing that he is being drugged by a candle fashioned out of a severed hand (an earlier, brief shot reveals that this so-called 'Hand of Glory' was cut from the corpse viewed in the undertakers during the search). In Freudian terms, the severed limb is uncanny because it creates a temporary uncertainty about the distinction between life and death, one of the film's central ambiguities. Take, for example, the trope of the automaton. Freud discusses Ernst Jentsch's observation that 'in telling a story, one of the most successful devices for easily creating uncanny effects is to leave the reader in uncertainty whether a particular figure in the story is a human being or an automaton'.[15] This device appears in many horror films, of course, in the form of clowns and mannequins which come to life, and it is prominent in *The Wicker Man*, especially during the scenes in which Howie conducts his exhaustive search for the missing girl. In one of these scenes, Howie discovers a figure draped in a sheet in a small wooden coffin-like box; he pulls away the cover to reveal a child's toy clown. The shot recalls Freud's remark that, while children do not balk at such 'doubles', for adults they become 'the uncanny harbingers of death' – as evidenced by the typically horrified audience reaction to Howie's gigantic wicker double at the end of the film. In a later search scene, Howie opens a wardrobe and a young girl falls out of it. After lying on the floor – apparently dead – for several seconds, the girl laughs, rises from the floor and runs briskly away.

In several of these uncanny scenes (particularly in the director's cut, which contains material omitted from the trimmer, but symbolically impoverished, cinematic release) we see Howie's immediate reaction in a mirror. The 'search scenes'

---

[15] Jentsch, cited in Freud, 'The Uncanny', p. 227.

involving the 'wardrobe girl' and the strange silent scene in the hairdressers, for example, both end with Howie turning towards a mirror. The mirrors at the end of the search scenes make visible – for those who have eyes to see – Howie's increasingly 'double' identity. In such mirror scenes, as Homi Bhabha explains, the:

> image of human identity and, indeed, human identity as image [...] are inscribed in the sign of resemblance. [...] This [...] is part of the West's obsession that our primary relation to objects and ourselves is analogous to visual perception. Pre-eminent among these representations has been the reflection of the self that develops in the symbolic consciousness of the sign, and marks out the discursive space from which the *Real Me* emerges initially as an assertion of the authenticity of a person and then lingers on to reverberate – The REAL ME? – as a questioning of identity.[16]

The mirrors in *The Wicker Man* indicate to the audience that the search scenes reveal less about the missing child than about Howie himself. In keeping with its traditional iconographic significance, the mirror symbolism here points up Howie's fundamental narcissism. It also indicates not so much the policeman's psychological disintegration (in fact, Howie is more exasperated than shattered by his uncanny experiences), but his bifurcation into subject and object – in the eyes of the audience, at least. These uncanny scenes not only heighten our curiosity as to the missing girl's status, but also undermine our certainty about Howie's own status as agent or puppet, subject or object. For the audience, these scenes undercut Howie's symbolic authority. Howie himself seems oblivious to his appearance in the film's mirrors, implying his unquestioning identification with his specular image, his stubborn refusal to 'see himself' objectively.

---

[16] Bhabha, 'Interrogating Identity', p. 6.

The trope of the mirror thus implies Howie's ethical failing: namely, that he does not avail himself of the many opportunities for 'self-knowledge', preferring instead to fully identify with his symbolic role, an identification pointed up by Howie's repeated assertions of his authority ('I am an officer of the law') and by his frequent appearance in full shot, so that we see him in his uniform. Full shots generally point up the social relationships between the characters in any frame;[17] the use of this technique therefore asserts the policeman's position of authority in relation to the islanders. Although Howie dismisses the islanders as 'raving mad', his own over-identification is itself presented as a kind of psychosis, recalling Lacan's well-known saying that a madman is not only a beggar who thinks himself a king, but also a king who thinks he is a king (or indeed a policeman who thinks he is a policeman).

If the mirror symbolism in the middle of the film reflects the audience's increasing doubts about the policeman's agency, it also invokes the archaic concept of the 'double', another prominent item in Freud's *ad hoc* inventory of things uncanny. When Howie first returns, exhausted and distressed, from his search of every house on the island, the landlord's daughter Willow (Britt Ekland) enquires: 'where are the other coppers?' (referring to the police backup Howie had hoped to summon from the mainland). Appropriately, Howie first appears in this scene reflected in the mirror behind the bar, which again suggests his entrapment in the film's play of mirrors. When he explains that he is unable to obtain backup because his plane will not start, the landlord cheekily comments: 'So, *he* spent his time instead turning the whole village upside down; no wonder *he's* worn out' [my italics]. The landlord's sarcasm infantilises the policeman, striking another blow at Howie's symbolic authority. Moreover, by referring to Howie in the third person, the landlord rudely reinforces the sergeant's doubleness as both investigating subject and (increasingly) manipulated object. In all of these ways, the islanders present the oblivious Howie with reminders of his own dual nature (a duality symbolised more obviously in his eventual adoption of the parti-coloured garb of the fool). While the

---

[17] Berger, *Media Analysis Techniques*, p. 30.

humorous, slapstick elements of *The Wicker Man* preclude its designation as a 'gothic film', these doubling effects contribute to a gothic sense of fragmentation and externalisation of identity, particularly during the house searching scenes. As William Day claims:

> Doubling [...] is not simply a convention, but is the essential reality of the self in the Gothic world. Once the protagonist enters that world, the [*sic*] identity begins to break up. The line between the self and the Other begins to waver, and the wholeness and integrity of the self begins to collapse.[18]

Howie, I should repeat, is unaware of his double identity, but the island's mirrors unerringly reflect his predicament.

Some of the film's other uncanny elements are more obvious. Freud emphasises that one of the central repressed beliefs that 'comes to light' in uncanny experiences is the belief in animism. For Freud, animism was the primitive belief system *par excellence*, one which has been repressed by Enlightenment rationality. Sergeant Howie frequently encounters evidence of the local belief in animal spirits and is informed at one point that the missing girl he is attempting to discover has transubstantiated into the body of a hare. The uncanniest moment, however – and the only one clearly recognised by Howie himself as uncanny – occurs at the end of the film, as Howie encounters his gigantic wicker double, which, like him, has been carefully prepared by the islanders for the final sacrifice.

Insofar as scenes of uncanniness dominate its denouement, *The Wicker Man* replicates many of the details in Freud's essay, heightening the audience's sense of Howie's psychic repression and bewilderment. We are also reminded here of Freud's remark that 'for many people the uncanniest thing of all is the idea of being buried alive'. Howie is, of course, burned, rather than buried, alive. Nevertheless, from Howie's encasement in his light aeroplane at the beginning of the film to his final enclosure in the

---

[18] Day, *In the Circles of Fear and Desire*, p. 2.

wicker effigy, the sergeant – so confident all along that he is an outside observer – is always already part of, identified with, *encased within*, the alien culture; as Royle puts it, the uncanny 'disturbs any straightforward sense of what is inside and what is outside'.[19] In this sense, the film's thematic climax, as Lorraine Rolston and Andy Murray observe, is not the burning itself, but Howie's encasement in the wicker effigy alongside the animals which symbolise his repressed instinctual drives; this is the moment at which 'Howie is confronted with the truth about himself'.[20]

So far I have argued that the film's uncanny episodes crystallise Howie's moral and psychological alienation. I would like to conclude, however, by briefly considering the impact of this theme of alienation upon certain sections of the film's audience. The directness of the film's allusions to Freud's 'The Uncanny' is hardly surprising when one considers the backgrounds and interests of those who worked on the project. The film of Anthony Shaffer's play *Sleuth* (Mankiewicz, 1972) appeared a year before the release of *The Wicker Man* and adumbrates the later film's concern with teasing plots, intrigue and psychological gamesmanship. Shaffer had also worked on Hitchcock's *Frenzy* (1972) before working on *The Wicker Man* and was therefore no stranger to psychoanalytic themes. Shaffer's brother Peter, author of the self-consciously psychoanalytic play *Equus* (1973), also collaborated on the writing, did a great deal of the research, and was present on set during filming.[21] Indeed, the detail of the girl falling out of the wardrobe during the search scene is presumably a joking reference to Peter Shaffer's first detective novel, *The Woman in the Wardrobe*.[22] As well as serving as the pretext for one of the film's in-jokes, *The Woman in the Wardrobe* also anticipates *The Wicker Man*'s presentation of Howie as lacking in self-knowledge, since its hero is an investigator who does not realise that he is the murderer. Clearly, in addition to its explicitly Freudian imagery, *The Wicker Man* shares with the Shaffer brothers' other works a concern with psychology, psychoanalysis

---

[19] Royle, *The Uncanny*, p. 2.
[20] Rolston and Murray, *Studying 'The Wicker Man'*, p. 18.
[21] Murray, 'Interview with Robin Hardy'.
[22] Shaffer, *The Woman in the Wardrobe*.

and repression. Like the film's use of Frazerian anthropology, these psychoanalytical preoccupations give the film a 'researched' quality and confer upon it a distinctly Modernist sense of depth (and even 'difficulty').

In this sense, it is easy to see the film's use of uncanny imagery as an auteurist – perhaps even elitist – bid for cultural capital, much like the use of mythopoetic and psychoanalytical topoi in other films of the period (those of Bernardo Bertolucci and Pier Paolo Pasolini spring to mind). However that may be, the filmmakers undoubtedly intended the film's uncanniness to strike a chord with audiences. The film's director, Robin Hardy, indicates that the 'bringing to light' of Pagan customs through individual perception is a central aspect of the film's attraction for audiences. Asked in an interview to explain the film's enduring appeal, Hardy replied: 'this film awakes in people a kind of tribal memory. It's full of echoes from our past, from our childhood, from the very things that are around us every day'. In an uncanny echo of Freud, Hardy adds that audiences are always interested in their 'collective past', 'particularly when they can find it all around them in the present'.[23]

No doubt Hardy is correct that this appeal to a putative 'collective past' constitutes a large part of the film's appeal to audiences. But it might be further suggested that this feature of the film appeals more strongly to some sections of the film's audience than to others. As Tanya Krzywinska notes, *The Wicker Man* was intended as a critique of pagan superstition, but it succeeds only partially in fulfilling that intention.[24] Despite its gruesome ending, *The Wicker Man* does not foreclose a positive reading of paganism. While all spectators must feel some sympathy for Howie at the end of film, they may also feel that the policeman is at some level responsible for his fate, for failing adequately to recognise his own implication in the order of the Other. Audience groups involved in the New Age, consciousness-raising movements of the 1970s might incline particularly strongly towards such a reading. Often drawing on Eastern philosophical, religious and psychological concepts, these

---

[23] Hardy, 'Interview', *The Wicker Man*, DVD.
[24] Krzywinska, *A Skin For Dancing In*, pp. 83-84.

countercultural movements typically emphasised the importance
of self-knowledge – the key insight which Howie lacks, and
which his uncanny experiences shockingly reveal. Thus the
directorial criticism of irrational and fascistic New Age-ism is
consistently undercut by Howie's experiences of the uncanny
sameness of the apparently alien Other. For much of *The Wicker
Man*'s audience, the film might be read not so much as a moral
indictment of New Age values but as a critique of an unreflective,
ethnocentrist establishment, such that Howie's desperate final
question to the islanders – 'Can't you *see*?' – rebounds on its
utterer. Thus, while the trope of the uncanny may guarantee the
film's cultural capital, it also subverts the psychic certainties of
its protagonist (or indeed, as I shall argue below, the filmmakers'
certainties as would-be creative protagonists), in ways that open
the film to oppositional readings among countercultural
audiences with a strong interest in psychology and/or
psychoanalysis.

The Freudian linkage of uncanniness and sexual repression is
key here. Of course, the film's subversive potential derives in
large part from its perspective on sexual repression. There are
many medieval analogues of *The Wicker Man*, in which an
unwitting Christian knight is subjected to sexual temptations by a
mysterious lady (indeed, the medieval precursors of *The Wicker
Man* remain completely neglected and could easily form the
subject of another study of the film).[25] In these traditional
Christian narratives, sexual continence and repression are
remunerable virtues. In *The Wicker Man*, by contrast, the hero's
repression leads to his death. This difference reflects not only the
shift from Christian essentialism to moral relativism but also,
more specifically, the negative connotations of 'repression' in the
'New Age' lexicon of the 1960s and 1970s. Whether or not one

---

[25] For example, the fourteenth-century poetic romance *Sir Gawain and the Green
Knight* is similar, in terms of narrative content and structure, to *The Wicker Man*.
It is a profoundly ludic text in which the Christian hero enters an alien, pre-
Christian culture and is subjected, unwittingly, to a series of sexual temptations
offered (apparently sincerely) by a mysterious lady, all of which he refuses. At the
end of the poem, the tribulations of the hero, including his sexual temptations, are
revealed to have been a 'game', in a way that resembles the ending of *The Wicker
Man*. Gawain's sexual continence is ultimately rewarded. See Cawley and
Anderson, eds., *Sir Gawain and the Green Knight*.

accepts the reality of 'repression', the 'repressive hypothesis', as Foucault put it, was particularly popular in this period, and even anthropological research was cited in popular justifications of 'free love'. For example, Margaret Mead and Bronislaw Malinowski's descriptions of carefree, pre-modern sexual jouissance[26] were sometimes invoked by certain sections of the counterculture as a model for the revitalisation of the West's ailing libidinal economy. Indeed, the popularity of the 'repressive hypothesis' in the 1970s was one of the principal impetuses for Foucault to write his *History of Sexuality*. The ludic uncanniness of *The Wicker Man* encourages countercultural identification with the carefree licentiousness of the islanders. For the countercultural audience, Howie's uncanny experiences have a monitory function, reminding a fallen, corrupt and authoritarian society of the repressed values of community and free sexual expression.

We have seen, then, that *The Wicker Man* makes extensive and rather explicit use of Freud's 'The Uncanny', to the extent that the essay must be regarded as a source for the film (and, for that matter, the novel). On a purely formal level, the film's uncanny details together constitute a vivid commentary on Howie's alienated state. Nor are they too obtrusive: while some of these uncanny tropes do give the film a somewhat 'studied' feel, the use of mirrors to show Howie's double nature, in particular, is subtly achieved. In the end, however, the force of the film's uncanniness escapes Hardy and Shaffer's control. We might conclude that Howie's experiences of uncanniness work against the director's rationalist imperatives in much the same way as they disrupt the sergeant's Enlightenment worldview. A focus on the film's uncanny moments permits a more critical or progressive reading of *The Wicker Man* than Hardy and Shaffer intended, since these eruptions of the strange undermine rationalism, revalorise alternative cultures, and pleasurably resonate with a countercultural audience eager to understand and even embrace the 'foreignness within itself'. This concern with uncanniness is not, as Hardy's comments imply, simply a

---

[26] Some key texts here are Malinowski, *The Sexual Life of Savages* and Mead, *Growing Up in New Guinea*.

universal human concern, but one which was particularly prevalent in the countercultural climate of the 1970s, in which the political radicalism of the previous decade gave way to new discourses of psychology, consciousness-raising and 'self-discovery'. The self-conscious use of uncanny motifs in *The Wicker Man* warns of the dangers of self-ignorance and repression, supporting Krzywinska's contention that the film unwittingly endorses countercultural values.

Bibliography

Berger, A., *Media Analysis Techniques* (Beverley Hills, California: Sage, 1998).

Bhabha, H., 'Interrogating Identity', in *ICA Documents 6*, ed. by L. Appignanesi (London: ICA Projects, 1987), pp. 5-11.

_____, *Nation and Narration* (London: Routledge, 1990).

Cawley, A. C and J. J. Anderson, eds., *Sir Gawain and the Green Knight, Pearl, Cleanness, Patience* (London: J. M. Dent, 1976).

Day, W., *In the Circles of Fear and Desire: A study of Gothic fantasy* (Chicago: University of Chicago Press, 1985).

Foucault, M., *The History of Sexuality Vol I, The will to knowledge*, trans. by R. Hurley (London: Allen Lane, 1979).

Freud, S., 'The Uncanny', in *The Standard Edition of the Complete Psychological Works of Sigmund Freud*, ed. and trans. by J. Strachey, vol. 17 (London: Hogarth Press, 1955), pp. 219-52.

Hardy, R., Interview, *The Wicker Man – Special Edition Director's Cut*. Dir. R. Hardy. Canal+ ([1973] 2002).

Hardy, R. and A. Shaffer, *The Wicker Man* (Feltham: Hamlyn, 1979).

Jancovich, M., *Horror* (London: Batsford, 1992).

Krzywinska, T., *A Skin For Dancing In: Possession, witchcraft and voodoo in film* (Trowbridge: Flicks Books, 2000).

Lyndenberg, R., 'Freud's Uncanny Narratives', *Proceedings of the Modern Language Association*, 112.4 (1997), 1072-86.

Malinowski, B., *The Sexual Life of Savages: In North-Western Melanesia*, 3rd edn. (London: Routledge and Kegan Paul, 1932).

Mead, M., *Growing Up in New Guinea: A study of adolescence and sex in primitive societies* (Harmondsworth: Penguin, 1942).

Murray, A. and L. Rolston, *Studying 'The Wicker Man'* (Leighton Buzzard: Auteur Publishing, 2002).

Murray, J., 'Interview with Robin Hardy', in *The Quest for 'The Wicker Man': Historical, folklore and Pagan perspectives*, ed. by B. Franks, S. Harper, J. Murray and L. Stevenson (Edinburgh: Luath, 2005).

Petrie, D., *Screening Scotland* (London: British Film Institute, 2000).

Royle, N., *The Uncanny* (Manchester: Manchester University Press, 2003).

Shaffer, P., *The Woman in the Wardrobe* (London: Evans Brothers, 1951).

Todorov, T., *The Fantastic: A structural approach to a literary concept* (Cleveland and London: Case Western Reserve University Press, 1973).

Weber, S. *The Legend of Freud*, 2nd edn. (Stanford, California: Stanford University Press, 2000).

Ziarek, E., 'The Uncanny Style of Kristeva's Critique of Nationalism', *Post Modern Culture* 5 (1995), <http://muse.jhu.edu/journals/postmodern_culture/v005/5.2 ziarek.html> [Accessed 22 June 2005].

The Wicker Man, The Uncanny, and the Clash of Moral Cultures

Stefan Gullatz

In a seminal paper entitled 'The Uncanny' (1919), Freud defines the eponymous phenomenon as something familiar in the subject's history that has, however, become de-familiarised by repression, so that the encounter with the uncanny object appears to strike a chord in the subject's unconscious, while conscious perception somehow remains uncomprehending.[1] The fear induced by this object reverberates with a fear of castration, the initial agent of repression. Freud cites the Sand-Man in E. T. A. Hoffman's fairy tale, whose threat to the hero's eyes connotes, Freud asserts, an underlying castration anxiety.[2] Freud's originary coinage forges an intimate link between 'uncanniness' and subjective experiences of fear sparked through confrontation with assumedly forgotten past desires and practices which nonetheless bizarrely reappear in the present as deeply disquieting revenants; hopefully, seen in these terms, it becomes apparent – even at this early stage – that *The Wicker Man*'s structuring premise makes it eminently readable as an 'uncanny' filmic text. However, in isolating the uncanny undercurrents of *The Wicker Man* (Hardy, 1973), we shall move beyond Freud's literal conception to encompass Lacan's notion of symbolic castration, the action by which the paternal metaphor of the Name-of-the-Father intervenes, subjecting the pre-existing Lacanian orders of the Real and the Imaginary to a radical revision.[3]

This chapter will demonstrate how the pervasive atmosphere of the uncanny in *The Wicker Man* can be adduced as a retroactive signification of its 'phenomenal surface', a process whereby the attention of the viewer is captured by a range of 'phallic' details – sticking out from a deceptively ordinary surface – that cast a different light on the passage of events. These details either introduce 'abyssal' double meanings (meanings dependant on

---

[1] Freud, 'The Uncanny'.
[2] See Freud, 'The Uncanny', pp. 230-31. See also Gullatz, 'Exquisite Ex-timacy'.
[3] For a detailed outline of the mechanism of retroversion in both subjectivity and signification, consider chapter 9 of Jacques Lacan's *Écrits, '*The Subversion of the Subject and the Dialectic of Desire in the Freudian Unconscious'.

repressed desire, which have never been made explicit) or, alternatively, create new meanings. In other words, the uncanny dimension of the film rests on the fact that the initial, 'naïve' audience perception of it is supplemented with desire.

Let us begin with a brief excursion into Nicolas Roeg's *Don't Look Now* (1973), shown in conjunction with *The Wicker Man* at its London premiere, in order to illustrate the role of the symbolic in generating a sensation of *das Unheimliche*. The former's symbolic dimension crystallises in a prophecy, issued by a mysterious couple of elderly ladies who warn John Baxter – an architect who is pursuing a re-construction assignment in a historic Venice church in the wake of the tragic death of his daughter – that he must leave immediately in order to avoid a danger to his life. The piercing blue eyes of one of the ladies are uncannily at odds with her blindness, suggesting that she is capable of 'seeing through time'. When Baxter is stabbed to death towards the end, the prophecy is fulfilled in a sudden outburst of murderous violence. This moment is 'overdetermined', insofar as it does not exhaust itself in the surface – the graphic assault – but also conveys a sense that Baxter has consummated his symbolic destiny, that his murder gives him his preordained place in the overall scheme of things. The film is extraordinary in maintaining a high level of suspense throughout, which is a direct consequence of the sinister atmosphere, the unbearable feeling of brooding anticipation created by the prophecy. Yet, when it finally comes true, we are still not able to categorise the event; we cannot evade its profoundly disturbing and disorienting effect, which is rooted in the uncanny sense of an abrupt suspension of time. At this point, when all the threads are woven together and everything is resolved, the film imposes upon us the truly traumatic sense of a radical dislocation, a blurring of the boundaries between meaning and absurdity, time and eternity, and life and death that is condensed in a single instant.

In Lacanian terms, *Don't Look Now*'s death scene describes the point where Baxter must acknowledge that the meaning that has been created in the 'capital Other' (the impenetrable, external circuit of the symbolic order), identifies his own most intimate truth. The moment of death is therefore paradoxically a moment of 'subjectification'. This, at first sight, provocative thesis is understood more clearly once we recall that Lacan had always been emphatically opposed to any notion of the subject as an autonomous self able to deliberately construct a narrative of his/her life. To Lacan, subjectivity is conceivable only with a view to the original symbolic castration of a narcissistic ego tightly circumscribed by being installed as an *object* in a pre-existing web of social and semantic structures the consistency of which is guaranteed by the Other – the locus of speech represented in *Don't Look Now* by the ladies' prophecy. The subject of psychoanalytic theory is, from the beginning, touched by a profound recognition of limitation and mortality. Accordingly, the haunting image of Baxter's death, his 'I' snuffed out, with lifeless flesh all that is left occupying its former position, could be seen as an almost archetypal condensation of the Lacanian self drained and 'mortified' by its *subjection* to an oracular Other.

In the classical *Oedipus Rex*, we discern the same deep resonance triggered in the Other the moment a subject realises his symbolic destiny as can be found in modern film texts such as *Don't Look Now* and *The Wicker Man*. Perhaps, then, a brief discussion of Sophocles' Theban Trilogy might in fact enhance, rather than digress from, this essay's proposed reading of Robin Hardy and Anthony Shaffer's celebrated horror classic.

In *Oedipus Rex*, the oracle's pronouncement that Oedipus will kill his father and sleep with his mother precedes a chain of events that serves to confirm this chilling prophecy. However, the crucial feature is not Oedipus' acting out of the prophecy as such, but rather the terrifying moment when he realises that he has fulfilled the 'word', the destiny that has been 'stalking' him. Only by fully identifying with the network of signifying traces that preceded him, prefiguring his existence before he was born, does he actualise himself as a subject. It is through this act of seeing himself through the eyes of the Other, of internalising his fate, that he installs himself in the symbolic order.

We could argue, in a first approach, that the Summerislanders – taunting Howie with his accession to 'martyr' status within the particular symbolic order the latter so assiduously aligns himself with – produce similar signifying effects as the oracle in *Oedipus*

Rex, and that both protagonists are linked insofar as their 'blinding', burning and banishment from the 'Kingdoms' (or in *The Wicker Man*'s case, perhaps 'fiefdom' is better) they inhabit and think they can effectively 'police' reduces them to nothing at all.

The prediction of the oracle, which gives Oedipus his unique identity, materialises the signifying mechanism of the symbolic order. Yet the phallic metaphor of *Oedipus Rex* is, in the final analysis, a 'fatal signifier', signalling the limitation and finitude of the symbolic subject, nothing but a void that is left-over when all organic substance has been subtracted. Oedipus' subjectification describes a trajectory from his fate – which is nothing but an absurd contingency in the real, a confluence of natural causes and effects – towards his tragic destiny, the inner kernel of his being. A very similar analysis can be applied to *The Wicker Man*'s central protagonist, who, despite his apparently 'mundane' status, is in this sense broadly comparable to a tragic hero. According to Lacan, by installing himself in the Other, where the answer to the mystery of his being and sexual identity are expected, the subject articulates an implicit question: 'What am I there?':

> It is a truth of experience for analysis that the subject is presented with the question of his existence, not in terms of the anxiety that it arouses at the level of the ego [...] but as an articulated question: 'what am I there?', concerning his sex and his contingency in being, namely that, on the one hand, he is a man or a woman, and on the other, that he might not be, the two conjugating their mystery, and binding it in the symbols of procreation and death.[4]

The abyss of this existential question, ostentatiously displayed in *Oedipus Rex*, also troubles Howie, who is, at *The Wicker Man*'s climax, about to face the forcible revelation of 'what I am' in the 'there' of Christian Heaven (assuming it is not 'nowhere').

---

[4] Lacan, *Écrits*, p. 194.

However, we must now accomplish an additional turn of the screw, we must look beyond Howie's adherence to his Christian identity to consider the way in which he is literally 'bound into' a symbolic order that is entirely foreign to him. For is it not the elaborate ruse of the islanders itself, the cunning trap they have laid out to lure Howie to his sacrificial death, that matches the structure of the oracle in *Oedipus Rex*? To see this, consider the fundamental incompleteness of the Summerislanders' symbolic network, marked by an 'empty site' at its core; to match their requirement for a substantial sacrifice following a prolonged drought they have their eyes set on a combined virgin, fool, and king for a day who came willingly. Howie is inserted into this vacant site and becomes a *subject* in the islanders' symbolic network, in the precise Lacanian sense of the term: he is made to see himself as an object in the eyes of the Other, represented here by the empirical others of the islanders. Of course, Howie never, in any way, identifies with this role on a narcissistic level, but if both *Oedipus Rex* and *The Wicker Man* reverberate strongly with a sense of the subject's original symbolic castration, it is in part because of these narratives' intuitive grasp of the way in which any socio-symbolic identity is *per se* alien.

If Howie has been walking around the islanders' trap with a false sense of security, this is because he failed to take account precisely of his own, subjective role. However, once Howie is placed inside the phallic statue of the wicker man and given to the ancient gods as a sacrificial offering, everything that has transpired must be subjected to a radical revision. This is apprehended by the viewer as an uncanny schism in the film's narrative, as if a hitherto 'invisible' parallel plot has suddenly emerged into full view. The audience is hereby provided with the ominous, 'true' answer to its desire for interpretation. Thus, the police investigation that seemed to be the substance of the film is reduced to a false appearance, while the true symbolic meaning of events comes into sight as if in a sudden epiphany: the ultimate object of Howie's search is himself. The islanders' machinations produce a meaning that identifies Howie, yet from which he is also radically de-centered. Thus, the outlines of an oracular pronouncement – curiously placed at the *end* of the narrative – come into sharp focus as Howie is identified with the phallic/fatal signifier that marks him as an objectified nothing, a void in the Other. The harrowing image of the burning effigy is therefore superimposed with a sense that Howie consummates his destiny only by having his subjective desire to find the missing girl diverted into the desire of the Other. Howie's sacrifice is an image of the uncanny par excellence: a re-staging of the subject's primordial access to meaning and identity that can be acquired only through symbolic castration.

In film, a sense of the uncanny is always produced by a dislocation, either in terms of a historic or a spatial dimension that is focalised in a single object, thereby reflecting the dislocation introduced into the subject by the phallic signifier.[5] The trajectory whereby Howie is constituted as a subject only by the imposed identification with an object that has always already been lost (himself) could be conceived as the 'main artery' of the film from which flow a range of secondary level uncanny superimpositions and dislocations.

The islanders' parochial culture has a surface appearance, which in many respects does not differ so much from what we would expect from an isolated island community in the West Highlands. Everyday life with its division of labour – fishermen, agricultural workers, an inn-keeper, a post-office official, a teacher, etc., who go about their daily business – captures the typical social life of a remote agrarian community, so that we often require a second glance before we get the impression that something is amiss. Yet, as Howie proceeds with his investigation exploring different layers of the island culture, he consistently comes across a small, phallic detail, a strange object that 'sticks out' and upsets the outward appearance of tranquillity. For instance, the islanders continue to bury their dead in the churchyard in the traditional fashion, yet there is the incongruous image of a tree sticking out from each grave, which is related to the Pagan idea of the transmutation of the corpse into another organic form of life, thus implicitly dismissing any Christian conception of a resurrection of the soul.

---

[5] This sentence and portions of the introductory paragraph have been adapted from Gullatz, 'Exquisite Ex-timacy'.

And as Howie visits the local school, we see the familiar image of a teacher facing her class of children neatly stacked up behind tidy rows of desks. Here, the phallic detail does not enter in terms of any visual effect, but rather on a discursive level. A student is a little embarrassed when she cannot answer the teacher's question on the symbolic significance of the maypole; the eagerness of the rest of the class to volunteer the explanation – that it is a phallic symbol – produces a hilariously comical effect, precisely because the surplus enjoyment that a social institution like a school is designed to keep at bay subverts institutional discourse, rendering the scene charmingly incongruous. Finally, while the merry pub scene close to the beginning may have been too much for uptight Sergeant Howie, the boisterous celebration is perfectly within the bounds of an island's social life. It is only the juxtaposition of this scene with the copulating humans and snails outside that renders it uncanny.

In all these instances, the protuberance of the phallic element that hints at a hidden excess of enjoyment is tied to the film's narrative of nature's exuberant, burgeoning fertility. This unbridled will to enjoyment drives the natural universe, as expounded both by the teacher and Lord Summerisle, who explains the islanders' return to the 'old Gods' to an incredulous Howie. The 'old Gods' supplement the ordinary, external appearance of the island community with the intimation of an uncanny surplus within the community, an object that exceeds it, that is 'in the community more than the community itself'. Effectively, the islanders pose a problem that is akin to the central theme of the *Invasion of the Body Snatchers* (Kaufman, 1978), where unfeeling alien organisms – embodying the register of drives – take on a human form and thus blend in perfectly with the rest of society. In *Body Snatchers* also, the uncanny effect hinges on the supposition of an excessively exuberant organic substratum that is deemed to lie beneath the outwardly ordinary aliens, which is underscored by the soundtrack which is composed of an eerie, thumping heartbeat and grotesque mucus related sounds suggesting the environment of an embryo in the womb. In *The Wicker Man*, however, there is an additional twist, insofar as the Pagan enclave that has somehow assimilated to the appearance of its mundane Christian host culture is not a spatially extraneous, but rather a 'temporal' Other. The blurring and superimposition of the two cultures is all the more uncannily strange because it confronts us with our own past, our own descent from pagan origins.

At its climax towards the end of the film, this temporal dislocation is ratcheted up to the point where the uncanny is transfigured into the sublime. Thus, just as we have productively traced the 'intellectual etymology' of uncanniness, so to better inform a reading of *The Wicker Man*, the same can be done with reference to seminal framings of 'sublimity'.

In *Lessons on the Analytic of the Sublime* (1994), Jean-Francois Lyotard re-frames the philosophies of Immanuel Kant and Edmund Burke with a view to their treatment of the sublime, aligning the sublime with the search for an 'absolute comprehension' transcending the strictures of conceptual thought bound to linguistic categories and empirical objects in space and time.[6] Spontaneous experiences of the sublime – through art or the contemplation of nature – would therefore denote a 'traumatic void'. Lyotard posits a confluence of the uncanny and the sublime which is captured by Thomas Huhn who defined the sublime as 'the uncanny attempt by subjectivity to feel something other than itself'.[7]

The boisterous, concluding scenes of *The Wicker Man* should be re-read in the light of these ideas. Consider Howie's research of historic paganism in the island's parochial library, which yields a book illustrating the masquerade of carnivalesque pagan rituals. There are hints that remnants of the May festivities survive in some areas, albeit stripped of their real substance involving human sacrifice, and just as he leaves the library and we are back outside, the illustrations from the book appear to have come miraculously alive, populating the streets in an astonishing display of pagan revelry. The display provokes the sublime effect of an 'absolute comprehension', because the superimposition of the book's symbolic explanations with the contemporaneous image of the costumed revellers hints at the supremely menacing possibility that the long lost real substance

---

[6] Lyotard, *Lessons on the Analytic of the Sublime*.
[7] Huhn, Review of Lyotard's *Lessons on the Analytic of the Sublime*, p. 91.

of these rituals, the surplus enjoyment of human sacrifice which is strictly forbidden by Western civilisation, describes a metaphysically real category. In *On the Genealogy of Morality* (1887) Friedrich Nietzsche has captured the terrible essence of joyous pagan rituals in a manner that seems closely related to the perspective taken in *The Wicker Man*:

> The Gods viewed as the friends of *cruel* spectacles – how deeply this primeval concept still penetrates our European civilization! [...] No cruelty, no feast, that is what the oldest and longest period of history teaches us – and punishment too has such very strong *festive* aspects![8]

Thus, some of the momentum and dramatic tension in *The Wicker Man* is created by the confrontation between its neo-Pagan and Christian perspectives. What then defines the key difference between the Christian and the Pagan horizons? According to Slavoj Žižek, the Pagan universe must be conceived as an organic whole that is sustained by the eternal recurrence of disturbed and re-balanced global forces. While the Pagan perspective identifies anything that contributes to maintaining the balance with Good, correspondingly any factor that causes a disruption of the homeostasis is seen as Evil. A natural disaster afflicting a community, affecting crops and livelihood, would therefore instinctively be linked to a disturbed balance of the universal organism, so that any redress of the situation will revolve around the restoration of the natural equilibrium. For example, Gods representing natural forces – such as Nuada, the Goddess of the Sun in *The Wicker Man* – would then have to be appeased with animal or human sacrifices. In perfect analogy to the conception of the universe as a balanced organism, society is conceived as an organic whole, a natural hierarchy in which each member occupies his assigned place. Any individual who is dissatisfied with his place would upset the global social balance and would therefore represent the supreme evil. Žižek argues that the

---

[8] Nietzsche, *On the Genealogy of Morality*, p. 46, p. 48.

emergence of Christianity designates a radical derailment of the Pagan balance, a decoupling of social organisation from any kind of organic conception. Christianity opens up the horizon under which ancient, monolithic hierarchies could be destabilised, under which social progress with an emphasis on the individual and individual rights became possible. According to Žižek:

> The very core of pagan Wisdom lies in its insight into the cosmic balance of hierarchically ordered Principles – more precisely, into the eternal circuit of the cosmic catastrophe (derailment) and the restoration of order through just punishment. [...] Christianity (and, in its own way, Buddhism) introduced into this global, balanced cosmic Order a principle that is totally foreign to it, a principle which, measured by the standards of pagan cosmology, cannot but appear as a monstrous distortion: the principle according to which each individual has immediate access to universality (of nirvana, of the Holy Spirit, or, today, of human rights and freedoms).[9]

We see this reflected in the way in which Howie, the Christian individual with a conception of individual rights (for instance those of the ostensibly missing girl), is pitted against an organic social group. In the following, we subject the distinct Pagan and Christian conceptions of evil to a closer scrutiny. Žižek, argues that the pre-Christian, Pagan universe is distinguished by the 'suffocating' absence of radical evil. To apprehend this, let us embark on a brief detour outlining the philosophical distinction between pathological and radical evil, in order to explain better the islanders' actions at the climax of the film.

In the *Critique of Practical Reason* (1788) Kant's notion of evil is still dependent on, and relative to, his construct of an ethical imperative.[10] Accordingly, he regards evil not as an

---

[9] Žižek, *The Fragile Absolute*, p. 120.
[10] Kant, *Critique of Practical Reason*.

intrinsic force, a 'Thing-in-itself' like the moral law, but a mere weakness, a pathological deviation from the pursuit of the categorical imperative. In other words, evil is but a 'pathological stain' on the moral law. As man is always bound to the moral law, he is imbued with an innate goodness, and evil arises only when, at some point, the sublimity of the law becomes tainted with the stain of passionate desire. By *Religion within the Limits of Reason Alone* (1793), Kant holds a more pessimistic view. He no longer regards evil as an occasional, pathological deviation, but rather as radical, as lying at the very roots of human nature:

> In view of what has been said above, the proposition, Man is *evil*, can mean only that he is conscious of the moral law but has nevertheless adopted into his maxim the (occasional) deviation thereof. He is evil by *nature* means but this, that evil can be predicated of man as a species – not that such a quality can be inferred from the concept of his species (that is, of man in general) – for then it would be necessary; but rather that from what we know of man through experience, we cannot judge otherwise of him, or that we may presuppose evil to be subjectively necessary to every man, even the best. Now this propensity must itself be considered as morally evil, yet not as a supernatural disposition but rather as something to be imputed to man, and consequently it must consist in maxims of the will which are contrary to the Law.[11]

We could point to the common intuition that however charitable in principle, most people are inclined to take a secret delight in the misfortune of others, even close friends, and are almost always disposed to indulge in a sense of triumph at the defeat of an enemy. In his bleak view of human nature, Kant posits an ingrained propensity for evil that is no longer simply a

---

[11] Kant, *Religion Within the Limits of Reason Alone*, p. 27.

pathological deviation, but a pathological stain on the very fabric
of the universe itself.[12]

The later Kant's perception of evil is paralleled by Friedrich
Schelling, the nineteenth-century nature philosopher and Idealist,
who came to regard evil as a dark force that emerges from a
'perverted unity of Existence and Ground'.[13] This notion is tied to
a definition of man as the unity of an obscure, natural Ground
that anchors his being with the light of Existence, by which
Schelling means his spiritual side. According to Schelling, Evil
cannot be apprehended by focusing on the two strands in
isolation, i.e. by considering only nature, the pre-human Ground
that has not yet achieved self-illumination, or a Spirit free from
material involvement. The possibility of Evil exists when
Existence and Ground, spirit and nature, are combined. A
necessary condition for sentient existence, nature must, however,
remain submerged as the underlying ground that facilitates being;
it has to be dominated by reason or light. If this natural unity is
perverted, and Ground (a neutral quantity of pure being in its pre-
spiritual state) is 'self-illuminated', raised to the level of spirit or
logos, it acquires the status of a will which 'has found itself', a
ferocious will which wills nothing but itself. According to
Schelling, this is the source of a perversion: in man, normal
animal egotism is 'spiritualised' expressing itself in the medium
of the Word. We are no longer dealing with an obscure drive but
with a Will which has finally 'found itself'.[14]

These notions can be elucidated through the context of
Schelling's philosophy of nature. Schelling was originally
influenced by the pantheistic philosophy of Benedictus (Baruch)
Spinoza, who equated the natural world with a divine substance,
but then departed from Spinoza by 'dynamising' his static
conception of the world as an all-encompassing object,
superimposing upon it Johann Gottlieb Fichte's dialectical

---

[12] For a comprehensive review of contemporary perspectives on the issue of
'radical evil', consider Copjec, ed., *Radical Evil*.

[13] Žižek, *The Indivisible Remainder*, pp. 63-7. In his analysis, Žižek relies on two
key texts by Schelling: *The Weltalter* (*Ages of the World*) (1811-15) and
*Philosophical Investigations into the Essence of Human Freedom and Related
Matters* (1809).

[14] Žižek, *The Indivisible Remainder*, p. 63.

construction of consciousness, of the thinking and willing 'I'. The key to Schelling's vision is this transference of the evolution of an individual consciousness onto the world as a whole which leads to the conception of an animated cosmos which is 'organic' at its core, even in all of its apparently non-organic manifestations (matter, gravity etc.). The world itself then becomes a quasi-subject participating in a mode of 'preconscious organisation', with a teleological orientation towards consciousness that is, however, only fully realised only in man. In his *Weltalter* drafts, Schelling then posits a kind of 'unconscious' within God, an archaic, preconscious rotary motion of drives that functions as the dark Ground into which he 'contracts' his being – and thereby becomes actual – yet from which he must then establish a proper distance in order to achieve the full light of freedom and self-identity.[15]

Thus, it becomes clear why evil definitely had to be of positive substance for Schelling, why he could not abide by the classical Aristotelian, or the early Kantian view, of evil as a mere negative, an absence of the good. In nature *per se*, self-recognition of Existence has not yet been attained – the 'Light of Existence' in nature prior to the emergence of man remains merely implicit. But because man experiences in himself the unity of spirit and nature, he is able to posit their difference. He is aware of 'being split between the obscure vortex of natural drives and the spiritual bliss of logos'.[16] As the only physical being with genuine freedom, man is placed at the apex of nature – his freedom replicates, for the first time, the freedom of the Absolute as such. Accordingly, he 'looks into the abyss', feeling within him motivations that pull him in the directions of good and evil equally, and through his inevitable (a-temporal and free) ethical choice, the nature of his character is determined. Both good and evil thus crystallise only in man as the singular point of unity of Existence and Ground, but Evil represents a perverted unity, or a perturbed tautology where 'centre is no longer centre'. Whereas Good designates a harmonious unity of Existence and its Ground

---

[15] This dialectic of contraction and subsequent 'rejection-expulsion' by a free Absolute describes the essence of Schelling's view of the stages, or ages, of the world in his *Weltalter* drafts.

[16] Žižek, *The Indivisible Remainder*, p. 64.

– a reasoned balance between the spiritual and the sensual (under the power of the spiritual) – Evil transforms this harmony into a fanatical disposition. The shift occurs when Ground becomes self-illuminated and usurps the *logos*, the rightful centre, when the hitherto 'unconscious' ferocity of nature is spiritualised and begins to express itself in the medium of the Word. The essence of radical evil, according to Schelling, is thus the 'purest' conceivable form of spirituality – a diabolical will which wills only itself, destructively opposing itself towards everything outside of itself, even Ground *per se*.

In the light of this complex philosophical framework, it can be seen that *The Wicker Man* presents a meditation on Christian and other attempts to apprehend the nature of Evil far more sophisticated than mere recourse to audience provocation and titillation via the onscreen depiction of 'shocking' pagan revels. Crucially, this philosophical hermeneutic allows us to see precisely what differentiates *The Wicker Man's* 'innocent' pagan revels from the sinister excesses of Hammer horror's satanic covens, exemplified, amongst others, by *The Devil Rides Out* (Fisher, 1968). In terms of Schelling's model of God, Summerisle's 'dark grounds' of preconscious desire – the pagan enclave's uncanny inhabitation of the ancestors' cosmological and geographical terrain – appear 'ethically neutral', given the strong sense that this community *exhausts itself* within a natural Ground claustrophobically enclosed, thereby disallowing any possibility of radical evil. By contrast, Terence Fisher's *The Devil Rides Out,* strongly influenced by Aleister Crowley's fundamental opposition to the monotheistic God, represents a Luciferian illumination of dark urges and basic instincts into a self-consciously evil disposition.

Returning to the psychoanalytic paradigm that formed this essay's point of departure, it should be noted that the Idealist concepts Ground and Existence conform closely to the Lacanian registers of the Real and the Symbolic, so Schelling's notions can be translated into Lacanian terms: Evil can occur only within the context of a symbolic universe, its possibility being opened up by a minimal distance separating the symbolic order from the real inscribed or re-duplicated therein. This creates the potential for a disjunction between the paternal metaphor of the Name-of-the-

Father and the actual, empirical person occupying its site. Thus, someone who is not the natural father may nonetheless perform the function of the paternal metaphor, i.e. the phallic signifier on which the symbolic universe is suspended: 'For that precise reason, evil can occur only within the symbolic universe: it designates the gap between a real entity and its symbolic *reduplicatio*, so that it can best be defined as a perturbed tautology – in Evil, 'father is no longer Father' or 'Centre is no longer centre'.[17]

Thus, only modern traditions facilitated by a monotheistic faith impute to man a kind of evil depth, absent from primordial communities that are closer to nature, that remain embedded in the circuit of the eternal return of natural cycles and have therefore not yet been projected onto a historical teleology. The pagan universe could therefore be defined precisely by the absent horizon of radical, or diabolical, evil. According to Nietzsche, 'man first became an *interesting animal* on the foundation of that *essentially dangerous* form of human existence, the priest, [...] and the human soul became *deep* in a higher sense and turned *evil* for the first time'.[18] If we take this analysis seriously, a factor not only in *The Wicker Man*'s uncanny atmosphere, but also its artistic integrity, suddenly comes into sight. Is not the joyful exuberance of the Pagan rituals of the islanders that involve the killing of a fellow human being, without, however, any trace of radical evil, existentially false? Paganism, in its original, historical form, will indeed have been 'something like that', which is not to suggest that the film reflects the practice with any ethnographic accuracy, but that it correctly apprehends the absence of a sense of radical evil. However, in modern, secular societies, the Christian conception of evil persists, informing a prevailing attitude towards violent crime that could not fail to filter through to any Pagan subculture. In other words, in a modern context, neo-Pagan ritualistic killings could never be undertaken without an accompanying sense of depravity. Examples that could be cited in support of this hypothesis include the neo-Pagan barbarism of Germany's National Socialism – a

---

[17] Žižck, *The Indivisible Remainder*, p. 66.
[18] Nietzsche, *The Genealogy of Morality*, p. 18.

fusion of modern industrial society with an archaic deification of Nature, now universally regarded as evil.

Yet the sublime-uncanny effect of *The Wicker Man*, which transports the original, *real* thing into our age, depends precisely on this falsity. Imagine what a lesser director from the Hammer Studios would have done to the film, if he had been commissioned to translate the script by Anthony Shaffer; how hard he would have found it to resist the temptation to attribute to the islanders a satanic Evil.

Bibliography

Copjec, J., ed., *Radical Evil* (London: Verso, 1996).

Freud, S., 'The Uncanny', in *The Standard Edition of the Complete Psychological. Works of Sigmund Freud*, ed. and trans. by J. Strachey, vol. 17 (London: Hogarth Press, 1955), pp. 219-52.

Gullatz, S., 'Exquisite Ex-timacy: Jacques Lacan vis-à-vis contemporary horror', *Offscreen* (2001) <www.horschamp.qc.ca/new_offscreen/lacan.html> [Accessed 4 June 2005].

Huhn, T., Review of Lyotard's *Lessons on the Analytic of the Sublime*, in *Journal of Aesthetics and Art Criticism*, 53:1 (1995), 89-91.

Kant, I., *Critique of Practical Reason*, ed. by M. J. Gregor (Cambridge: Cambridge University Press, 1997).

_____, *Religion Within the Limits of Reason Alone*, trans. by T. M. Greene and H. H. Hudson (Chicago: Open Court, 1934).

Lacan, J., *Écrits: A selection* (London: Routledge, 1977).

Lyotard, J.-F., *Lessons on the Analytic of the Sublime; (Kant's Critique of Judgment)*, trans. by E. Rottenberg (California: Stanford University Press, 1994).

Nietzsche, F., *On the Genealogy of Morality and Other Writings*, ed. by K. Ansell-Pearson and Carol Diethe (Cambridge: Cambridge University Press, 1994).

Schelling, F. W. J, *Die Weltalter, Fragmente. In den Urfassungen von 1811 und 1813*, ed. by Manfred Schröter (Munich: Biederstein, 1979).

_____, *Philosophical Investigations into the Essence of Human Freedom and Related Matters*, in *Philosophy of German Idealism*, ed. by Ernst Behler (New York: Continuum, 1987).

Žižek, S., *Tarrying with the Negative: Kant, Hegel and the critique of ideology* (Durham, NC: Duke University Press, 1993).

_____, *The Indivisible Remainder: An essay on Schelling and related matters* (London: Verso, 1996).

_____, *The Fragile Absolute: Or, why is the Christian legacy worth fighting for?* (London: Verso, 2000).

Notes on contributors

Gail Ashurst is an Associate Lecturer in English at Manchester Metropolitan University, where she is completing a doctoral thesis in cult film audiences. Her current interests include cinema, and the psychodynamics of the cinematic experience. She is active in the field of audience research and has been producing and editing since 1998 a fan journal, *Nuada*, which is devoted to *The Wicker Man*.

Belle Doyle completed her PhD at the University of Sheffield in 1999. Following this she ran the South West Scotland Screen Commission and the Robert Burns Centre Film Theatre for five years. She now runs the Locations Department at Scottish Screen, the national agency for film in Scotland.

Benjamin Franks is a Lecturer in Social and Political Philosophy at the University of Glasgow's Crichton Campus in Dumfries. His book on anarchisms, *Rebel Alliances*, is due to be published by AK Press (Edinburgh) in late 2005.

Stefan Gullatz received his M.Phil from Cambridge University and completed his PhD at St. Andrews University. He specialises in the philosophy of psychoanalysis. He is particularly interested in the Lacanian tradition and related philosophies. He recently completed a study of C.G. Jung and the theory of the archetypal unconscious.

Robin Hardy is the author of a number of novels, including *The Education of Don Juan* (1980), and plays, most notably *Winnie*, which opened at the Victoria Palace in London in 1988. He has also contributed journalism to *The New York Times*. As a feature filmmaker, Hardy wrote and directed *The Fantasist* (1986), based on a Patrick McGinley novel. He is the co-writer of *The Wicker Man* novel with Anthony Shaffer, and the director of the classic 1973 film of the same name.

Stephen Harper is a Senior Lecturer in Media Studies at the University of Portsmouth. His special interest is in media

representations of mental health and gender studies. He is author
of *Insanity, Individuals and Society in Late-Medieval English
Literature* (Mellen, 2003) as well as several articles on media,
gender and mental health.

Mark Jones is a Senior Lecturer in English at the University of
Wolverhampton, where he teaches contemporary literature and
culture, and also contributes to Film Studies courses. He has
written on 1960s literature, science fiction, crime fiction,
pornography, and popular music.

Jonathan Murray teaches in the Centre for Visual and Cultural
Studies at Edinburgh College of Art. He has published several
scholarly articles on Scottish film culture, with a book-length
Researcher's Guide to Scottish Cinema, prepared in collaboration
with Scottish Screen, forthcoming in 2005. His other research
interests include contemporary British cinema and twentieth
century Scottish history and culture.

Justin Smith is a Senior Lecturer in Film Studies at the
University of Portsmouth, where he is also completing a PhD on
Cult Films and Film Cults in British Cinema, 1968-86. He has
written widely on film fandom, reception and exhibition cultures.

Melissa Smith is a doctoral candidate at McMaster University in
Hamilton, Ontario. Her research focuses on the impact of
epidemic disease on early modern drama. She was Assistant
Editor of *Reading Early Modern Women: An Anthology of Texts
in Manuscript and Print, 1550-1700* (Routledge, 2004).

Lesley Stevenson completed her PhD, on the representation of
traditional music in Scottish tourism, at the University of
Glasgow in 2005. She is currently a Lecturer in Tourism and
Leisure at Liverpool Hope University College.

Steven J. Sutcliffe is a Lecturer in Religious Studies at the
University of Edinburgh. He specialises in contemporary religion
and in the history of the study of religion, and is editor of
Religion: Empirical studies (Ashgate, 2004), author of *Children*

of the New Age: A history of spiritual practices (Routledge, 2003) and co-editor of *Beyond New Age: Exploring alternative spirituality* (Edinburgh University Press, 2000).

INDEX

agrarian 40, 75, 78, 80, 194
Aloi, Peg 58
alterity (otherness) ... 43, 93, 181,
  183-84, 191-94, 196
American Werewolf in London,
  An 79
anarchism 3, 58, 65-66, 68-70
Annett, Stephen 45
anti-authoritarianism 2, 27-28
anti-capitalism 3, 58, 65
Antliff, Allan 65
Anwoth 116, 135
audience 1, 4, 7, 10, 18, 27-28,
  31-32, 37-40, 42-43, 46-49,
  51-53, 58, 65-67, 75, 81, 87,
  98, 107, 131-32, 136, 139-40,
  160-61, 163, 165, 168-69, 174-
  86, 190, 193, 202
authenticity 7, 25-26, 179
authoritarianism...3, 58-59, 61,
  65, 185
authority......3, 11-13, 20, 22, 28,
  40, 42, 58-62, 64-67, 69, 94-
  95, 104, 160, 167, 180
Baader-Meinhof group 40
Bacchilega, Cristina 103
Baker, Michael 108, 110
Baker, Roy Ward 139
Baldwin, James 21-22
Bannock, Mary 142-43, 145,
  152-53
Barclay Securities 124
Barker, Roy Ward 94
Barr, Charles 31
Barra 12
Bartholomew, David . 10, 33, 57,
  60-61, 65, 91, 125, 127, 130,
  133, 137
Bartsow, Anne Llewellyn 77
Baxter, John 147, 190-91
BBC Scotland 115
Beech 143-46

Bentley, John 124-25
Bertolucci, Bernado 183
Beveridge, Craig 23
Bhabha, Homi 175, 179
Boorman, John 79, 108
Boulting, John 124
Boyd-Perkins, Eric 127-28
Boyle, Danny 20
Braveheart 34, 109
Brigadoon 14, 29
British Lion.. ..... 124-25, 128-29,
  139
British Tourist Authority 111
Broome 62
Broughan, Peter 24
Brown, Allan 13, 33, 45, 57,
  75, 111, 124-28, 130-33, 141
Brown, Callum 44
Bruce, David 16-17
Buchanan, Ash 83, 101, 128,
  131, 134
Burke, Edmund 196
Burnt Offering 48, 52
Burrowhead 116
Butler, Judith 4
Butler, Richard 109
Byrom, Michael 158
Cadfael 110
Campion, Jane 140
Canal+ 8, 136
capitalism ... 3, 40, 59-60, 62, 66-
  67, 69-70, 76-77, 82, 84, 87
Captain Kronos: Vampire
  Hunter 139
carnival 29, 43, 132, 158, 196
Carrie 4, 86
Carter, Angela 4, 101-02
Caton-Jones, Michael 24
Caughie, John 13, 30
celibacy 2, 39
Christ, Carol 99

Christianity.... 2, 6-8, 37-53, 57,
    61, 64-65, 68, 70, 77, 82-83,
    85, 91, 96-97, 103, 130-31,
    146, 148-49, 167, 170, 174,
    177, 184-85, 193, 195, 198,
    202
Christie, Bill 113, 115-16
Cilento, Diane 125-26, 135
Cinefantastique ..50, 57, 60, 125,
    127, 129, 136
Cixous, Helene 4, 92-93, 95
Clemens, Brian 139
colonialism....1-2, 11, 16-20, 22-
    24, 29-30
Comical Tragedy or Tragical
    Comedy of Mr. Punch, The ...6,
    157, 162, 168-69
Communion................39, 61, 82
Communism.....................59, 66
conservatism..... 3, 43, 58-59, 61,
    65-66, 70, 91
Cook, Pam 24-25
Corman, Roger 128-29
Corrigan, Timothy................ 123
Cowper, Geraldine 135
Coyne, Michael 21-22
Creed, Barbara 97
Creetown 113
criminality.........79-82, 142, 158,
    203
Crowley, Aleister 202
cult film 5, 49, 51-52, 58, 75,
    111, 119, 123-25, 129-30, 133,
    136-37, 140-41
cult, religious.......... 46-47, 57-58
cultural production 6, 17, 53
Culzean Castle..................... 107
Daily Mail, The 3, 66
Daly, Mary 99
Davies, Jude 65
Day, William 181
de Beauvoir, Simone ..91, 97, 99,
    104

De Palma, Brian 4, 86
deconstruction....... 2, 25, 31, 175
Deeley, Michael 128
Deliverance.................... 79, 108
democracy.............. 3, 59, 65, 67
demotic 38, 43, 58
détournement 65
Devil 6, 157, 168, 202
Devil Rides Out, The....... 94, 202
diegesis 113, 133
dissonance................. 5, 133, 136
Doane, Mary Ann 4, 102
Don't Look Now. 7, 86, 128, 147,
    190-91
Donner, Richard................. 4, 76
Druidry..................... 46, 48, 146
Dumfries . 1, 4, 8, 39, 49, 111-12,
    125, 159
Dumfries and Galloway Tourist
    Board.............................. 111
Ealing studios 11, 13
Eco, Umberto........... 123-24, 137
Ekland, Britt....111, 125-26, 131,
    135, 151, 180
Ellangowan Hotel 113, 115
EMI 128
Empire (film magazine)........ 111
Enlightenment.... 3, 58, 149, 181,
    185
Episcopalianism.............. 61, 148
Equus 51, 182
evil....... 7, 66, 69, 71, 83, 93, 97,
    112, 198-204
Ewan, Dr 143-45
Exorcist, The 4, 86
fairy tales 93, 100-02, 137
fascism 57, 59, 153, 184
femininity.......4, 80, 85, 92, 100-
    04
feminism...4, 50, 92, 97, 99, 101-
    02, 104
Fetchit, Stepin 21
feudalism.................... 14, 18, 62

Fichte, Johann Gottleib......... 201
Field of Dreams.................... 108
film noir................................. 93
Financial Times, The............ 129
Fisher, Terence.............. 94, 202
Fitzpatrick, Jeanne................. 59
Flannery, Seamus............ 125-26
folk medicine......................... 47
folklore....................2, 9, 47-48
Folklore Society..................... 47
Fool............. 10, 12, 63, 167, 180
Forsyth, Bill............... 13, 16, 27
Foucault, Michel.......... 177, 185
Frazer, James....6, 38, 47-48, 50,
   132, 146, 159, 174, 183
Freud, Sigmund ...6, 7, 149, 173-
   78, 180-83, 185, 187, 189
Friedkin, William............... 4, 86
Friends of the Earth............... 78
Gaiman, Neil..... 6, 157, 162, 168
Galloway.4, 8, 107, 110-12, 116,
   119, 125
Galloway Gazette, The 107,
   110, 112, 119
Gardner, Gerald...................... 46
gaze, the......5, 80, 86-87, 92, 98,
   108-09, 119, 164
gender...... 1, 3, 4, 27, 38, 70, 76,
   80, 91-94, 98, 100-04
Gibson, Mel.......................... 109
Giovanni, Paul...... 127, 133, 157
Golden Bough, The......6, 38, 47-
   48, 50, 132, 159, 174
Goldenberg, Naomi......... 99-100
Gollan, Mary........................ 116
Green Man Inn, The........ 76, 81,
   101, 113, 133, 163, 165
Green, Joe.............. 44, 161, 168
Gross, Kenneth........ 161-62, 166
Guardian, The...................... 115
Hair....................................... 43
Hallam, John......................... 130
Hammer Studios................... 204

Hardy, Robin... 1, 7-8, 10, 37-39,
   41, 48-51, 53, 57-58, 61, 70,
   75, 91, 107, 123, 125-27, 129-
   30, 132, 139-41, 143-46, 148-
   54, 157, 159, 174-75, 183, 185,
   191
Harries, John........... 160, 165-66
Haskell, Molly.......................97
Hate Mail..................... 3, 66-70
Hay, Brian............................112
hedonism.............................2, 40
hegemony........ 10, 15-16, 18, 20
hermeneutics.............37, 47, 175
hierarchy............... 3, 60-61, 197
Higginbottom, Judith........ 51-52
Hitchcock, Alfred...........79, 182
Hitler, Adolf.....................50, 57
Hoffman, E. T. A. 189
Hollywood Reporter, The......129
Holocaust......................57, 154
homoeroticism....................3, 80
Hopps, Stewart.....................127
horror...4-6, 8, 11, 50, 76, 86-87,
   89, 91, 93-95, 104, 123, 135-
   36, 139-40, 147, 151, 154, 174,
   176, 178, 191, 202
Hough, John 95
Houston, Robert 21-22
Howie, Sergeant Neil....2-3, 6-7,
   12, 18-20, 28, 33, 39-43, 51-
   52, 61-65, 68-71, 76, 79-85,
   87, 92, 95-99, 102-03, 111,
   113, 130-37, 142-54, 157-60,
   162-70, 174, 177-85, 192-198
Huhn, Thomas......................196
Hutchings, Peter............... 94-95
Hutton, Ronald.................. 47-48
I Know Where I'm Going!.......25
ideology.....1-2, 4, 10-11, 14, 17-
   18, 23, 27-28, 31, 67, 78, 93,
   95, 103-04, 153-54
imperialism............................22

INFORM (Information Network Focus on Religious Movements) 47
International Society for Krishna Consciousness (Hare Krishnas) 46
Internet 66, 78, 111, 113, 115-17, 119, 130
Invasion of the Body Snatchers 195
Irigaray, Luce 99, 102
Jackson, Ellen-Raïssa 30
Jancovich, Mark 123, 174-75
Jentsch, Ernst 178
Jews (and Judaism) 142, 149, 154
Jonestown Massacre 57-58
Judy ... 157, 160-61, 163, 165-66, 168-69
Kant, Immanuel 196, 199-200
Katz, Leslie 161-62, 166
Kaufman, Philip 195
Kemp, Lindsey 134-35
Kemp, Philip 11-12
Kermode, Mark 52
Knox, William 21-22
Krzywinska, Tanya ... 40, 50, 67-68, 96-97, 183, 186
Lacan, Jacques ...7, 79, 177, 180, 189-93, 202
Lady Chatterley's Lover 43, 152
Laing, R. D. 15
Last Great Wilderness, The 15, 28, 79
Last Supper 39, 82
Laurie, John 21
Lawrence, D. H. 43, 152
Leach, Robert 157, 161, 168
Lee, Christopher 5, 10, 14, 50, 52, 62, 67, 125, 127-29, 131-32, 134-35, 177
Leech, Kenneth 45

legitimacy 58-61, 65, 175
Lennon, John 44
lesbianism 100
liberalism 3, 58-59, 61, 66-67, 70-71, 149
libertarianism (anti-market)....*see* anarchism
libertarianism (free-market).... 44
Local Hero 13-14, 27
Locke, John 58-59
Lucas, George 139
Lust For A Vampire 95
Lyotard, Jean-Francois 196
Macbeth, Lady 93
MacGregor, Alder... 40, 134, 163
MacGregor, Willow 3, 83-84, 97-99, 101, 127, 131, 133-35, 144, 147, 151-52, 165, 180
Mackendrick, Alexander ... 1, 11-13
Mackenzie, Compton 11-12
Mackenzie, David 15, 79
Madonna (Virgin Mary) .. 39, 99, 104, 152
Maggie, The 1, 13-14
magic 8, 48, 53, 150, 174
Mahoney, Elisabeth 115-16
Malinowski, Bronislaw 185
Mankiewicz, Joseph, L. 182
Marcuse, Herbert 70
Marshall, Calvin B. 13
Marshment, Margaret 93
Martin, Bernice 44
martyrdom 2, 40, 82
Marwick, Arthur 43-44
masculinity 3, 79
matriarchy 87-88, 100
May Day (commemoration) .. 66, 69, 82-85, 115, 131-32, 157, 164, 196
maypole 26, 40, 84, 103, 146
McArthur, Colin ... 17, 19, 23, 29
McCormick, John 32

McCrone, David 23, 35
McKean, Dave 6, 157
McTaggart, Police Constable ....
    39, 64, 130, 143, 148
Mead, Margaret 185
Medea 93
Michie, Alistair 17
mimesis 102-03
Minnelli, Vincente 14
misogyny 77
modernity 14, 20
Molloy, James 59
Monarch of the Glen 32-33
Moore, John 65
Moore-Gilbert, Bart 44, 49
morality 2, 6, 8, 15, 46, 77, 83,
    86, 91, 93, 97, 160, 169, 173,
    182, 184-85, 199, 201
Morgan, Nigel 109
Morris, Aubrey 135
Morrison, May 64, 70, 83-84,
    133, 145
Morrison, Myrtle 133
Morrison, Rowan ... 4, 41, 64, 76,
    80-83, 85-86, 88, 113, 133-35,
    144-45, 150, 158, 163-67, 169,
    174
motherhood 84
Mulvey, Laura 4, 97-98
Murray, Andy 182
Murray, Jonathan 16, 39, 49,
    182
Musgrove, Frank 44
narcissism 179
National Socialism.... 57-58, 154,
    204
naturalism 26-27
Neale, Steve 3, 80
New Age 37, 40-41, 57, 66,
    183-4
Newton Stewart 111
Nietzsche, Friedrich 197, 203
Ninian, St. 112

novelisation 5, 139-41, 143
Nuada 72, 130
Nuada (deity) 197
nudity 40, 43, 48, 99, 144, 164
Nuremberg Rally 57, 153
O' Mara, Kate 101
Oban Times, The 117
occult 2, 40, 45-46, 67
Oedipus Rex 7, 191-93
Oh, Calcutta! 43
Omen, The 4, 76, 86-87
Pagan Federation 47
Paganism 4-8, 15, 26, 37-43,
    45-53, 57-58, 65, 67-69, 82,
    85-87, 96-97, 100, 103, 111-
    12, 117, 131-32, 136, 146, 150,
    154, 164-65, 167, 174, 177-78,
    183, 195-98, 202-04
Palmer, Paulina 102
parthenogenesis 43, 84-85, 99,
    103
Pasolini, Pier Paolo 183
patriarchy 1, 3-4, 59, 69, 75-
    76, 83-88, 91, 94-96, 99, 102-
    03, 149
Peckinpah, Sam 15
Petrie, Duncan 14-15, 25-26,
    31, 175
phallic symbolism 7, 84, 103,
    132, 189, 193-95
Piano, The 140
Pitt, Ingrid 100, 125-26, 135, 143
Plato 60
Plockton 107, 116
Polanski, Roman 76, 147
policing..... 3-4, 6, 23, 40, 62, 64-
    65, 69-70, 75, 78-83, 85, 87,
    131, 136, 142, 144, 147-49,
    163, 174, 179-80, 183
politics 1, 3, 11, 19, 28, 33, 40,
    44-45, 58-59, 154, 186
Porton, Richard 65

postcolonialism 2, 20-22, 30, 33, 175
Powell, Dilys 129
Powell, Michael 25
Presbyterianism 39, 148
Pressburger, Emeric 25
Pritchard, Annette 109
prophecy 7, 145, 190-91
Psycho 79
psychoanalysis ... 7, 174-75, 177, 182-84, 191, 202
psychotherapy 15, 44
puberty 82, 174
Pulcinella 158, 160
Punch, Mr. 6, 26, 157-63, 165-70
Quest for 'The Wicker Man', The 9
Quixote, Don 96
racism 6, 22, 154
Radway, Janice 48
Ramsay, Lynne 20
Rank 124
Rapunzel 100-01
Ratcatcher 20
Reagan, Ronald 59
Reeves, Michael 94
Riefenstahl, Leni 153
Riley, Roger 108, 110
Rivere, Joan 102
Rob Roy 24, 26, 28, 30
Robinson, Phil Alden 108
Roeg, Nicolas 7, 86, 128, 147, 190
Rolling Stone 44
Rolston, Lorraine 182
Roper, Tony 130
Rose, Miss 3, 28, 30, 40, 64-65, 81, 84, 96, 99, 145, 148, 150, 158, 166-67, 174
Rosemary's Baby 76
Ross, Herbert 108
Royal Hunt of the Sun 51
Royle, Nicholas 175, 182

sacrifice 2, 4, 6-7, 12, 20, 40, 48, 57, 62-63, 82, 84, 87-88, 100-01, 111-12, 146, 150, 157-60, 163-65, 167, 169-70, 174, 181, 197
Sangster, Jimmy 95
Saunders, Nicholas 45
scapegoat 3, 66, 159
Schelling, Friedrich 7, 176, 200-02
Scientology, Church of 46
Scotland 1, 8, 10-11, 13-34, 45, 70, 77, 79, 107, 111-13, 117, 119, 127, 143, 148, 174-75
Scotsman, The 112
Scott, Ridley 108
Scottish Tourist Board 109
Scullion, Adrienne 23
Seaton, A. V. 112
Seed, John 49
semiotics 81, 92
sex 2, 40, 44, 60, 68, 81, 84, 111, 131, 133, 149, 153, 195
sexual repression 81, 150-51, 177, 184
Shaffer, Anthony 38, 49-52, 57, 60-61, 65, 70, 91, 125-27, 129-32, 136, 139-41, 143-46, 148-54, 174-75, 182, 185, 191, 204
Shaffer, Peter 51, 182
Sharp, Alan 24
Sharp, Cecil 133
Shepperton Studios 124-25, 128
Sillars, Jane 2, 26-32
Skye 107
Sleuth 51, 182
Smith, Madeline 100
Snell, Peter 124-25, 127-28
Sobchack, Vivian 87
socialism 70, 149

Sorcerers, The......................... 94
Sorrel 143, 145-46
spectacle 51, 80, 98, 175, 197
Spikings, Barry 128
Spinoza, Benedictus (Baruch)
.... 201
spirituality. 6, 8, 64, 99, 150, 152
St. Ninian's Cave..... 112-13, 116
Star Associated 124
Star Wars 139
Steel Magnolias 108
Stirling 109
Stonehenge 40
Straw Dogs 15
Street, Sarah........................... 13
structuralism 2, 12, 30, 49
sublime, the.................. 196, 204
Summer Isles 116-18
Summerfield, Penny 48
Summerisle (fictional setting) . 3,
    7, 11-12, 18-20, 28, 33, 38, 40,
    50, 52, 60-62, 64-65, 68-71,
    78-85, 87, 102-03, 107, 111,
    113, 116-18, 131-32, 134, 143-
    44, 146, 148, 157-58, 163-67,
    169-70, 175-77, 180-81, 184-
    85, 192-95, 198, 203-04
Summerisle News.................. 130
Summerisle, Lord 4, 10-11,
    18-19, 29, 39, 41-43, 51, 57,
    61, 63-64, 67, 70, 85, 87-88,
    99, 101-02, 104, 117-18, 131-
    32, 134-35, 143-46, 149, 154,
    160, 164-67, 169-70, 177, 195
Sunday Telegraph, The 129
Sunday Times, The 129
Sunters, Irene....................... 133
superstition 12, 50, 57-58, 183
symbolism...... 2, 5, 7, 40, 51, 81,
    92-93, 132-33, 135, 150, 157,
    159, 178-80, 182, 189-95, 197,
    202-03
Tanera Mhor 118

Texas Chainsaw Massacre, The
.... 79
That Sinking Feeling 16
Thelma and Louise 108
Todorov, Tzvetan 175-76
Tooke, Nicola....................... 110
totalitarianism..................... 3, 59
tourism....... 4-5, 78, 107-12, 115,
    118-19, 130, 142
tragedy............ 52, 137, 190, 192
*Tragical Comedy or Comical
    Tragedy of Punch and Judy,
    The*..................................... 157
Trainspotting 20
transgression............. 40, 64, 101
Triumph of the Will 153
Turnbull, Ronald 23
Twins of Evil........................... 95
uncanny, the 6-7, 173-85, 189-
    96, 202
Unification Church (Moonies) 46
Universal Studios 139
Urry, John.................... 5, 108-09
Vampire Lovers, The 94-95,
    100
Van Doren, Carlton 108
Vault of Horror, The 139
virginity........ 63, 83, 87, 99, 131,
    150, 152, 167
Waggett, Captain Paul....... 12, 31
Waters, Russell..................... 135
Waxman, Harry 125, 127
Weber, Max 3, 59-63, 65, 67,
    70, 177
Western Isles 107
whimsy 26-28, 32
Whisky Galore! 1, 11-14, 31
Wicca.............. 38, 46, 48, 65, 77
Wicker Man Week 115-16
Wicker Man, The (film)...... 1-20,
    25, 27-31, 33, 37-38, 42, 44-
    47, 49-53, 57-58, 61-62, 65-67,
    75-77, 79, 84, 86-87, 91-98,

100-04, 107-08, 110-13, 115-
19, 123-25, 127-30, 136, 139-
41, 145, 147, 154, 157-60, 162,
164-65, 167-69, 174-79, 181-
85, 189-93, 196-97, 202-03
Wicker Man, The (novel) ...5, 61,
70, 139-42, 147, 154
Wickerman Festival ..5, 112, 119
Wigtown Bay 112
Wilder, Bill............................. 118
wilderness........ 15-16, 19-20, 24-
26
Williams, Raymond 38
witch hunts 95
Woman in the Wardrobe, The .....
182
Wood, Robin 86
Woodward, Edward 125, 127,
130, 174
Wren, Richard 131
Wright, Jake 127
Yelland', Sue......................... 127
Žižek, Slavoj 7, 197-98, 200-
01, 203